COMPUTER SCIENCE, TECHNOLOGY AND APPLICATIONS

ICT PERFORMANCE AND ROBUSTNESS INVESTIGATIONS

SOME ETHICAL AND HUMAN BEHAVIOR ASPECTS

COMPUTER SCIENCE, TECHNOLOGY AND APPLICATIONS

Additional books and e-books in this series can be found on Nova's website under the Series tab.

COMPUTER SCIENCE, TECHNOLOGY AND APPLICATIONS

ICT PERFORMANCE AND ROBUSTNESS INVESTIGATIONS

SOME ETHICAL AND HUMAN BEHAVIOR ASPECTS

JÓZEF BOHDAN LEWOC
EDUARD BABULAK
AND
DAVID AL-DABSS
EDITORS

nova science publishers
New York

Library of Congress Cataloging-in-Publication Data

ISBN: 978-1-53614-916-6

Published by Nova Science Publishers, Inc. † New York

CONTENTS

Preface		**ix**
Acknowledgments		**xiii**
Chapter 1	The Approach to Ethics Aspect Assessment *Jozef B. Lewoc, Pasha Bekhrad, Mike Fitzgibbon, Iwona Chomiak-Orsa and Eric Leitgeb*	**1**
Chapter 2	The Approach to Human Behaviour Aspect Assessment *Jozef B. Lewoc, Pasha Bekhrad, Mike Fitzgibbon and Eric Leitgeb*	**5**
Chapter 3	A Line of ICT Systems and Networks Designed and Developed in Wroclaw, Poland *Jozef B. Lewoc, Pasha Bekhrad, Iwona Chomiak-Orsa, Antoni Izworski, Bogdan Kasierski, Mike Fitzgibbon, Antonina Kieleczawa, Eric Leitgeb, Jozef Patkiewicz, Mieczyslaw Rozent, Halina Strzelecka, Wojciech Szubert and Edward Ziaja*	**9**

Chapter 4 The Line of the Emerging ICT Systems under Performance Investigation **15**
Jozef B. Lewoc, Pasha Bekhrad, Mike Fitzgibbon, Iwona Chomiak-Orsa, Antoni Izworski, Bogdan Kasierski, Antonina Kieleczawa, Eric Leitgeb, Jozef Patkiewicz, Mieczyslaw Rozent, Halina Strzelecka, Wojciech Szubert, Andrzej Tomczyk and Edward Ziaja

Chapter 5 Robust Design of Computer Control Systems **203**
Jozef B. Lewoc, Pasha Bekhrad, Mike Fitzgibbon, Iwona Chomiak-Orsa, Antoni Izworski, Bogdan Kasierski, Antonina Kieleczawa, Eric Leitgeb, Jozef Patkiewicz, Mieczyslaw Rozent, Halina Strzelecka, Andrzej Tomczyk, Wojciech Szubert and Edward Ziaja

Chapter 6 Case Studies of Ethics and Human Behaviour under Investigation: The Line of the ICT Systems and Networks **221**
Jozef B. Lewoc, Pasha Bekhrad, Mike Fitzgibbon, Iwona Chomiak-Orsa and Eric Leitgeb

Chapter 7 Conclusion **251**
Jozef B. Lewoc, Pasha Bekhrad, Mike Fitzgibbon, Iwona Chomiak-Orsa, Antoni Izworski, Bogdan Kasierski, Antonina Kieleczawa, Eric Leitgeb, Jozef Patkiewicz, Mieczyslaw Rozent, Halina Strzelecka, Andrzej Tomczyk, Wojciech Szubert and Edward Ziaja

About the Editors **257**

About the Contributors **263**

Index **279**

Related Nova Publications **285**

PREFACE

There is, in general, no doubt regarding the ethical and human behaviour aspects of the research work of any type. The researchers are thought of working for the society and are low paid. However, in the practice of the science and technology, they should work, first of all, for system designers who need their support in designing, developing and implementing the systems under investigation. Unfortunately, this is not a popular case in the area of the Information and Communication Technology (ICT), where the support of the system and network researchers for the system and network designers, developers and operators is very limited if any.

Considering that, the team of authors of the book (the Team) decided to present the design experiences gained during designing, implementing and operating some line of the computer systems and networks in Poland (the Country). The Country was selected purposefully: due to the political reasons, various embargoes were imposed on the importation of modern equipment and methods of the computer industry, and the Team needed very severely a good support from the researchers to fulfil the design and development tasks successfully. However, in the ICT domain, relatively new one in the human life and, thus, needing the significant support of the Science in every country, this support was a minute one, in practice. In well developed countries, possessing surplus hardware and software components, the need of the support was also observed but could be bypassed through using surplus supplies or by learning on the design errors. This bypass was much less available in the Country in severe economic conditions and the political conditions of so called Cold War.

Some malicious persons could call the book Polish centric. The remarks hereinabove testify that it would be correct. In addition, the editor of the Book could state even more, the book could be called the editor centric since all case studies discussed herein were referred to the projects led by the editor, at least on some decisive phase. Due to that, the editor being the leading author of the Book, possessed the biggest possible knowledge and experience in the domain of the case studies.

In addition, the editor was educated and upgraded in the Country (Poland) and realised that any citizen of the Country had to contribute an equivalent of some 10 loaves of bread into his toys, the computer hardware and software needed for him to acquire the knowledge and skills and not wasting the money. The knowledge and skill level was such high that the editor could make fun on the big heads of the University of Cambridge Computer Laboratory, and that was a real fun for the editor. Therefore, he recognised that he could never pay his debt to the people of the Country and worked mainly on Polish case studies though, for a quarter or so last years, he worked for international scientific and technical organisations, exclusively.

But could the editor be blamed for working on the case studies he knew best, the ones from the country, he loved? Due to it, he could solve the problems of the international interest also. So the book based on the Polish or the editors exemplification may and should be a more interesting item than those based on the international domain, i.e., actually, carrying small if any detailed knowledge of the real life.

Some other witty Reader may accuse the Book of describing ICT history. Here, we have to remind that: *Historia est mater studiorum (Historyis the mother of knowledger).* And this is very well shown in the case of adoption of the open system approach to investigate presently computer systems and networks, elaborated more than fifty years ago and, from that time, found as being an inadequate ones. Such approach should not be applied in any actual case, where there are standard flow control methods saving against system or network overload and saturation; the severe threats informed (erroneously) by the system or network "investigators". It is not necessary, even more, it is harmful to cite such references since it would be an advertising of such publications and granted undue citations for them.

Thus, the objective of the book is to present the line of the ICT systems and networks, under design and operation from the late 1960-ies and finishing when this book was written, and to present the requirements for the system and the basic support available then from the Science. The research aspects under consideration were, first of all, the performance evaluation and, for the systems of the XXI-st century, the robustness evaluation, interesting most the system designers, implementers and operators.

Jozef B. Lewoc

ACKNOWLEDGMENTS

This Book has been written under the auspices of the Working Group 03, Nota (Non technological aspects of automation and ICT), of the Technical Committee 9.5, TECIS (Technology, Culture and International Stability), of IFAC (International Federation of Automatic Control). The substantive support of IFAC is thankfully acknowledged.

The linguistic support provided by Anna Krotkiewska-Zagorska to the Authors of this Book 2 is thankfully acknowledged also.

In: ICT Performance … ISBN: 978-1-53614-916-6
Editor: Józef Bohdan Lewoc et al.

Chapter 1

THE APPROACH TO ETHICS ASPECT ASSESSMENT

Jozef B. Lewoc**, Pasha Bekhrad, Mike Fitzgibbon, Iwona Chomiak-Orsa and Eric Leitgeb

1. INTRODUCTION

The basic sciences that investigate human conduct in various domains of life are known as ethics and human behaviour (HB). It seems worthwhile to present here some relevant theories of ethics and human behaviour described in the literature.

2. THEORIES AND METHODS OF ETHICS

Hersh (2015) describes a number of theories and methods of ethics, some of which are itemized below.

* Corresponding Author's Email: jblewoc@wroclaw.home.pl.

According to Beaucamp and Childress (2001), ethics is often discussed in terms of four ethical principles: *beneficence* – the active promotion of acts that benefit others); *non-maleficence* – the avoidance of harm; *autonomy* – the defence of individual rights against the state; and *justice* – the fair and impartial distribution of social benefits and burdens. In addition, Gilligan (1982) recognizes an *ethics of care*, described as a context-based approach to preserving relationships.

Other important approaches to ethics include:

- deontological approaches - those that are based on independent moral rules and duties, which focus on the morality of actions themselves as opposed to their consequences;
- consequentialist approaches – those that are concerned with the consequences of actions;
- virtue ethics – person- or character- based approaches, incorporating those supporting actions that build good character (Koehn 1995); and
- narrative ethics - those that focus on personal or community identity and events, stressing the importance of systems and processes (Sorlie et al., 2004).

3. Theories and Methods of Human Behaviour

The first factor to be considered is that of *needs*, originally conceived of by Abraham Maslow in 1943, wherein he described a model of a *hierarchy of needs* (Maslow 1970). Alderfer (1969), in an extension of Maslows' hierarchy, suggests that there are three categories of needs: existence, relatedness and growth. Mclelland (1961) defines three types of motivational needs: achievement, authority/power and affiliation motivation.

Other theories and models are beyond the scope of the present section.

REFERENCES

Alderfer, C. P. (1969). An empirical test of a new theory of human needs. *Organisational Behavior and Human Performance* 4(2), p. 142-175.

Beachamp, T. L. and Childress J. F. (2001). *Principles biomedical ethics*, 5th edition. Oxford University Press.

Gilligan, C. (1982). *In a different voice*. Harvard University Press, Cambridge, MA.

Hersh, M. (Ed). (2015). *Ethical Engineering for International Development and Environmental Sustainability*, Springer-Verlag London.

Koehn, D. (1995). A role of virtue ethics in the analysis of business practice. *Business Ethics Quarterly* 5(3), p. 533-539.

McClelland, D. C. (1967). *Achieving society*. Simon and Schuster.

Maslow, A. (1970). *Motivation and personality*. Harper and Row, New York.

Sorlie, V., Kihlgren, A., L., and Kihlgren, M. (2004). Meeting ethical challenges in acute care work. *Nursing Ethics* 11(2), p. 179-188.

In: ICT Performance …
Editor: Józef Bohdan Lewoc et al.
ISBN: 978-1-53614-916-6

Chapter 2

THE APPROACH TO HUMAN BEHAVIOUR ASPECT ASSESSMENT

Jozef B. Lewoc**, Pasha Bekhrad, Mike Fitzgibbon and Eric Leitgeb

Though this book presents various approaches to Ethics and Human Behaviour, it seems worthwhile to adopt a single approach to the initial assessment of various solutions from the Ethical and Human Behavioural points of view. All of the authors of this book live in Judeo-Christian settings, and so this book is intended, primarily, for people living in the contexts of these religions. It seems worthwhile to adopt, for an initial assessment, the methods assumed for Ethical and Human Behavioural appraisal that are valid in this domain. Such appraisal in the Judeo-Christian domain is based on the Decalogue, or Ten Commandments, presented below in the form of the old English found in the Hebrew Bible:

1. I am the Lord thy God, thou shalt have no other gods before me
2. Thou shalt not take the Lord's name in vain
3. Remember the sabbath day

* Corresponding Author's Email: jblewoc@wroclaw.home.pl.

4. Honour thy father and thy mother
5. Thou shalt not kill
6. Thou shalt not commit adultery
7. Thou shalt not steal
8. Thou shalt not bear false witness
9. Thou shalt not covet thy neighbours wife
10. Thou shalt not covet thy neighbours goods

For the purposes of this book, as well as for life in general, if one uses the Decalogue in full for the assessment of ethics and behaviour, the task becomes unfeasible. The individual Commandments are in contradiction of one another and some hierarchy of their importance is needed in order for them to be used for the evaluation of human behaviour and ethics. The Judeo-Christian faith offers no support here, providing no such hierarchy. For the book's purposes, therefore, there is a need to reduce the number of mutually inconsistent Commandments to some consistent minimum that enables one to use the Decalogue consistently and effectively.

A reasonable synthesis of the Ten Commandments would imply that, to behave ethically and appropriately, a human being must not harm any other human being. Thus, they may be substituted by one Commandment:

- Thou shalt not harm your colleagues, with the border condition: In this global village, the world, we all are colleagues of each other.

The word "colleague" helps in accepting the only one Commandment: even Nazis, SS or Communist NKWDs (members of the Interior Ministry of the Soviet Union) accepted the rule that their members should not harm other members of the murdering organisations. The border condition is something that is missing in the Hebrew and Christian faiths; the idea that you may not harm anybody in any way was, unsuccessfully, being shown by specification via a big number of examples. This was, of course, unsuccessful due to unavoidable contradictions within the Commandments' specifications and the inherent incompatibility of the Decalogue.

Thus, in this book, before an accurate analysis of Human Behaviour and Ethics can be achieved, we shall do some initial assessment based on the Commandment.

In: ICT Performance …
Editor: Józef Bohdan Lewoc et al.
ISBN: 978-1-53614-916-6

Chapter 3

A LINE OF ICT SYSTEMS AND NETWORKS DESIGNED AND DEVELOPED IN WROCLAW, POLAND

Jozef B. Lewoc*, Pasha Bekhrad, Iwona Chomiak-Orsa, Antoni Izworski, Bogdan Kasierski, Mike Fitzgibbon, Antonina Kieleczawa, Eric Leitgeb, Jozef Patkiewicz, Mieczyslaw Rozent, Halina Strzelecka, Wojciech Szubert and Edward Ziaja

1. INDUSTRIAL DEVELOPMENT OF LOWER SILESIA AND WROCLAW (LOWER SILESIA) AFTER THE WORLD WAR II

After World War II, Lower Silesia, which was a part of pre-war Germany, was connected to Poland in accordance with the Yalta agreement (Farlex 2017). In Lower Silesia, many Polish people who had

---

* Corresponding Author's Email: jblewoc@wroclaw.home.pl.

been driven out of their homes, settled and rebuilt the post-German industrial infrastructure. Soon after liberation of these areas, important Polish industrial plants were established, such as Pafawag (a Polish railway wagon factory), Archimedes (a Polish agricultural machine manufacturing plant), Dolmel (an Electric machinery plant), Diora (a Radio equipment factory), Elwro (the first Polish manufacturer of computers). The industrial plants continued and expanded the production range of former German industries and were very successful on the scale of not only Poland or Comecon (Council for Mutual Economic Assistance) countries. Soon, Lower Silesia became one of the top industrialised regions of Poland.

The industrialisation processes for Lower Silesia were not easy. The time was just after the end of the World War II, and the so called Cold War had begun. In an attempt to stop the imperialist efforts of the Soviet Union ruled by Stalin, developed democratic countries tried to block the proliferation of the hi-tech equipment to Comecon countries, instituting various embargoes. This resulted in that, in Lower Silesia, the citizens had to develop their own solutions comparable to those available in the West. This was possible primarily due to the education and upskilling systems developed in Lower Silesia. The systems were based on the pre-war systems run mainly in Vilnius and, even more so, in the Lvov regions. On one hand, the primary and secondary education systems were oriented towards student education and upskilling/improvement of a Renaissance-type character: this created young people who could cope with and solve a broad range of problems, not limited to some narrow specializations. On the other hand, higher education and upgrading were primarily oriented toward solving practical problems. The graduates could attack even those difficult problems generated in real life. And they did it successfully, developing the industries in Lower Silesia.

It should be emphasised here that, on the whole, the embargo policies failed. First of all, the necessity to develop local solutions resulted in development of the regions' own human resources, capable of substituting the equipment and know-how covered by the various embargoes. Of even more importance was that, in Lower Silesia, the embargoes generated a protest or even a fury: in this region almost all families were expelled from their homes in the East and suffered a lot from the murdering and double-faced Eastern System. They were worst affected by, and struggled with the Communists' system; and found it hard to believe that they were now being punished with embargoes as Communists. Their protest and fury manifested itself in their consent for a harder work, in solidarity among Polish people and in obstinacy to develop solutions of equal quality to those available in the West. (J. B. Lewoc and M. Hersh 2018).

2. Development of ICT Solutions in Wroclaw

The beginning of the computer era used to be counted from the instant that the ENIAC computer was turned on in the Pennsylvania University in 1946. This computer, called by the press the gigantic brain, generated hopes connected with a significant improvement of the human life. However, this was not to be realised in Poland as a Comecon country; soon, embargoes were imposed on computers which, in theory, made it impossible to import computers into Communist countries. In practice, paradoxically, the Soviet Army had no problems with bypassing the embargoes, buying the most modern electronics for their fighter-jets and missiles via Finland which tried to protect its independence. But for the civilian applications, good computers could not be imported.

Due to the considerations mentioned above, the Polish power decided to establish the first Polish computer manufacturer in Wroclaw. The factory was founded in 1959 (13 years after the ENIAC computer was turned on). Soon, in spite of various embargoes that had been imposed, and an absence of computer components like ferrite core memories, Elwro started to manufacture better and better computers, starting from a first vacuum-tube machine, UMC-1; transistor-based computers such as Odra 1003, 1013; tabulating machines Odra 1103; and a modern interrupt-driven Odra 1204; ICL Series 1900 - compatibles: Odra 1304, Odra 1325, Odra 1305, to their Unified System computers R-32 and R-34 (compatibles of 360/System and 370/System computers of IBM).

However, while computers were the essence of ICT, they could not help to directly improve the living standards of the people. For this, application systems were needed. This book analyses the processes of the design, development and use of a line of successful application projects led by a single leading designer (refered to as the Leader). It should be noted that, due to the various embargoes, the Leader had always only at his disposal computers and peripherals that were obsolete for at least five to ten years, compared with those that were available in Western countries. Therefore the questions of performance needed for individual systems were even more important than in the West. In addition, the results of performance evaluations obtained from developed countries could hardly be applied to the Leader's project due to the significant differences in performance characteristics of the computers and peripherals available in the Leader's country.

A significant variety of projects were led by the Leader. These included a steel-bar mill traffic control system, a radio-astronomy centre control system, a regional power control board system, a SOSAPI operating system, a power industry VDU system, a power industry training simulator, a microprocessor-based power control board system, an interuniversity communication network, an internal network measuring system, an approximate network performance evaluation tool (Anapaest), and a power plant database. The robust design of control systems, designed and developed during the period from 1968 till 2017, made it possible to assess the help that was available from the theoretical sciences, to the system design and development practitioners. In many cases, no such support was available, and the Leader's design and development teams (the Teams) had to solve the practical performance and robustness evaluation problems by themselves. The book discusses these actual performance (and robustness) problems and presents the available theoretical methods and tools for performance (and robustness) evaluation. In general, the available analytical methods are criticised due to inappropriate research assumptions, making them inapplicable in practical work. The methods worked out and applied by the Teams are presented for each of the individual cases. For performance evaluation, there were simulation methods based on actual structures of the applications. However, at the end of the design and development process, an approximate performance evaluation tool (Anapaest) was proposed. For robustness evaluation, a feasible μ-function (robustness measure) evaluation method for such computer systems that could only be built of older components only was shown.

The missing theoretical science support for ICT system design, development and operation was not a single specific case and, therefore, it was a matter of engineering ethics and human behaviour concerns; this book is devoted to such aspects.

Conclusion

Various formal and informal embargoes imposed on ICT hardware and software by Western countries resulted in Comecon countries, including Poland, having to develop their own computers and applications. This resulted in such ICT equipment and software being obsolete in comparison with those available in the West. Because of this, the ICT system designers and developers needed a support from the theoretical sciences in assessment of performance (and robustness). This support was missing in practice. Therefore, it seems interesting to study the ethical and human behaviour aspects for the case studies for the period of circa 50 years.

Reference

Lewoc J. B. and Hersh M. (Eds). (2018). *Ethics and Human Behaviour in ICT Development*. Springer-Verlag, in print.

In: ICT Performance … ISBN: 978-1-53614-916-6
Editor: Józef Bohdan Lewoc et al.

Chapter 4

THE LINE OF THE EMERGING ICT SYSTEMS UNDER PERFORMANCE INVESTIGATION

Jozef B. Lewoc*[*]*, Pasha Bekhrad, Mike Fitzgibbon, Iwona Chomiak-Orsa, Antoni Izworski, Bogdan Kasierski, Antonina Kieleczawa, Eric Leitgeb, Jozef Patkiewicz, Mieczyslaw Rozent, Halina Strzelecka, Wojciech Szubert, Andrzej Tomczyk and Edward Ziaja

1. ABBREVIATIONS

A	number of individual measurements
AI	Analogue inputs
SVDU	Alphanumeric Visual Display Unit
ARU	Automatic Restart Unit
A_i	set of closed routes beginning at the i-th link

[*] Corresponding Author's Email: jblewoc@wroclaw.home.pl.

B_i	set of closed routes passing via the i=th link but not beginning at that link
C	constant value
C_n	Constants, n = 1,…,13
CCU	Cluster control unit
C_i	set of routes parallel to the s-th closed route in the i-th link
CE	Control engineer
D	Number of process control IR-s
D	Number of digital input bytes
DI	Digital inputs
DCE	Data Communication Equipment (set of communication network switches)
DS	Dummy scheme
DTE	Data Terminal Equipment, set of network subscribers
d_k	k=1,…,u – network subscribers
D_s	s-th closed route throughput
e	mean transmission time
$\bar{e}_{I,s}$	mean service time for the closed routes encountered by the s-th route at the i-th link
EOT	End of Transfer
G_C	common-medium network concentrator transfer function
G_S	star network concentrator transfer function
h	hesitation traffic intensity
$h_s(i)$	link preceding the i-th link in the s-th closed route
H	set of IR numbers of peripherals capable of block transfer
i	server index
IASE	Power System Automation Institute (from Polish Instytut Automatyki Systemów Energetycznych)
IN	set of communication network input links
IPB	Inter-Processor Buffer
IR	interrupt request
IR_k	k-th interrupt request
l_3	phase rotator counter
I_s	set of links passed by the s-th closed loop

k	interrupt request index, data concentrator index
k'	index of interrupt request dependent on k-th interrupt request
K	set of interrupted IR-s
KR	Number of keyboards
KRBD	Keyboard
K_{CE}	CE pushbutton number set
L	number of interrupt requests (important events)
m	mean thinking time
$\overline{m}_{I,s}$	mean thinking time for the closed routes encountered by the s-th route at the i-th link
MIPS	million instructions per second
$MIPS^h$	million instructions per second taking hesitations into consideration
N_{CE}	full sojourn time for IR_k request; $k \in K_{CE}$
ODM	Regional power distribution board (from Polish Okregowa Dyspozycja Mocy)
R_s	s-th closed route round trip delay
r_s^*	maximum possible round trip delay in the s-th route
s	closed route index; s=1,…,n
s_k	Sojourn time of the IR_k request
S	Number of displays; set of all closed routes
SAPI	Automatic information processing system (from Polish System Automatycznego Przetwarzania Informacji)
SI	Standard Interface
SIAL	Industrial process control peripheral interface
SMA	Automation Module System (from Polish System Modulow Automatyki)
SOSAPI	Operating system of automatic data processing system (from Polish System Operacyjny Systemu Automatycznego Przetwarzana Informacji)
SUB	set of links (hops) within the communication network
SVDU	Semi-graphic visual display unit
t_H	extension of 11 second mean instruction execution time due to hesitations

t_k	k-th concentrator delay time
$\bar{t}_{I,s}$	mean cycle time of closed routes encountered by the s-th route at the i-th link
TI	number of telemechanic interfaces
TO	Time Out
T_s	s-th closed route cycle time
v	speed; power of S set
V	number of VDU-s
VDU	Visual Display Unit
WAN	Wide Area Network
w_k’	console writing blocked time
y	mean waiting time
$\bar{y}_{I,s}$	mean waiting time of closed routes encountered by the s-th route at the i-th link
$\chi_{k,i}$	k-th interrupt request service time at i-th server
w_i	I = 1,…,o – set of communication network switches (nodes, routers, gateways)
$\chi_{k,i}$’	k-th interrupt request cumulated service time at i-th server
χ_{ko}	k-th interrupt request service time at CPU
$\chi_{ko}*$	k-th interrupt request service time at CPU for the end of message
χ_k^1	in-cycle k-th interrupt request service time at CPU
χ_k^2	end-of-cycle k-th interrupt request service time at CPU
γ	basic server (CPU) busy time
$\bar{\gamma}$	mean basic server (CPU) busy time
γ_u	computer time fraction available to user programs
γ^*	maximum possible basic server (CPU) busy time
η_{ko}	current waiting time realisation for k-th interrupt request
$\overline{\eta_{ko}}$	mean k-th interrupt request waiting time
η_{ko}^*	maximum possible value of waiting time for k-th interrupt request
λ	intensity of pseudo-random number of exponential distribution
λ_k	k-th interrupt request distribution intensity

λ_k*	k-th interrupt request distribution intensity for complete messages
$\lambda_{k'/k}$	distribution intensity of time between k'-th and k-th interrupt request arrivals
λ^h	total offered hesitation load
λ_k^h	hesitation input stream density for the k-th peripheral
ν_k	k-th IR sojourn time at the basic server, the foreground fraction
ν_k^*	maximum permissible IR_k sojourn time at the basic server
ν_k^{Max}	maximum possible sojourn time of the k-th IR
ν_k^{COO}	*IR_k* request coordinator sojourn time
ν_k^{MOD}	*IR_k* request model sojourn time
$\Sigma\gamma$	total basic server (CPU) busy time
$\Sigma\eta_{ko}$	total k-th interrupt request waiting tim
θ	pseudo-random number of exponential distribution
θ_k	minimum interval length of k-th interrupt request distribution
θ_k*	inimum interval length of k-th interrupt request distribution for complete messages
τ_k^0	initial value of next arrival instant for k-th interrupt request
τ_k^n	next arrival instant for k-th interrupt request
$\tau_k^{n''}$	buffered next arrival instant for k-th interrupt request
ζ_I	current queue length for i-th server
ζ_I'	current queue length for requests waiting service of i-th server
ζ_I^*	maximum queue length for i-th server

2. Steel-Bar Mill Material Traffic Control System

The first Polish industrial application of ICT was developed for the steel bar mill department of the metallurgical plant in Warsaw. The department was a modern one, intended for milling of round or square bars of noble steels.

2.1. System Description

The general organisation of the steel-bar mill is presented in Figure 1. The steel mill described here processed noble-steel billets into square or round bars. The system under discussion was of an informational/logical character and its objectives were to trace the bar milling process and to make it possible to run the process in a rather simple and fast manner.

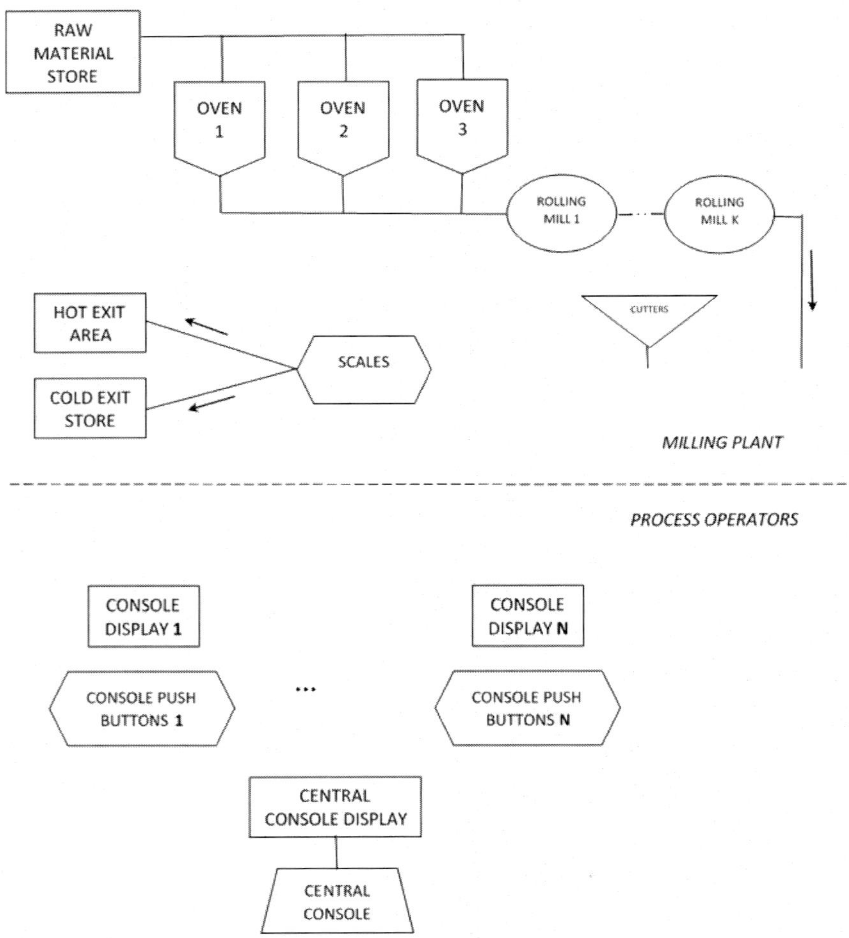

Figure 1. General organisation of the steel-bar mill.

During the production process, billets were transferred from the raw material store to the heating ovens 1 – 3 where they reached the milling temperature (above 1000°C). Heated-up billets passed from the ovens onto the reversible roller table that led them to the sequential rolling mills 1 – K, whereat the process medium was elongated and profiled to the required dimensions through milling and cutting. The finished product was weighed and transferred to the cold exit store (the cooling bank) or to the hot exit area (intermediate store prior to further processing). The milling lane was more than 200 m long and the equipment in the final part of the steel-bar mill enabled to achieve the rod run speed of 7 m/s. The processing actions were automated and required operator interventions (with the consoles 1 – N, provided with pushbuttons and numerical displays) only when the manufacturing process technology changed.

However, the rod-steel mill was destined for manufacture of noble-steel rods for small-lot commissions and the manufacturing process technology needed to be changed quite often, and the operators' interventions had to be frequent. Any operator had to recognise the end of the lot being milled and to set the equipment in a relevant centre for milling of the subsequent lot. The recognition of the end of lot was a difficult thing since billets or rods of various steel grades did not differ at all one from another; this necessitated high time spacing between sequential lots. Such a solution decreased, of course, the throughputs of the mills and, therefore, in the new facility, it was decided to introduce the automatic milling process for the tracing and detection of the ends of lots.

Due to various economic – technological considerations (including the fact that modern Polish interrupt-driven computer, Odra 1204 was to be available soon), it was concluded that the most effective system could be the one based on a digital computer installed in the central console house. It was the first computer automation system designed and developed in the country. The following objectives were defined for the system:

- to store the information concerning the milling process, entered once per a shift via the paper tape reader,

- to collect signals of billet or rod passages from operators or automatic sensors (photo-relays) and, on this basis, to determine the material distribution on the milling lane,
- to display the processing information at individual operators' stations, in accordance with the current material distribution along the milling lane,
- to measure the billet temperature values after leaving the heating ovens and before entry into the second milling cage, and to indicate possible deviations to the control engineer (dispatcher),
- to read and record the weight of the output material and of the final product,
- to produce manufacturing reports.

2.2. The Analytical Model

The computer system structure of the material traffic control system for the Bar-Mill of the Warsaw Metallurgical Plant is depicted in Figure 2.

In the system under discussion, the Central Processing Unit (CPU) interacted with the process under control via 5 units called channels 0 – 4.

The Channel zero constituted an internal part of any Odra 1204 computer and handled so called software interrupts (e.g., program errors). In addition, in the steel-mill system, a timer was included in the channel 0 to verify the appropriate action of photo-relay pairs and to check the material flow direction. For this purpose, at individual passages from various process nodes, photo-couple pairs were installed. The timer defined the time limit for the system to wait for the signal from the other photo-relay of the pair. The sequence of signals from the sensors determined the direction of the material flow at the photo-couple pairs. One signal only was an indication of no movement or a failed signal of the sensor.

Channel 1 connected the three well-known peripheral modules to CPU: the paper tape reader (TR), paper tape punch and the console teletype. During normal operation, this channel generated the interrupt signals informing of the TR readiness for reading a block and of completion of transfer via the channel.

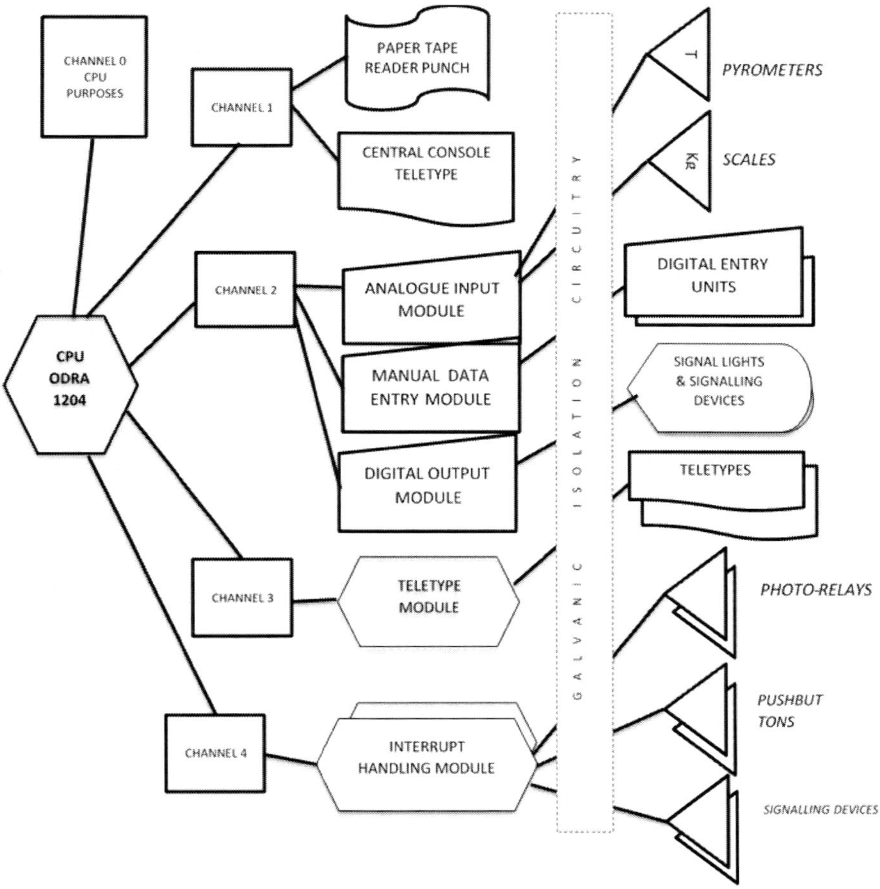

Figure 2. Computer system structure.

Via Channel 2, the CPU interacted with the analogue input module (AI), the manual data entry module and the digital output module. The AI module handled the cooperation with the relay-type selector, A/C converter and digital clock. Upon reception of initiating signals (from push-buttons for weights and from pyrometers for temperature values), the relevant measuring point numbers were sent to the selector, the points were selected and the measuring results converted into the digital code. Afterwards, the converter-ready interrupt was generated and called the relevant processing program. In addition, the module internal digital clock generated routine interrupt request signals used for time updating.

The manual data entry module served for cooperation with four digital entry units enabling manual inputting of information to the CPU. Via this module, the operators could generate interrupt requests resulting in reading the relevant data entry units. The transfers completed after circa 100 ms each and resulted in calling the relevant program handling the information read-in.

The digital output module served for outputting the process information to the steel-mill operators. The output devices included lights and signalling devices (including digital displays). The digital output module did not generate any interrupt requests.

Channel 3 enabled interworking of CPU with four teletypes operating in block transfer mode (similar to the paper tape reader and punch). Individual characters generated so called hesitation signals requesting transfer of the next character, using the technique called memory-cycle-stealing (a character was output during the instruction memory cycle, through prolongation of the cycle, allowing it to output the data character). After completion of a transfer of a complete data block, the relevant teletype generated the end-of-block interrupt request resulting in the movement of the teletype transfer queue.

Channel 4 was the process Interrupt Request (IR) handling the channel. The channel informed the CPU of important process events such as a billet or rod entry to the next processing station (the signals generated by photo-relays), operators' commands (from pushbuttons) and signalling device activation.

The galvanic isolation circuitry's purpose was to separate CPU and computer peripherals from the processing environment. They served their purposes very well but they were, logically, transparent devices and produced no IR-s nor Hesitation Requests (HR-s).

The basic request streams and the service time distributions for the steel-mill system are described below.

2.2.1. Software Interrupt Requests

The requests occurred when program failures happened, leading to the system switch-off (trip) requiring a restart. Therefore, they could not be considered in normal operation of the system.

2.2.2. Timer IR-s

Here, the instant of the timer IR was determined by the instant of reception of the signal of the first photo-relay of a pair installed in a given passage between processing stations. If the timer service station was empty when such an event occurred, it resulted in the next timer request after.

2.2.2.1. Note

The service time values were determined by the CPU service programs. Their distributions were stepwise, reflecting the finite number of paths through the programs, determined by the conditions in the rod steel-mill. It would be unfeasible to describe the conditional distributions for the overall plant. However, it was feasible to find the maximum possible generations of the service times and it was a honest assumption that the service times were equal to their possible maximum values; such an assumption corresponds to investigation of the system performance in the worst conditions possible to be generated in operation. In practice, such conditions could be produced and the system should operate appropriately in these worst conditions and the performance values at such conditions were the most interesting ones from an engineering point of view.

Therefore, in this book, the assumption that the program service times could be approximated by the durations of the longest paths possible in normal operation of the system was accepted for all service programs.

2.2.3. Paper Tape Reader IR

The paper tape reader in the steel-mill operated in so-called block transfer mode, whereby a portion of data was read in one instruction, without any IR-s generated inside the instruction period. After the next character was read by the reader, the latter generated an HR signal and the character value was entered into the core memory during the next available memory cycle, thus increasing the next instruction time of one memory cycle. Therefore, to ensure a safe performance evaluation, it was assumed that the instruction times were extended to all possible delays due to HR service for all peripherals operating in the block transfer mode (paper tape reader, paper tape punch, four digital entry units and four teletypes). This resulted in increasing of all theoretical service program times by ca. 0.5%.

After the portion of data was read-in, the reader generated the End-Of-Block (EOB) IR that called the reader data service program, with (as mentioned above) the constant processing time (here: 0.9 ms).

The next block transfer mode read IR could happen only after the minimum paper tape change operation (minimum duration here: 10 seconds) and after the expiry of a random variable describing the operator's thinking time (of the exponential character and the mean value λ_D, here: $\lambda_D = 240$ s). Thus, the input stream for the paper tape reader RI-s was defined by a random variable between the instant than an IR was generated and the instant that the next IR was generated. This random variable had the exponential distribution with the minimum interval during which no next paper tape reader IR could be generated.

2.2.4. Converter Ready IR

These IR-s were generated after a constant time (here: 20 ms) after relevant IR-s of pyrometers or read weight pushbuttons were accepted by the CPU. Service program times were constant, as mentioned above.

2.2.5. Read Digital Entry Unit IR-s

The IR-s were generated by the input store operators after completion of loading of production lots onto the roller feeders. The time spacing between two successive IR arrivals for one of the four digital entry units was described by the random variable of the exponential distribution with a minimum interval (the interval length was equal to the minimum time needed to complete the material lot involved and the expectance of the exponential part was λ_E, here set to 240 s)).

2.2.6. Teletype IR-s

Teletype operations were initiated by IR-s generated by the operators' end-of-lot pushbuttons. The distribution of the time between the instants that the successive IR-s from the relevant teletypes were produced was exponential (here: the expectancy was 240 s) with the minimum interval of the length of the shortest message transmission time (here: 1 s).

2.2.7. Photo-Relay IR-s

The photo-relays that were installed in pairs, as mentioned above, to increase the system reliability and/or to detect the bar or billet movement direction, were the basic material traffic sensors, detecting passes from one to the next processing station. There were K photo-relay pairs (here: K = 16). In normal processing conditions, all material pieces moved in one direction. The reverse movement was connected with material separation problems and resulted in less severe CPU load, thus less interesting from a performance evaluation point of view. For the first photo-relay of the k-th pair (k=1,...,K), the time between successive IR-s had the exponential distribution implied by the operators' actions, with an expectancy, $\frac{1}{\lambda_k}$, calculated from the maximum possible bar-mill throughput and local constraints, with the minimum interval I_k' implied by the time needed for the transition of one billet or bar under the k-th photo-relay pair. For the first photo-relay of a pair, the k-th IR service time, μ_k' (here $\mu_k' = 0.15$ ms) was small (activation of the timer in the channel No. 0 – to set-up the time limit for the IR from the second photo-relay of the given pair (k)). The time that the relevant IR was generated by the second photo-relay of the pair was defined by a constant value, λ_k'', after the instant that the IR of the first photo-relay was generated; this was determined, in the most severe case of the material traffic, by the maximum speed of the material piece at the photo-relay pair. In this case, the IR service time, μ_k'', was longer, covering recalculation of the material pieces at the two neighbouring processing stages (here, $\mu_k'' = 0.8$ ms).

2.2.8. Push-Button IR-s

The pushbuttons generated IR-s informing of some operators' commands to be entered into the CPU. The IR input stream was defined by the time between successive IR's, being a random variable of the exponential distribution of expectancy λ_p (here: λ_p = 240 s for each p = 1,…,P, were P was the total number of pushbuttons that could generate IR-s), with the minimum interval of constant duration I_p defined by local technical constraints (here: I_p = 10 s).

2.2.9. Signalling Device IR-s

The signalling devices producing IR-s were the ARDOFOT pyrometers signalling that a hot billet temperature may be measured. The time between successive instants that the IR-s were generated was defined by a random variable of the exponential distribution of expectancy determined by the maximum bar speed at the pyrometer, λ_a, a = 1,…, A, where A = ARDOFOT pyrometer number (here: A = 2 and λ_a = 4 s for a = 1,2), with the minimum interval of a constant value I_a, a = 1,2 (here: I_a = 4 s).

2.2.10. IR Service Priority System

The computer system was used, primarily, for material traffic control purposes and all sources of IR-s were of the same importance for the overall functioning of the steel bar mill. On the other hand, all CPU service programs were short and the system designers did not see any reason for interrupting some material traffic control programs by any IR-s requiring a more prompt response.

Considering this, it was decided to apply a non-pre-emptive priority system. In such a system, any IR accepted by CPU was served till the end and any IR-s received during that service time were handled on the rule: First-In-First-Out (FIFO).

Note: The non-pre-emptive priority system was an approximation only. In the CPU, Odra 1204, like in other digital computers, occurrences of IR-s were stored in 1-bit memories of the interrupt register. The time instant values when IR-s occurred were not stored in standard computers.

Therefore, the IR-s were found on the basis of some sequence. Usually (and in Odra 1204), it was done from the beginning of the interrupt register (Channel 0 interrupts) to the end (Channel 4 interrupts). Such operating regime is called round-robin mode.

2.3. Basic Performance Characteristics of the Steel-Bar Mill Computer System

The designers of the computer system (two young engineers) were interested in the complete distribution of each IR that may occur during operation in severe traffic conditions. However, such a solution was not feasible and it was decided to introduce some basic characteristics and measures of performance of the system.

First of all, the system must have operated in the real-time, i.e., it had to be capable of reception of each IR_i, $i = 1,\ldots,I$, where I was the total number of interrupts connected to the system, before the next IR_i for the same interrupt occurred. A convenient measure for this real-time operation requirement were the numbers of lost requests (not accepted before the next occurrence of IR_i during an operation period of length τ, $l_i(\tau)$). This measure was a pass / fail type: if, for any i and any τ, $l_i(\tau) > 0$, the system was not capable of operation in real-time, then it must have been redesigned or liquidated.

The maximum possible CPU busy time was the next measure of the system performance, of interest for the designers. For the system, the CPU busy time, τ_B, must have had a distribution concentrated on a finite interval, T_B; this was a prerequisite for the system operating in real-time. The knowledge of T_B was important for assessment of a possible system structure and function range expansion, without violation of the real-time operation requirements.

The maximum possible queue lengths of the timer, Q_t, converter, Q_c, manual data entry module, Q_m, and teletype module, Q_{tt}, made it possible to assess the operational quality of the devices.

Odra 1204 was a scalable multi-programmed computer and there were rather wide possibilities of expansion of the computer system configuration (e.g., core memory of a bigger capacity, external memories) and, at the same time, there was a demand for local computing power for, e.g., technological and managerial programs. Such programs could and were, in fact, executed at the lower priority level. To evaluate how it was possible to extend the system functionality of such secondary programs, it would be beneficial to evaluate the mean CPU busy factor, $E_B = \frac{T_B}{T}$, where E_B was the busy factor expectance, and T_B was the expectance of the busy period during the time period T. E_B was a secondary measure of the system performance.

The system designers tried to find support for evaluation of the characteristics and measure from mathematical science. It was in 1969.

2.4. Queuing System Aids Available for the Steel-Mill Project (until 1969)

The recognised father of the theory of queues, Agner Krarup Erlang, a Danish engineer who published his first paper in the field in 1909 (A.K. Erlang 1909). Later on, this branch of mathematics developed fast (University of Windsor 2013) and, in 1969, when the two steel rod-mill traffic control system designers were interested in investigating their solutions, the monograph by Lajos Takacs was considered the book available for the designers, describing best the then-current development of the theory of queues (L. Takacs 1962) (R. G. Miller 1964).

The control system designers appreciated very much the fact that the theory of queues investigated systems of requests for service, waiting in queues for service. However, the devil was in the detail.

2.4.1. The Input Stream

The reference book (L. Takacs 1962) described principally the case of single server systems corresponding to the steel-bar mill system, where the CPU was the single server of all requests for service (interrupt requests) generated by the plant under control. However, the definition of the input stream, i.e., the server load with the requests for services in the reference book, was unacceptable for the real-life conditions of the steel mill. In the book by L. Takacs, as well as in all works on the theory of queues known to the designers of the steel-mill material traffic control system at that time, the service request loads from any input sources were defined by the request for service inter-arrival times, the independent stochastic variables of the exponential distribution. The assumptions of the statistical independence and the exponential character of the times between successive arrivals of requests for service made it possible to substitute all the sources of requests for service by a single one, also of an exponential distribution of the inter-arrival times. This made it possible to simplify, to a high extent, calculation of the dependent variables investigated by the theory of queues.

However, the assumptions did not hold in the material traffic control system:

- For the first photo-relays of the pairs installed between the mill process stations, the IR inter-arrival time distribution was exponential (which modelled rather well the thinking time of the relevant operator) with the minimum interval corresponding the minimum time that was needed for a billet or bar to pass through the process station, and not exponential.
- In no case could the minimum interval of the distributions be ignored since the distribution of the service time for the first photo-relay of any pair had to be concentrated within the relevant minimum interval; this was the primary real-time operation requirement for the system under investigation.
- For the second photo-relays of the pairs, the requests for services arrived after a time period determined by the maximum speed of billets or rods at the relevant process stations after their arrival (an approximation ensuring the performance conditions at the heaviest conditions of the system service load); therefore, the independence of the inter-arrival times could not be assumed.

- For the paper tape reader and punch, and for the teletypes, the next arrival of any request for service, IR, happened after a time period after the instant that the service of the relevant previous IR was terminated; the time period being described rather well by a random variable of the exponential distribution (approximating well the operator's thinking time) with the minimum interval (describing the peripheral inoperability period after completion of the previous service action). This action should not be approximated by one determined from the instant the previous IR service was completed until the instant that the next IR arrived, since the mechanism governing there was the earliest known realisation of a protection of computer systems against losing requests for service, known as the flow control.

2.4.2. Service Times

For the queuing systems investigated in the book by L. Takacs, the exponential service was assumed in the basic Markov cases. This assumption was false for the steel-bar mill system since:

- Most services realised by programs and service time distributions were discrete. Taking into consideration that the steel-rod system should be investigated at the worst service conditions, the service times could be assumed as constant and equal to the execution time of the longest path in the relevant program.

2.4.3. Primary Stochastic Variables under Study

The primary stochastic variables under study in the book by L. Takacs were: the waiting time of a customer (IR), the queue size and the server busy time. The stochastic variables were interesting for the Designers also. However, though the researchers were interested very much in full distributions of the primary stochastic variables, they were not able to find them; therefore they limited their research to a characteristic of the distributions, the expected value (the mean value).

In the book An Introduction To Probability Theory and Its Applications (W. Feller 1957, 1971), recognised as the best monograph on the probability of that time, William Feller warned against making use of the mean value for the queuing systems. He showed (Volume II, Chapter VI, § 9) some cases that the variance values for a simple queuing process were many times higher than the mean values (e.g., the variance values of 225 and 1900 for the expected values of 5 and 10, respectively). This meant that distributions of such random variables had long tails and could not be characterised well by their expected values. In addition, the Designers were interested, first of all, in the intervals in which the random variables were concentrated. The rule was: an engineer must know that the random variables may not exceed some values. And, at the assumptions of the queuing theory of that time, the basic random variable, the waiting time of a customer (IR) was not concentrated in any finite interval.

The only primary stochastic variable being studied for which the expected value was interesting for the Designers was the server busy time. This mean value would make it possible to assess the computing power that could be assigned to extra tasks of technological computing to be executed at a lower pre-emptive resume priority level with respect to the basic steel-bar mill system tasks described above.

Perhaps the most important variable characterising the steel-bar mill system capability of the real-time operation was the number of lost requests (IR). In no case should it be confused with the number of lost arrivals being studied by Agner Krarup Erlang (A. K. Erlang 1909). The number of lost IRs that was of interest to the Designers decided of the system success or failure: if it were bigger that 0, the system could not work in real-time and should be dismantled. So, if a single IR were lost, the distribution of the billets and rods along the process lane, stored in CPU, would be distorted, resulting in high recovery costs exceeding any savings provided by the system.

The queuing system methods available then (and now) made it not possible to assess this variable.

Some other references available for the Designers at that time were: (B. Avi-Itzak and P. Naor 1964, D.P. Gaver 1967, L. Kleinrock 1967, G.K.

Manacher 1967, J. E. Shemer 1967, L. Takacs 1960). All of them refer to the domain of the computer science but they repeat the inadequacy of assumptions of queuing theory, discussed above.

2.4.4. Final Comments

After World War II, the Wroclaw school of mathematics was led by Professor Hugo Dyonizy Steinhaus whose approach to applications of mathematics may be depicted by the following example: some biologists asked him for help in counting live bacteria under a microscope. The task was difficult since bacteria were moving. Professor Steinhaus advised: etch a grid and count the number of crossings, and he then provided some mathematics enabling calculation of the sample size. But, what he was proud of was the idea of the grid he devised by him. The Professor and his school of mathematics applied a similar approach to upgrading and educating mathematics students: they prepared people with wide Renaissance knowledge, able to solve problems irrespectively of whether they were strictly mathematical. And such mathematicians were the ones actually needed in the pioneering era of Polish computers, in the conditions of various unjust embargoes imposed on computer systems and components by well developed countries.

An excellent example of such a mathematician was the one who was allotted the task of preparation of magnetic drum manufacture. The magnetic powder needed for drums was not available in the market. So he bought magnetic tapes, immersed them in acetone and dried, thus obtaining the needed powder (R. Zuber 2017).

Having a staff of such powerful mathematicians was a prerequisite of the success of the first Polish manufacturer of computers (Elwro) established in 1959, that launched production of the first Polish computer in 1962 and the very then-modern, interrupt-driven computer Odra 1204, applied in the steel-mill system in 1967, discussed in the present cection.

Odra 1204 was a milestone, terminating the Information and Communication Technology (ICT) pioneering era in Elwro. Unfortunately, at the end of the era, the character of the Wroclaw school of mathematics changed dramatically. The successors of Prof. Steinhaus were not apt at solving the general problems of the customers, limiting their interest to strictly mathematical ones.

2.4.4.1. An Example

Deep-sea fishermen visited a Prof. Steinhaus successor several years later, asking for help with the assessment of shoal sizes on the basis of shoal diameters recorded. The successor replied that, basing on the diameter measurements, it was not possible to assess shoal sizes and during a big conference on applications of mathematics, laughed at the fishermen for not being capable of formulation of a mathematical problem, (Szeligi, 1977).

Most probably, Prof. Steinhaus with the fishermen would have analysed probable shapes of shoals and would have produced some approximations of the shoal sizes. In addition, in the conditions of the Communist economy, the fishermen had to do some work, most probably hard, to arrange for money for the mathematical support and laughing at them was very, very inappropriate.

2.4.4.2. A Performance Evaluation Example

The same successor took a look into the description of the steel-bar mill system, developed by the performance evaluation project leading designer (the Leader) and commented: The input stream is Poisson, the service is exponential; there is nothing to do – the problem has been solved. This was completely false – see the simplified analytical model above in the present Section. Till now, after 50 years, the problems presented in this section have not been solved by the queuing system theory, and the attitude of the successor is a proof of another inappropriate approach of some mathematicians: making up systems under investigation fit to the assumptions, making it possible for the mathematicians to 'solve' the problems.

Considering the fact that the queuing system theory was not helpful in investigating the steel-mill system performance, the Leader decided to do it using the system simulation (Monte Carlo) methods.

2.5. Simulation Aids Available for the Steel-Mill System (till 1969)

The queuing system methods failed not only in the case of the steel-bar mill system, and so many researchers used the computer simulation techniques. At the turn of the nineteen-sixties, the basic book available for the designers and describing the available simulation aids and/or methods was *The Monte Carlo Method: The Method of Statistical Trials* (A. P. Buslenko et al. 1967).

For performance evaluation of various computer systems, a method called the event-driven simulation, formulated several years later, was used in most cases. The method made use of the *next event instant table*, defining the instants of the next occurrences of important events such as request arrivals, or completions of service, or a service phase. The main simulation program looked for the nearest event instant and operated the model referring to the event. When the model passed control back to the main program, the procedure was repeated up to the end of the simulation run.

Simulation of random variables of various distribution was based upon the so-called generator of the pseudo-random numbers of the Uniform distribution. To ensure high simulation quality, measured by the quotient of the simulated object time and the simulation time, especially for the case of computer control systems where, in general, the events were frequent and the service times low, the pseudo-random number generator must be very fast.

Buslenko enumerated several pseudo-random number generators of which the additive ones were the most often used due to their high speed. However, for the basic generator of this type, realising the algorithm:

$$x := x_0 + x_1;\, x_0 = x_1;\, x_1 := x_2 \qquad (1),$$

the subsequent realisations of the pseudo-random were highly correlated, which was harmful to the simulation results. However, due to a mistake in the program preparation process, the algorithm was changed to:

$x := x_0 + 2x_1; x_0 = x_1; x_1 := x_2$ (2)

The algorithm (2) worked very well: the figure of 2 eliminated the correlation between subsequent realisations of the pseudo-random numbers, and the generator remained almost so fast as that realising the algorithm (1). The multiplication by 2 was realised with the short instruction of movement to the left. The algorithm (2) was popular among Wroclaw researchers and practitioners involved in computer simulation.

With regard to generation of random variables, Buslenko specified a method called *the sectional approximation of the distribution density* described below for the Poisson distribution:

A finite interval of the random variable should be divided with the a_k numbers into n sections so that the probability of hitting the interval (a_k, a_{k+1}) was equal to $\frac{1}{n}$. Thus:

$$\int_{a_k}^{a_{k+1}} f(x)dx = \frac{1}{n}$$

for the Poisson distribution of intensity: λ: $f(x) = \lambda e^{-\lambda x}$; therefore:

$$\int_{a_k}^{a_{k+1}} \lambda e^{\lambda x}\, dx = \frac{1}{n}, a_1 = 0 => a_{k+1} = -\frac{\ln(e^{-\lambda a_k} - \frac{1}{n})}{\lambda}; \; k = 1, \dots, n \quad (3)$$

A program realising (3) computed the distribution density table which was read together with the simulation program data and used by the random variable computing routine during simulation runs. The routine fetched the pseudo-random number of the Uniform distribution, r, the highest bits of which constituted the address, k, in the density table. The variable being generated, v, was determined from the formula (4):

$v := a_k + (a_{k+1} - a_k)\, r_1$ (4)

where a_k and a_{k+1} were the successive entries of the table and r_1 was another pseudo-random number of the Uniform distribution, in the interval (0,1).

At the turn of the nineteen-sixties, no event-driven simulation systems were available for designers. This represented no major problem: the Leader, who was supposed to investigate the steel-mill system performance, designed some 40% of the specialised system hardware and some 60% of its software, and performed roughly 50% of hardware testing/commissioning and software debugging work. Therefore, he was predisposed to the simulation of the system he had a detailed knowledge of. In addition, the steel-mill material traffic control systems were originally Polish, designed by a local metallurgical industry design office, and it would be very improbable to find similar simulation models. And even if any such models existed, they would be protected by informal embargoes imposed by many Western researchers during the Cold War era.

On the other hand, the general-purpose simulation aids like the table of important event instant processing program (the main loop) and the random number generators proposed by N. P. Buslenko et al. (1967) were simple and described in a comprehensive way, and a professional computer control system designer and programmer could attack the problems without any qualms. Such an individual approach to system simulation could be beneficial to the quality of the simulation process, since it made it possible to devise faster programs.

The steel-mill control system performance evaluation/prediction was not foreseen in the project. Therefore, it had to be performed on the voluntary basis (the Polish notion of *praca spoleczna* - work for the society - seems to be much more appropriate here) and the Leader decided to do it within the framework of his graduation project in mathematics, undertaken in the University of Wroclaw.

2.6. Simulation Model Developed by the Leader

2.6.1. Introductory Remarks

The only computer available for the Leader for simulation studies was the same Odra 1204 that was applied for development of the rod-steel mill material traffic control system itself. Due to the expert knowledge of assembler language programming possessed by the Leader, it was realistic to develop the simulation system (Simulator 1) with use of the Odra 1204 assembly language JAS (Wikipedia 2012) thus enabling the achievement of a much better simulation quality than had been possible, even with a very efficient high level language compiler Algol 1204 (K. Jerzykiewicz and J. Szczepkowicz 1970), developed some time later.

2.6.2. General Structure of Simulator 1

The general structure of the steel-mill material traffic control system is depicted in Figure 3.

The initial action routine, X_{in}, when entered, read the simulation input data and organised the current version of the control system simulation experiment. This covered the relations between the $\{\tau_1^n, \ldots, \tau_L^n\}$ vector components (IR-s of next important component instants) and the parameters of the distributions of the times between arrivals of requests for service. The initial value of the $\{\tau_1^n, \ldots, \tau_L^n\}$ vector needed be also defined since the simple zeroing of all its component could produce IR traffic conditions that were impossible in normal operation of the process under simulation.

The routine M_0, the main loop of Simulator 1, modelled the service by the basic server (the central processing unit) and evaluated the parameters of this service. The main loop operated on the random vector $\{\tau_1^n, \ldots, \tau_L^n\}$, computed the required characteristics on the basis of the sequence of realisations of this vector.

The commencement of service of the *k*-th *IR* ($k = 1, \ldots, L$) was modelled by the M_k subroutine that determined the required the *k*-th *IR* service time and computed the new realisation of the $\{\tau_1^n, \ldots, \tau_L^n\}$ vector. This made it possible to simulate dependent IR streams, as in the case of photo-relay pairs, or multi-phase service, as for the paper-tape reader and punch or teletypes. In addition, the subroutines verified if no signals were lost, and tested the possible multiphase service. The required service times, generated in the IR simulation subroutines, and the values of the $\{\tau_1^n,\ldots,\tau_L^n\}$ vector made it possible to assess, in the main loop, the quality of service realised by the basic server (CPU). Therefore, in the main loop, the sojourn times of the individual IR-s at the basic server were computed, and the actions enabling assessment of the relevant service characteristics (the maximum sojourn times, sojourn time summarising, IR number counting). The main loop, M_0, was executed through the defined simulation time period and the final actions, X_{out}, were fulfilled next. The latter consisted of the editing of the results and outputting them in a form suitable for further analysis.

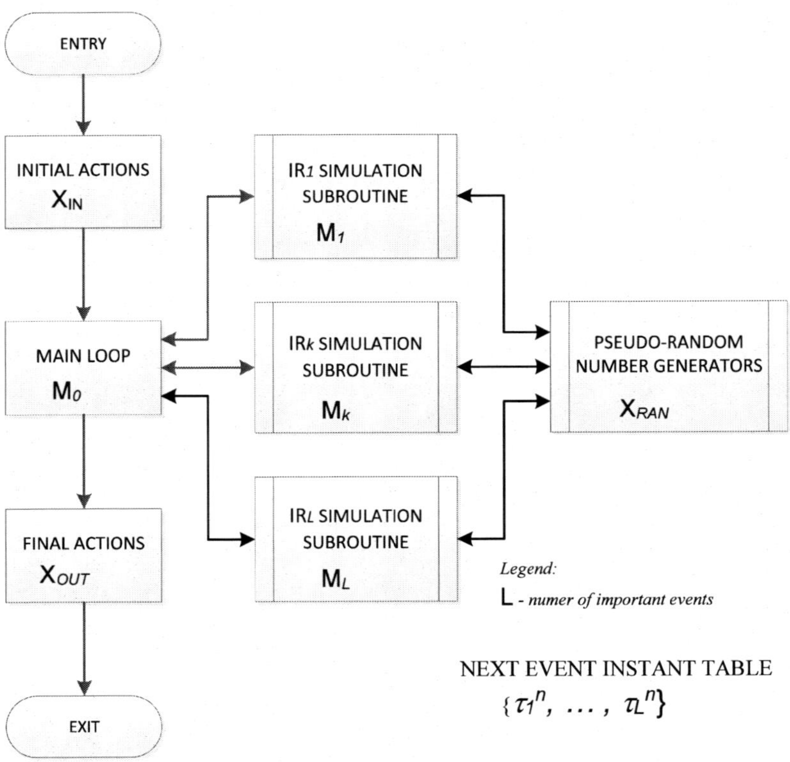

Figure 3. General diagram of Simulator 1.

The modular structure of Simulator 1 made the investigation of the system configurations under design a rather easy task. An appropriate version of the main loop, the initial actions and the final actions could be chosen and the IR simulation routines should be set up, writing, possibly, some subroutines not included in an earlier library. Then, the selected program set could be entered into the internal computer memory and operated on the data determining the input stream parameters and service times. Modification of the data made it possible to investigate the service quality for changed input streams or service times thus enabling comparisons of various configurations, to define the intensity limits for input streams for which the system under investigation would still meet the requirements for the real-time operation, or the allowable service times for individual IR-s (i.e., the limits within which the system tasks may be expanded).

The algorithms that would be executed by individual components of Simulator 1 have been presented below.

2.6.3. The Main Loop of Simulator 1

The flow diagram of the main loop of Simulator 1 is depicted in Figure 4.

The main loop simulated service by the steel-bar mill material traffic control central processing unit, and performed statistics that enabled it to assess the service quality. The basic objective was to verify that the computing power of CPU made it possible to operate in the real-time, i.e., that for $k = 1,\ldots,L$, the IR_k sojourn time was lower than some positive limit, ν_k^*, defined by the process under control.

In the steel-bar mill material traffic control system under investigation, all IR-s were of the same urgency, and service times were rather small. Therefore, the simplest possible service mechanism available for the Odra 1204 computer could be applied – the non-pre-emptive priority discipline. For this mechanism, service of any request IR_k could not be interrupted even if a request of a higher priority, IR_m, $1 <= m < k$ arrived. Therefore, the sojourn time of the k-th IR at the basic server (CPU), ν_k, was equal to the sum of the service waiting time, η_{ko}. and the service time, χ_{ko}.

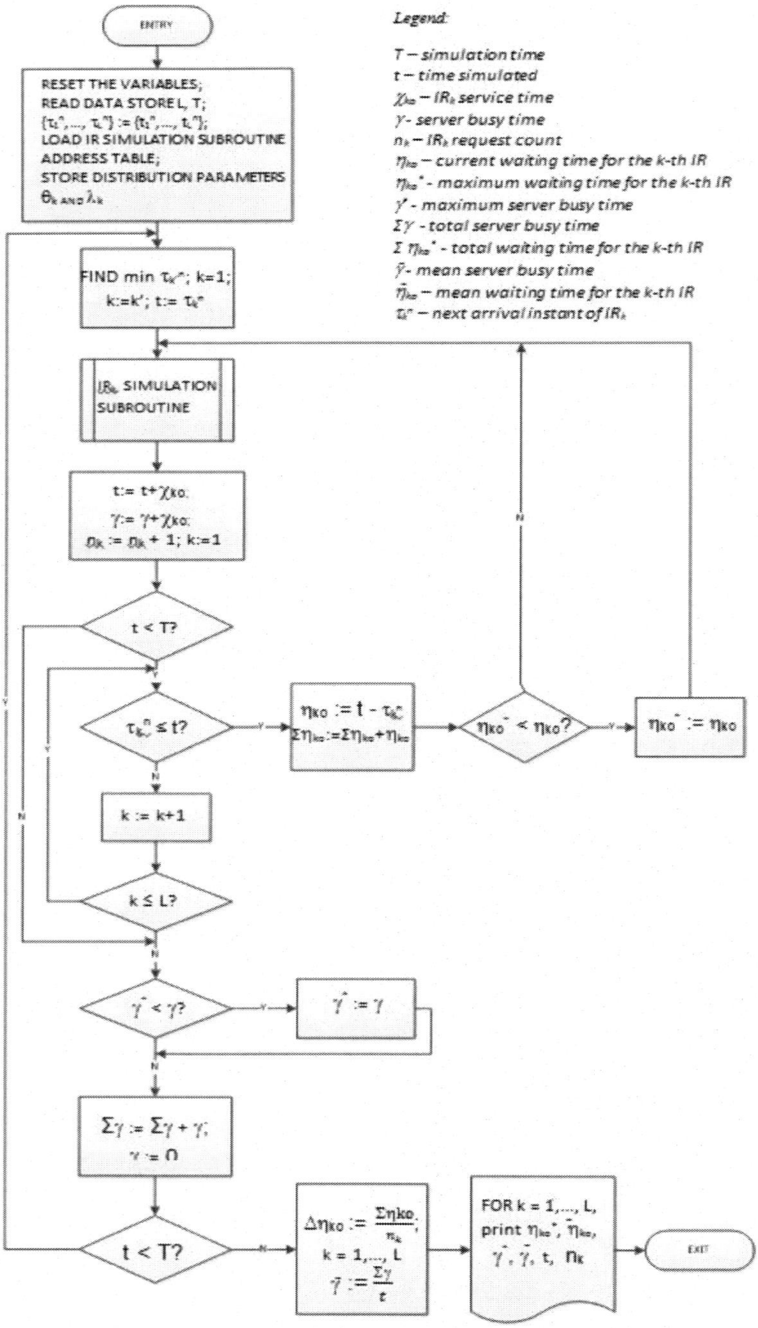

Figure 4. The main loop of Simulator 1.

The service time distributions were given so it was necessary to assess the service waiting times in order to deteremine the sojourn times. Taking this into consideration, the objective of the main loop algorithm could be reduced to computing the maximum waiting times for service of CPU, η_{ko}^{*}. In accordance with the assumptions specified in this sub-chapter, the algorithm should calculate, additionally, the mean waiting times for the IR-s, the mean occupancy and the maximum busy time of the basic server.

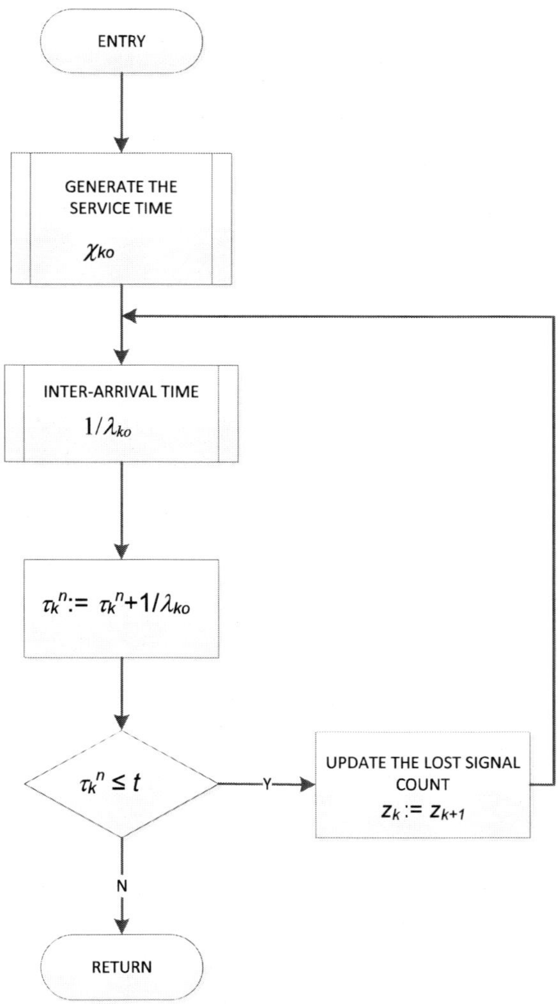

Figure 5. Simulation of IR-s of independent input streams.

The initial action routine reset the Simulator, and read and stored simulation run data: the number of IR-s, simulation time, next event instant vector-table, defined the simulation configuration, and the parameters of the distributions of the variables determining the next arrival of the same or other IR (of exponential distributions with minimum intervals).

The flow diagram of simulation of the Interrupt Requests of independent input streams is depicted in Figure 5.

The main loop proper found the IR number to be simulated through the analysis of the next event instant vector, and called the relevant simulation subroutine. After the return, the time simulated, server busy time and the interrupt request time were updated.

Next, the requests that could have arrived during service of the *k*-th one were looked for. The main loop did not model this on a FIFO (First In First Out) basis, but used a round-robin mechanism, where the IR-s were scanned in the sequence of their numbers.

After elapse of the simulation time, Simulator 1 computed the mean waiting times, the mean server busy time and printed the simulation results.

2.6.4. IR_k Simulation Subroutines

2.6.4.1. Single-Phase Service, Independent Input Stream

The simplest case of the IR simulation routines (single-phase service, independent input stream) is shown in Figure 5. The routine generated a realisation of the service time and of the inter-arrival time (or times, if some IR_k requests had been lost; in such case, the lost signal count was updated).

2.6.4.2. Interrupt Requests with Dependent Input Streams

Examples of IR-s of that type are two subsequent photo-relay pairs or teletype interrupt requests where some *k*-th *IR* arrival determined the arrival instant of some other *k'*-th *IR*.

The flow diagram of the IR simulation algorithm for the dependent input stream case is shown in Figures 6.a (initial part), 6.b (middle part), and 6.c (final part).

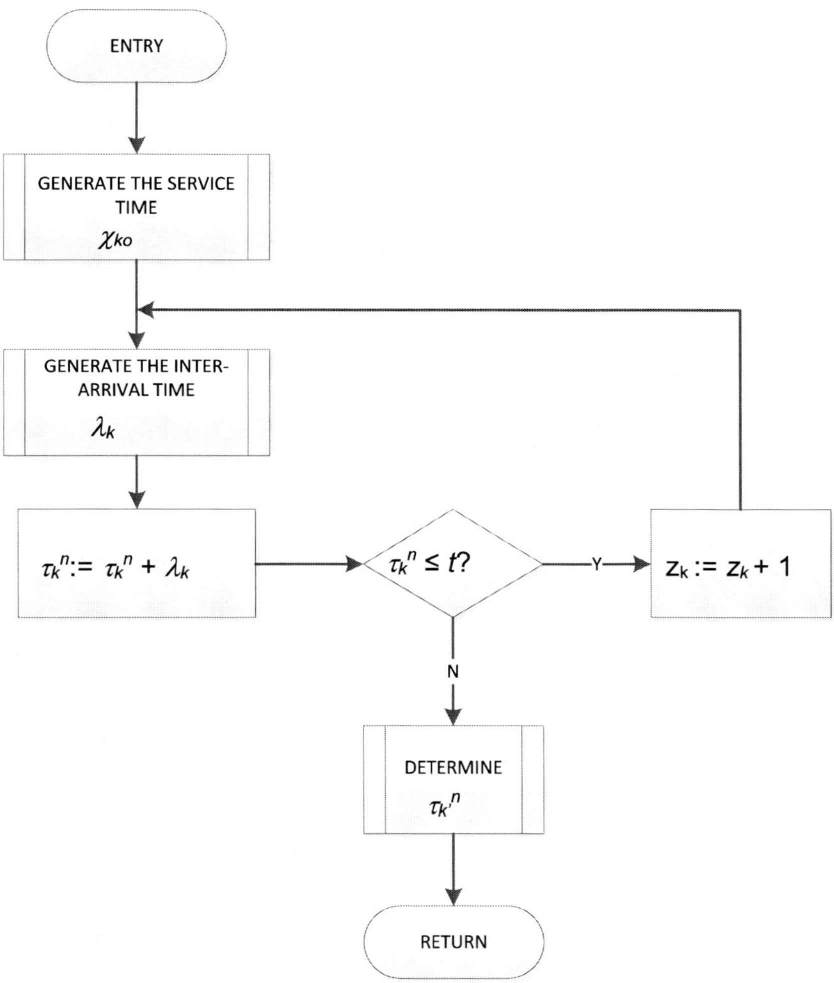

Figure 6a. IR simulation algorithm for the dependent input stream case (initial part).

The algorithm is the same as that used for the independent stream case (see Figure 5 above) except for the box "Determine $\tau_{k'}^n$" at the subprogram end. The box determines the time to the arrival of the *k'*-th *IR*. For the *k'*-th component of the next event instant vector that was smaller than the simulation time, the buffered value of the *k'*-th *IR* was set to that of the *k*-th *IR* plus the generated value of the time between arrivals of the *k'*-the and *k*-th *IR*-s. In the other case (no buffered *k'*-th *IR*), the next event component of the *k'*-th request was defined in such a way.

The *k'*-th simulation subroutine computed the buffered value of the next *k'*-th *IR* instant, checked for a signal loss and, possibly, incremented the *k'*-th IR lost signal count, and substituted the actual instant by the buffered one, and set the latter to 'infinity' (a value bigger than the simulation period, *T*).

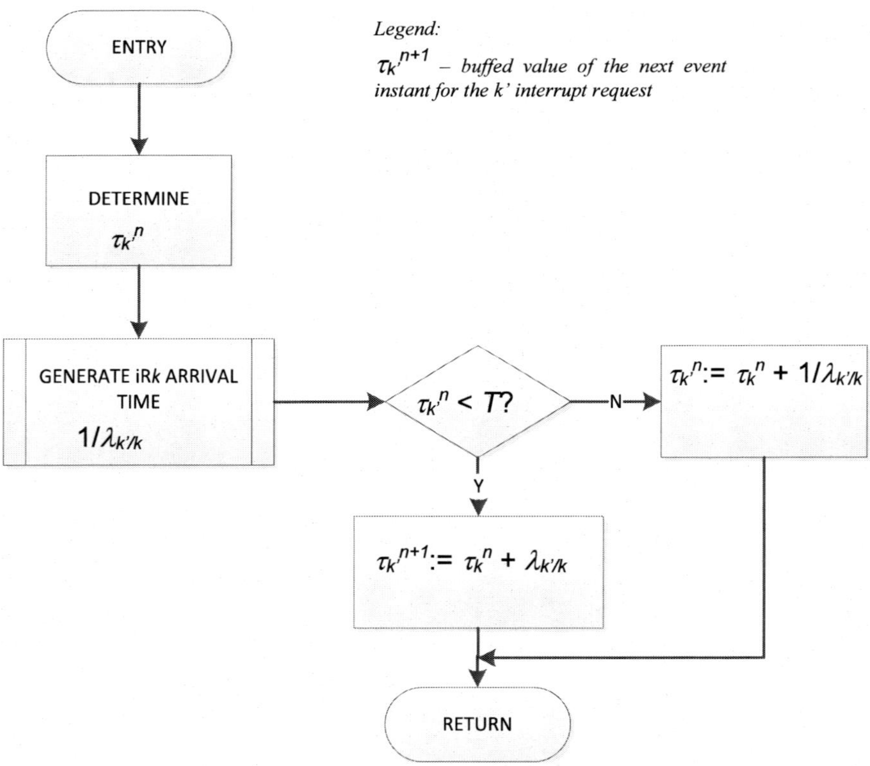

Figure 6b. IR simulation algorithm for the dependent input stream case (middle part).

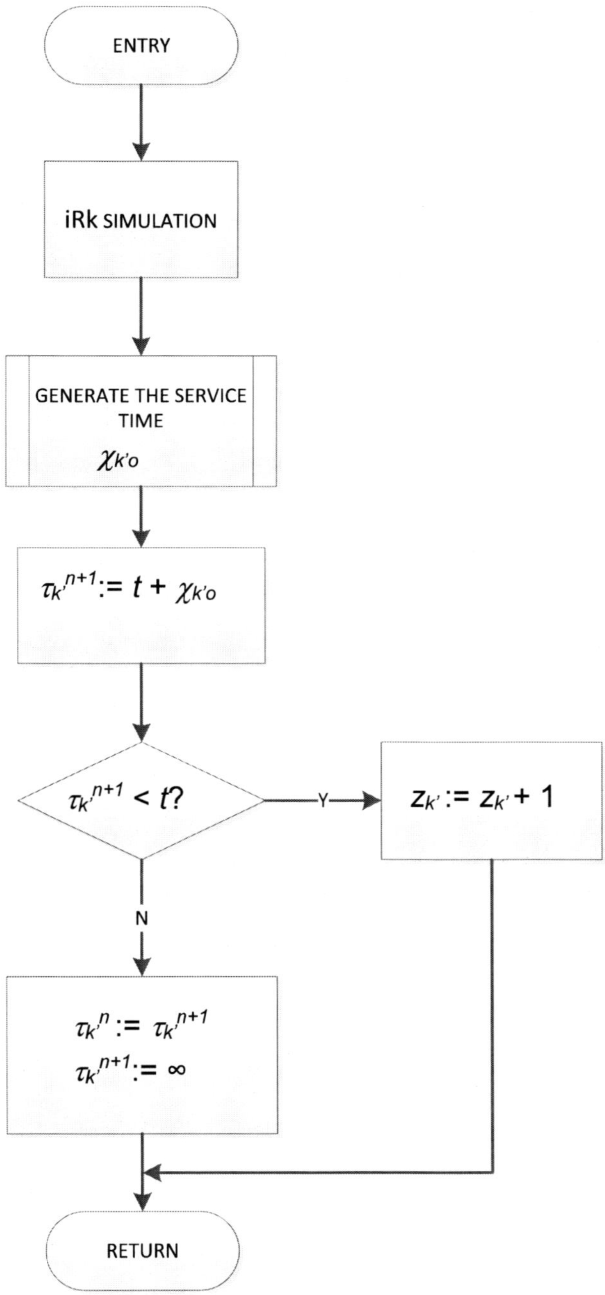

Figure 6c. IR simulation algorithm for the dependent input stream case (final part).

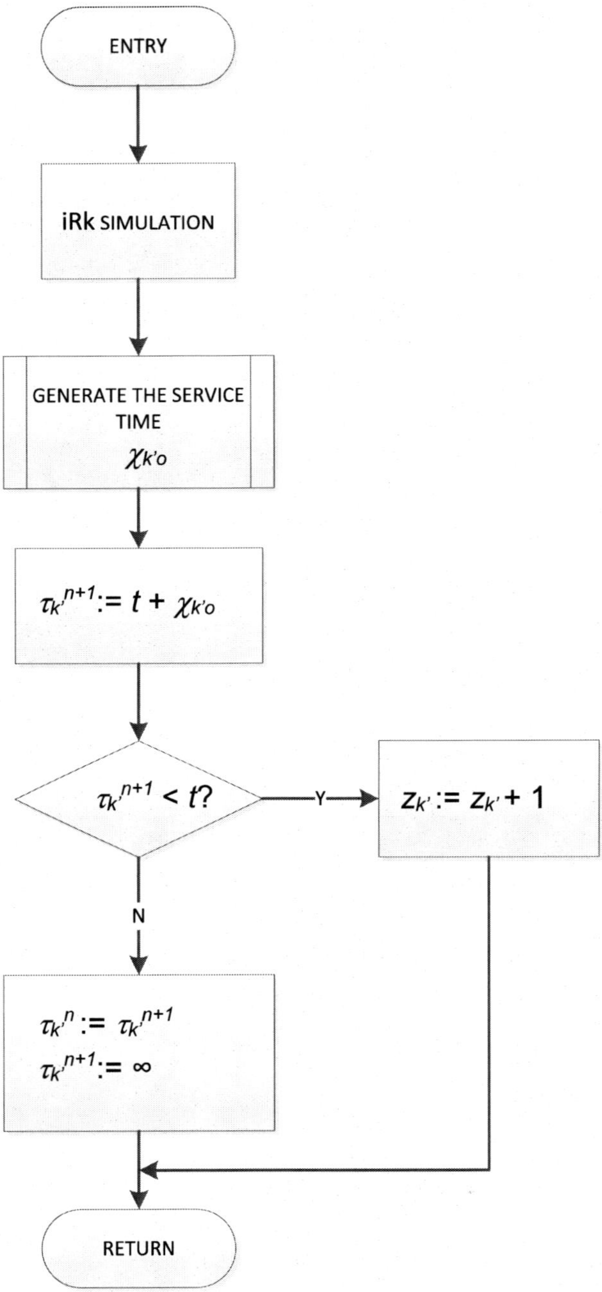

Figure 7a. Simulation of IR-s and secondary servers: group service (the initial part).

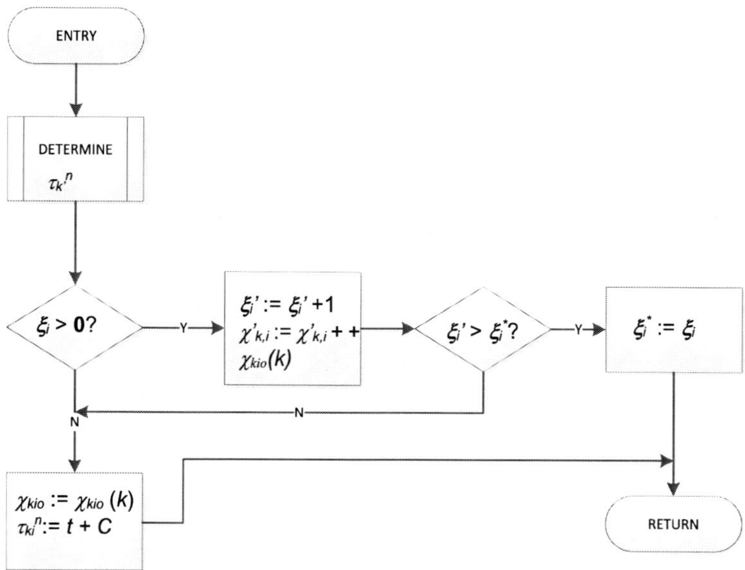

Figure 7b. Simulation of IR-s and secondary servers: group service (the middle part).

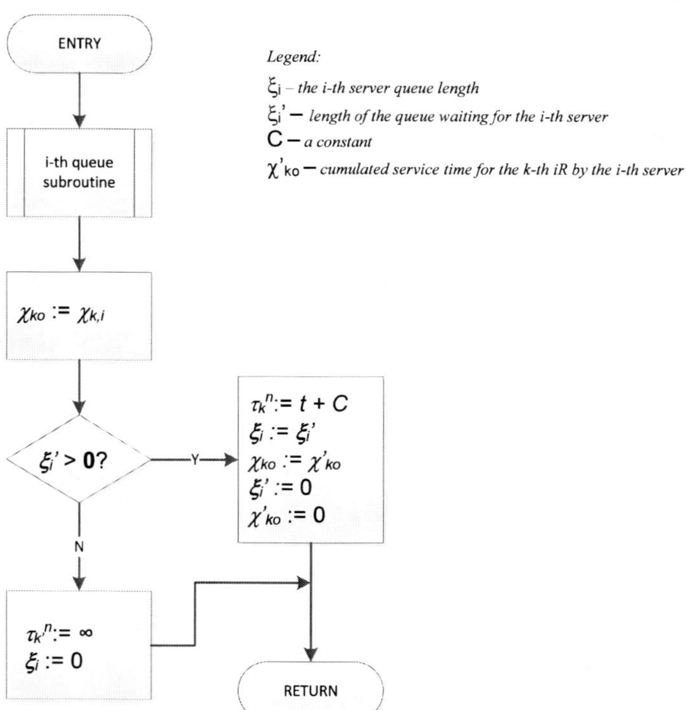

Figure 7c. Simulation of IR-s and secondary servers: group service (the final part).

2.6.4.3. Simulation of IR-s and Secondary Servers – Group Service

In the steel-bar mill, a transit of a billet or bar from one process station to the next one was signalled by photoelectrical sensors (photo-relays) installed in pairs for the detection of the movement direction and for increasing detection-system reliability. The traffic flow control problem was solved as follows: The photo-relay signals operated individual flip-flops in the external interrupt systems. When the first signal was detected, it would be stored and some delay would be provided to enable operation of the other sensor. For this purpose, the CPU timer was used. After some time, the IR of the other photo-relay would arrive, detected and stored by the CPU. The IR associated with the signal resulted in the determination of the movement direction, and updated the material distribution. There was a single timer in the CPU and, thus, a queue for service was organised.

The flow diagram of the algorithm is presented in Figure 7a (the initial part), 7b (the middle part) and 7c (the final part). The first part presents the standard procedure of the k-th *IR* simulation routine. Next, the next instant of the k'-th *IR* was determined. If the i-th server was busy, the request was entered into the queue waiting for the i-th server of th k-th *IR* and the queue length was updated; if not, it was entered into the i-the server service station.

The i-th queue subroutine moved the possible queue of the requests waiting for the i-th server, or reset the i-th server service station queue.

2.6.4.4. Simulation of IR-s and Secondary Servers – FIFO Service

The steel-bar mill material traffic control system checked the hot billet temperature prior to successive passages to the primary mill and was used to indicate possible deviations to the central steel-mill control engineer and the mill operator. The temperature values were measured with radiation-type pyrometers installed along the milling lane.

The flow diagram of IR-s and secondary server simulation algorithm for the FIFO case are presented in Figures 8.a (the initial part), 8.b (the middle part) and c (the final part).

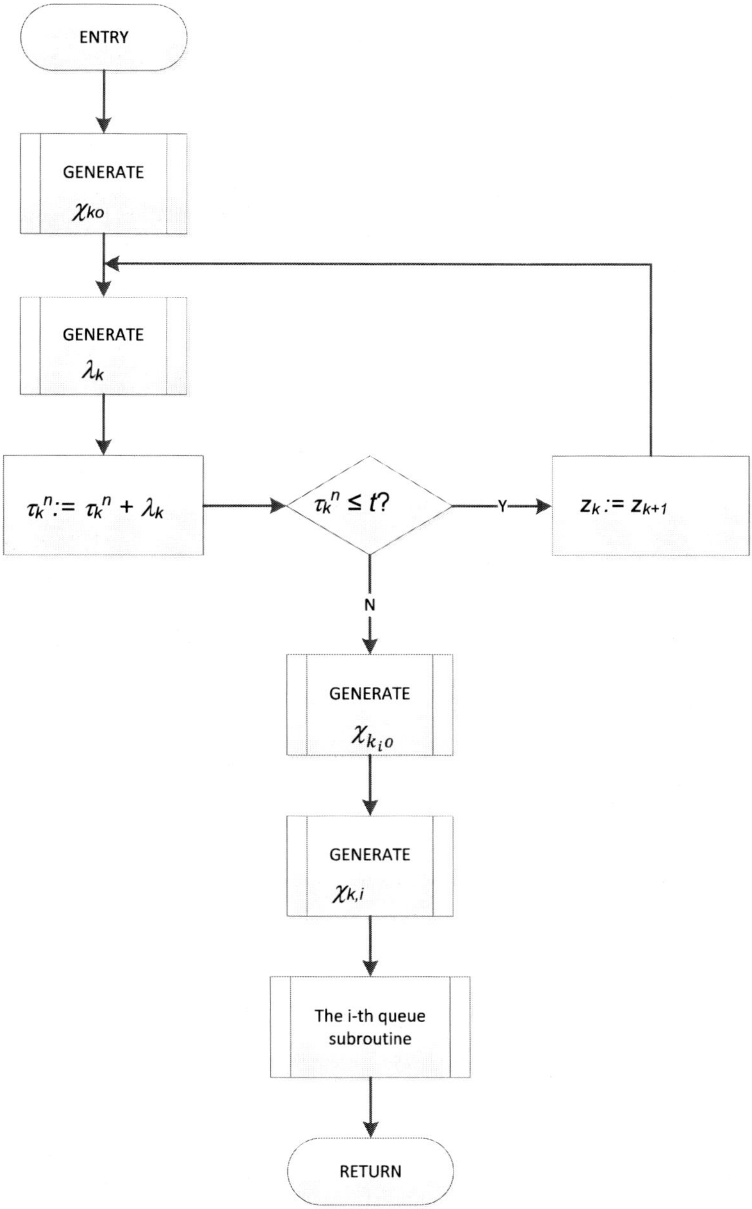

Figure 8a. The flow diagram of IR-s and secondary server simulation algorithm for the FIFO case (the initial part).

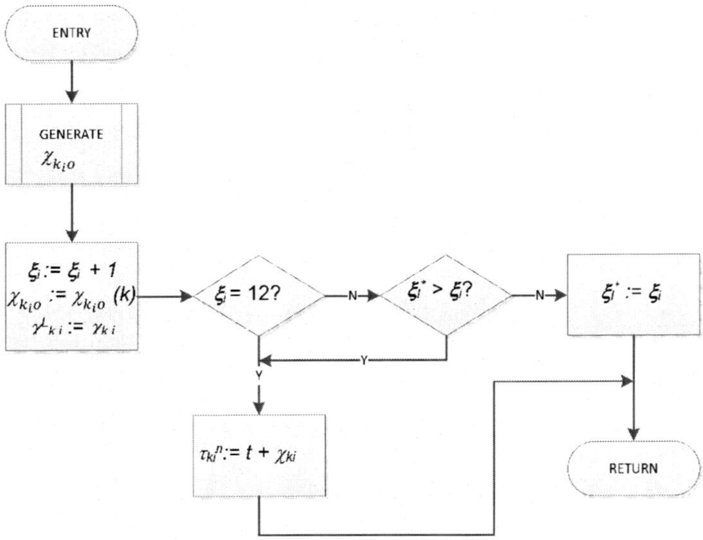

Figure 8b. The flow diagram of IR-s and secondary server simulation algorithm for the FIFO case (the middle part).

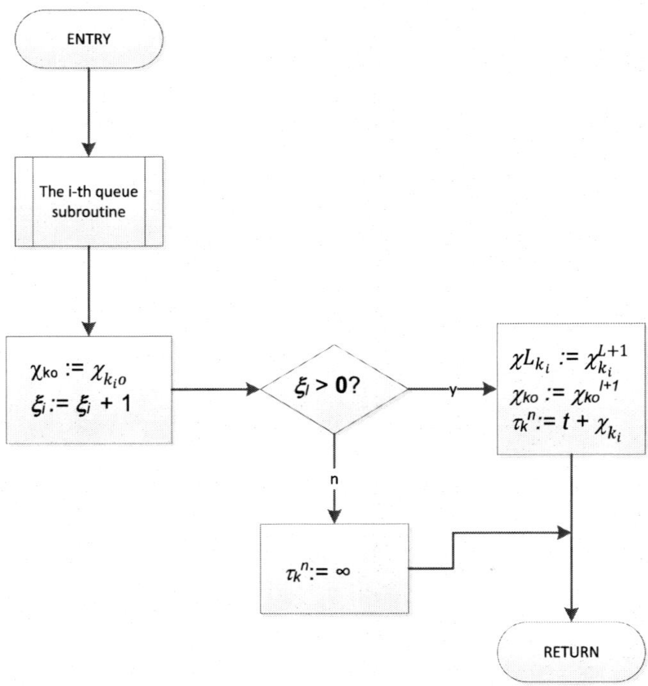

Figure 8c. The flow diagram of IR-s and secondary server simulation algorithm for the FIFO case (the final part).

In the first part, the algorithm simulated the standard IR-s of independent input streams. Next, it generated the value of the k_i-th IR service time by the basic server (CPU), where the k_{io} is the number of the secondary request indicating the end of service of the *k*-th *IR* by the *i*-th secondary server. The subroutine updated the maximum queue length for the i-th secondary server and computed the next event instant for the k_i-the IR. If there was a queue for the i-th server, the queue was shifted by 1 position and the next event instant vector component for the k-th IR was increased by the k_i IR service time or, in the other case, was set to 'infinity' (a value bigger than the simulation time, T).

2.6.5. Final Remarks

The cases A up to D describe all service mechanisms applied in the steel-mill material traffic control system. The sequences of conditional events in other applications may be more complex. However, the rule used in generating such streams was the same: the basic event sequence was generated and, by jumping to relevant subroutines, the dependent stream realisations were obtained. With regard to service by the secondary servers, the two models discussed above were most popular in computer control systems (omitting the case where one secondary server served only one IR; this case is covered by Section b above).

When designing and developing computer control system simulation programs, an important rule should be kept in mind: the programs should map the reality in detail but, at the same time, they should be as simple and fast as possible in order that various possible hardware and software configurations may be investigated within a limited program operation time. A single program run needed thousands or even hundreds of thousands of main loop passes, so it was valuable to think about the necessity of use of any instruction. The subroutines could not be too long so that they, complete with the program data, could be located in the working memory since the use of external memories would increase the simulation time to a great extent.

2.6.6. Random Number Generators

The generators of pseudo-random numbers of the Uniform and Poisson distributions, applied in the steel-bar mill control system simulation project, are discussed in the subchapter: Available simulation aids above.

The two basic random number generators applied in the simulation project for the steel-bar mill computer control system are described below.

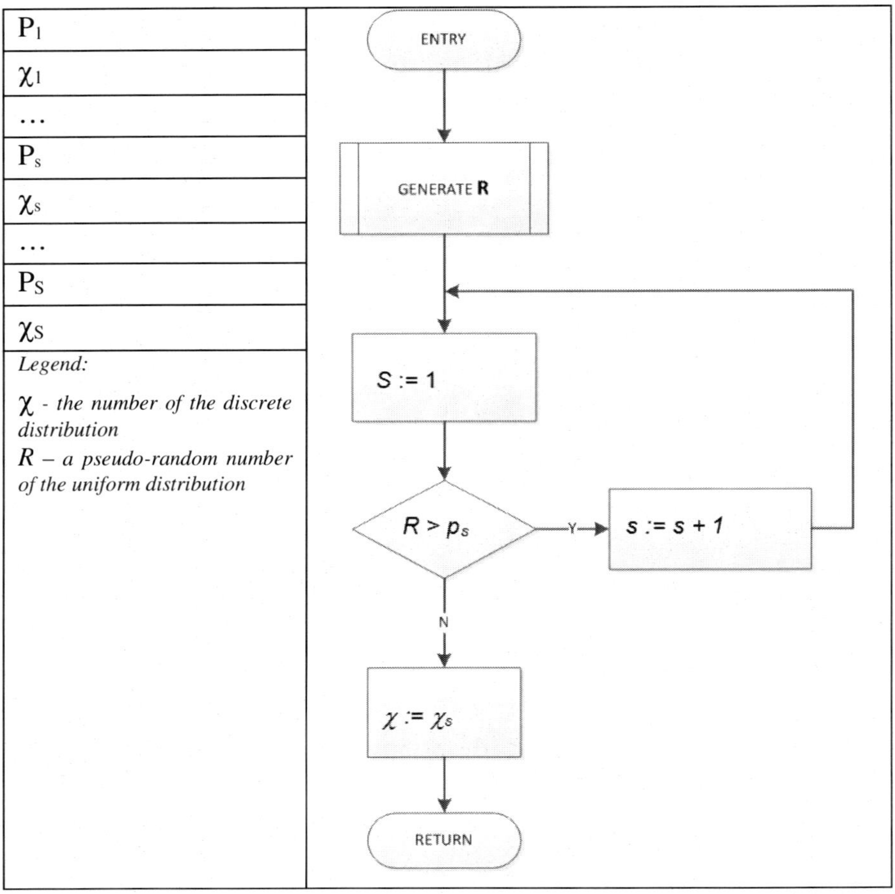

Figure 9. Flow diagram of discretely distributed numbers.

2.6.6.1. A. Generator of Random Numbers of Arbitrary Distributions

For the steel-bar mill under investigation, the service times and some IR inter-arrival times were of discrete distributions and even could be constant. For instance, the times between arrivals of the real-time clock were constant, for sure. The service times for the basic server (program operation time in CPU) were, in general, of the discrete distributions. The random (or, more accurately, the pseudo-random) numbers of discrete distributions were generated with use of the algorithm presented in Figure 9.

A pseudo-random number of the Uniform distribution, *R*, was generated and the discrete distribution table was looked through, trying to find p_s not less than *R*. The service time value corresponding to the p_s value found was the service time generated.

2.7. Steel-Mill Material Traffic Control System Simulation Project Results

2.7.1. Simulation Results

The basic simulation results for two exemplary cases and the simulation time, *T*, equal to 1 hour and 10 hours are shown in Table 1. The operation time of the program amounted to ca. 8 minutes and 1 hour, respectively.

Table 1. Exemplary simulation time results

Simulation time	Maximum CPU busy time	Mean CPU busy time	Maximum queue length				Lost signal count
			Timer	Converter	Teletype module	Manual data entry module	
T	γ^*	$\bar{\gamma}$	ξ_2^*	ξ_3^*	ξ_5^*	ξ_6^*	z_k
1 hour	30 ms	1.02%	9	2	3	1	0
10 hours	30 ms	1.01%	9	2	3	1	0

2.7.2. Exemplary Verification of Meeting the Sufficient Conditions for Operation of the Steel-Mill Material Traffic Control System

2.7.2.1. The Condition That No IR Is Lost

This condition was verified in all IR simulation subroutines. On the model, no signal loss was detected.

2.7.2.2. An Example of Complex Multi-Phase Service of the First Photo-Relay, FA', of a Pair

The IR of the photo-relay would be received and identified by CPU (the first service phase). Next, the CPU activated the timer to measure a time interval during which the IR from the second relay of the pair would arrive. The service by the timer (server 2) constituted the second phase of the second photo-relay, *FA''*. After the delay was measured, the timer produced a $IR_{17,2}$, the reception and identification of which and updating of the material distribution constituted the third phase of IR_{17} service. The last phase consisted in a transfer of the information to the operator via the channel 2 (server 3). The time of the above process should not be bigger than 1 s (a correct process observation condition). Thus, the sufficient condition for the real-time operation for IR_{17} may be given by (5):

$$\nu_{17}^{*} + \eta_{2}^{*} + \chi_{17,2}^{*} + \nu_{0}^{*} + \eta_{3}^{*} + \chi_{17,3}^{*} \leq t_{17}^{4} = 1\ s \tag{5}$$

For the timer, the maximum waiting time $\eta_2^* < 100$ ms and $\chi_{17,2}^*$=100 ms.

For the timer, the service time was constant and equal to 100 ms ($\eta_3^* \leq 100$ ms).

For the transmission channel 2 (server no. 3), the maximum waiting time for service did not exceed the maximum block transfer time for this channel ($\chi_{17,3}^*$ <50 ms).

The channel 2 service time was, in practice, zero but there was some delay between transmission of data from CPU and displaying it on the relevant operator station. So:

$\chi^*_{17,3} < 50$ ms.

Thus, to verify if (5) was met, the sojourn times of *IR 17* and *IR 0* (the timer), ν^*_{17} and ν^*_0, respectively, should be assessed.

The sojourn time of any IR at the basic server was not longer that the maximum server busy time. Therefore:

$$\nu^*_{17} \leq \gamma^* = 30 \text{ ms}$$

$$\nu^*_0 \leq \gamma^* = 30 \text{ ms}$$

and:

$$\nu^*_{17} + \eta^*_2 + \chi^*_{17,2} + \nu^*_0 + \eta^*_3 + \chi^*_{17,3} \leq t^4_{17} \leq 0.5\, s$$

Therefore, the condition 5 was met.

Similar investigations were conducted for all IR-s of the steel-mill material traffic control system and it was found that the system met all sufficient conditions for the real-time operation and that there was a large reserve of time for possible extra tasks that could be executed at a lower pre-emptive resume priority level.

2.8. Final Remarks

2.8.1. Remarks Concerning Simulation

The simulation proved to be an effective technique for the investigation of the steel-mill material traffic control system since:

a) It made it possible to map the mass service system rather accurately. It was unnecessary to make any major simplifications with regards to the service structures and mechanisms; the actual structures and mechanisms could be investigated directly (e.g., the multi-phase service).

b) It made it possible to evaluate various system quality measures. This had a special importance for investigation of the steel-mill material traffic control system since this required measures other than those evaluated when investigating queuing systems (e.g., the "maximum" waiting or sojourn times were much more important than the expected values of the random variables).

c) It was rather easy to solve the conditional event problems. This feature was important for the analysis of the system under investigation since some signals from the facility were strongly correlated, reflecting the interconnections between processing centres.

d) Investigation and comparison of various possible system configurations were relatively simple. After defining the queue discipline that was often imposed by the process under control, or by the general organisation of the control system, the basic server simulation program could be developed and any structural modifications needed only some numbering changes or modifications of the IR or secondary server simulation subroutines.

e) It was rather easy to generate random variables of complicated distributions and, therefore, oversimplifications for the input streams and service times were unnecessary.

f) The accuracy of the method, satisfactory for the computer control system analysis, could be achieved within a reasonable computer operation time.

g) Some confirmation of the investigation project quality was that the Leader's graduation work covering the control system investigations was evaluated as very good and the Leader was granted the M.Sc. degree in Mathematics with distinction (J. B. Lewoc, 1971).

h) The simulation project helped very much in understanding the operation of the system being modelling. It was surprising how much better the designers could then understand how their own programs worked. And they could find rather good approximations for the basic system measures themselves. They used this knowledge in future projects.

2.8.2. Remarks Regarding the Theory of Queues

The then-current level of the theory of queues made it impossible to investigate the steel-mill material traffic control system since:

2.8.2.1. The Input Stream

The basic assumption of independent inter-arrival times was not true for the system under investigation and probably for any actual computer control system due to correlations resulting from the process under control. The exponential distribution of the inter-arrival times was not a good approximation for the system under investigation nor for any computer control systems; in the case under study and in many other cases, the distribution was an exponential one with a minimum interval, mapping the operator's thinking time and the period that the work station was busy with the previous item under processing.

2.8.2.2. Service Times

The assumption of independent service times was not true in the system under study and in other control systems since there were several secondary servers where the service time was determined by various IR-s. In general, service times were not exponential but discrete, mapping the character of computer programs. The multi-phase service occurring in the system under study and in other computer control systems could not be investigated with the queue theory available at that time (1971).

2.8.2.3. System Performance Characteristics and Measures

The queue theory of that time could not determine distributions of the control system's characteristics and measures. The only characteristic that could be evaluated was the expected value of some random variables. W. Feller indicated that expected value was not a appropriate characteristic due, to the high variance values of variables occurring in queuing processes. This meant that the distributions of the variables searched had long tails, and it was impossible to verify if the system met the real-time requirements. In fact, at the standard assumptions of the queuing theory, the distributions of the variables being searched for were not concentrated in finite intervals and, therefore, the real-time operation conditions could not be verified nor met.

2.8.2.4. Some Reasons for the Inadequacy of Queuing Theory

The basic reason for queuing theory inadequacy was formulated several years later by Jan Oderfeld, presented at the conference Applications of Mathematics in Szeligi: The primary objective of numerous mathematical studies was some scientific award, and not solving a real problem (J. Oderfeld 1977, private message). And the solving of virtual queuing theory problems made it possible to present more formulae than the verification of meeting of the real-time requirements by actual computer control systems, thus creating bigger chances for being granted scientific awards.

Another reason for the inadequacy of queuing theory was the position presented by the Hugo Steinhaus successor, presented above in this sub-chapter. It consisted of perverting the characteristics of real mass service systems in order that they could be investigated by the known queuing theory methods. This position made it possible to pretend that the researchers involved did a useful work, analysing actual mass service systems though their results falsified the actual operating conditions of the systems under investigation.

2.9. Initial Assessment of the Ethical and Human Behaviour Aspects

The capacities of queuing theory available to the computer control system designers until the end of the nineteen-sixties did not allow for adequate investigation of system performance. Therefore, the queuing system experts knowingly harmed their colleagues that were designing and developing the actual systems as well as prospective users of the systems investigated with these inadequate methods. Therefore, their conduct and behaviour should be assessed as unethical and inappropriate.

The computer simulation experts provided the aids that enabled rather easy performance evaluation of computer control systems. It may be stated that, due to their work, they made it possible to investigate computer control systems in an adequate way and to avoid system failures. Therefore, they did not harm anybody and their behaviour should be assessed as ethical and appropriate.

The Leader also harmed nobody due to his volunteer work (work for the society), protecting against possible losses due to possibly inadequate performance of the steel-mill material flow control system. Thus, his conduction and behaviour should be assessed as highly ethical and appropriate.

2.9.1. A Digression

<<The system start-up and commissioning period was rather long. Firstly, the system was sent to the steel-mill too early as was a popular habit of various representatives of PoP (the Power of People) controlling projects formally or not and waiting impatiently for their (undeserved) benefits: money, promotion and, most of all, the glory of the main system creators. Due to that, the initial hardware testing and start-up actions, and program debugging lasted much longer than it would have been usual in the test laboratory of the system manufacturer, ELAM. Secondly, the metallurgical plant changed the system assumptions several times and the designers plus the commissioning brigade had to develop new versions of the systems. At the end, in 1971, a 72-hour trial run was organised and the system passed it. Since the plant automation department, assuming the unavoidable failure of the project, denied earlier access to attend the commissioning and start-up work needed to learn the system operation and maintenance, the plant managers were afraid of the future useful operation period; they refused to take over the system and referred the case to an arbitrage Authority. The Authority rejected the suit in total, blamed the

plant for obstructing technological progress, and recognised the system taken over. The metallurgical plant withdrew the case and paid the full contract price. The arbitration award was really surprising since the primary reason for constructing the metallurgical plant was to provide a so-called large-scale industry to the working class of the capital city of Warsaw, and the plant was the apple in eye of the Polish United Workers' Party Central Committee ruling the Country (Poland) at that time.>>

3. Radio-Astronomy Centre Control System

3.1. Description of the Radio-Astronomy Facility and Control System Tasks

The radio-astronomy centre facility was to be equipped with a big instrument for the investigation of sky radiation on the frequencies from several hundred megahertz up to a few gigahertz. In such applications, signals at very low levels in comparison to very high noise-levels should be received, with the implied application of special reception methods (correlation-type receivers) and highly developed parabloloid antenna systems. Construction of big paraboloids was very costly and, therefore, the instruments were based on arrays of smaller antennas located at some distances one from another (up to several kilometres), some of which could be shifted (translated). The antennas operated as an interferometer and, on the basis of multiple observations at various positions of the translational antennas, the map of the sky area under investigation was developed.

The interferometer was a very big instrument and automating of its control as well as data collection and processing operations were necessary for the conduct of large-scale scientific experiments. The following basic objectives were defined for the computer control system:

A. To scan the correlation-type receiver inputs and the calibration system outputs upon a clock (frequency-standard) signal.

B. To process the measuring data on-line and to output the results onto magnetic tape.
C. To compute the delay required for balancing the optical paths from the source to the correlation-type receiver (via various radio-telescopes) and to enter the appropriate delay cable sections into the signal track.
D. To compute the required signal phases and to operate the phase rotator.
E. To process the measuring data and to output the simplified results onto magnetic tape.
F. To output the information concerning the instrument condition and the observation course upon the operator's demands.
G. To receive alarm signals from antenna drives (limit position violation) and to output the relevant information for the operator.
H. To conduct the diagnostics of the receivers and drives.

3.2. Control System Hardware Configuration

The proposed configuration of the control system is shown in Figure 10.

The central processing unit of the system was provided with the Input/Output channel enabling simultaneous transmission from/to several peripheral devices. To the channel, there were connected well-known peripherals (output teletype, operator console, paper type reader and punch, magnetic tape unit). In addition, the process control channels operated with the Input/Output channel, enabling the connection of various devices for interworking with the facility.

The analogue input unit served for the selection (upon receiving a signal from the central processing unit) of individual measuring points, the conversion of the analogue values into digital ones, and their entry into the working memory.

Via the digital input unit, the data on the antenna coordinates (hourly angle, declination), positions of characteristic calibration circuits, time and antenna operating modes were input into CPU memory. The external interrupt module transferred the signals from the clock to the CPU, synchronising operation of the system and the complete instrument, as well as from the antenna motor drives (antenna approaching or violating the horizontal position). Via the digital input module, the control and information signals developed by the central processing unit (calibration circuit control, pre-setting the starting positions of the antennas, direct antenna motor control, switching of the delay cables and phase rotator control) were output to the radio-astronomy facility.

3.3. Performance Requirements and the Software Configuration Idea

The performance evaluation project was executed at the undertaking of the initial stage of the overall radio-astronomy facility, and the detailed requirements for the real-time operation could not be defined yet: the detailed structure of the instrument itself, the receiving systems, the calibration circuitry, etc., were not developed in detail. In spite of that, the idea of the instrument's operation made it possible to define the basic requirements.

Table 2. Control program specification

No.	Program description	Functionality	IR stream	Service time	Permissible sojourn time
1.	Clock subroutine	Clock signals synchronised operation of the system. Updated clock routine time controlled and verified antenna operation, controlled the calibration and measuring circuits and initiated delay and phase rotator pre-set computing.	Determined. $\lambda_1 = C_1$	Constant. $\chi_{1o} = C_2$	10 ms. (service must be completed before the analogue input unit takes the measurement).

No.	Program description	Functionality	IR stream	Service time	Permissible sojourn time
2	Analogue input subroutine	It was initiated after completion of a subsequent measurement. It read a measuring value, performed the limit tests on it (taking into account the phase calibration) and outputted to individual channels (6 analogue points each) the current delay and phase rotator pre-sets.	Determined. After each 10 ss, a sequence of 24 requests in 20 ms distance.	After each 6 measurements: $\chi_{2o} = C_3$ For the other measurements: $\chi_{2o} = C_4$	20 s. (service must be completed before taking the subsequent measurement).
3	Phase rotator subroutine	It computes the phase rotator pre-sets for next 10 s and delays for next 30 s.	Determined: $\lambda_3 = 10$ s.	After each 30 s: $\chi_{30} = C_5$. In the other cases $\chi_{30} = C_6$.	10 s.
4	Magnetic tape (MT) subroutine	It performed actions connected with the end of data transfer onto MT or with detection of a MT data error	Poisson of intensity λ_4.	$\chi_{40} = C_7$.	1 s.
5	Monitor subroutine	Reading and processing information being output by the Input/output teletype.	Inter-character-block time of exponential distribution of λ_5 parameter.	For a single character: $\chi_{50} = C_9$. For complete message:	1 s.
			Inter-character time: exponential with parameter μ_5 and minimum interval C_8.	$\chi_{50} = C_{10}$.	
6	Output teletype subroutine	Teletype queue update.	Poisson of intensity λ_6.	$\chi_{60} = C_{11}$.	1 s.
7	Alarm subroutines	Alarms caused testing and preparing information to be output onto the console.	Poisson of intensity λ_7.	$\chi_{70} = C_{12}$.	1 s.
8	Reduction subroutine	Initial measurement result processing.	Determined by the last measurement of a cycle.	$\chi_{80} = C_{13}$.	10 s.

The measuring value collection and processing were to be realised within 10 second cycles originated by the digital clock. The radiation intensity measurements at two coordinates, together with the auxiliary values for calibration, were to be integrated during the measuring cycle and, after the values were read in by the computer, the integrators were zeroed. A very important thing was to maintain a possibly constant measuring cycle since this guaranteed the correctness of the data obtained on the basis of long observation. Another requirement was to complete each data reduction cycle prior to the completion of the next measuring cycle (10 s long).

Computing the delays and the phase rotator pre-sets would also be completed within the 10 s cycle. Excepting these, the system response times for the interrupt requests of the well-known peripherals should be kept within reasonable limits (say: 1 s).

The basic requirements dictated some solutions of the system software organisation. First of all, the clock (frequency standard) interrupt requests (IR-s) had to have the highest possible pre-emptive resume priority, in order that the busy condition did not result in measuring cycle changes. For this same reason, the IR-s from the analogue input unit should have the next priority in the sequence. The priorities of further tasks would be defined during the design process.

Since the proposed central processing unit was a multi-programmable computer, it was proposed that, when the instrument operated in interferometer mode, the programs specified in Table 2, operated in CPU. In the table, the character of the IR streams calling the individual programs, the service character assumed, and the requirements for the real-time operation were described also.

3.4. Queuing System and Simulation Aids Available for the Radio-Astronomy Dish Control System (Till 1970)

The extended feasibility study of the radio-astronomy centre control and data processing system was worked out during the last year of the commissioning period for the steel-mill material traffic control system, and most queuing system and simulation aids were the same as for the first case study described in this book. Since the antenna control system was to operate on a pre-emptive resume priority basis, the Leader did a survey of such system disciplines: B. Avi-Itzak and P. Naor, 1961, 1963; B. Avi-Itzak, 1963; A. Cobham, 1954, 1955; L. Durr, 1069; M. Eisenberg, 1971; C. R. Heathcote, 1960; N. K. Jaiswal, 1961; L. Kleinrock and R. P. Finkelstein, 1967; P. Mevert, 1968; C. E. Skinner, 1967; H. White and L. S. Christie, 1958. Unfortunately, all the references repeated the inadequate assumptions discussed for the steel-mill material traffic control system above.

The simulation aids available for the radio-astronomy dish control centre were exactly the same as those available for the steel-mill system.

3.5. Simulation Model Developed by the Design Team

The general architecture of the radio-astronomy dish control system modelling program (Simulator 2) is shown in Figure 11.

Simulator 2 was composed of the main loop including: the initial action block defining the simulation conditions; the main loop proper, controlling and coordinating the simulation run; and the final action block editing and outputting the results. The main loop interacted with a set of subroutines, simulating the basic and radio-astronomy oriented peripherals of the system. Simulator 2 was developed during the extended feasibility study of the control system and the final distributions of the control variables were not known; thus only four subroutines made use of the generator of pseudo-random numbers. Figure 11 shows also the most important (for the simulation run) table (called also a vector) of the next arrival instants, $\{ \tau_k^n ; k = 1,\ldots,L\}$.

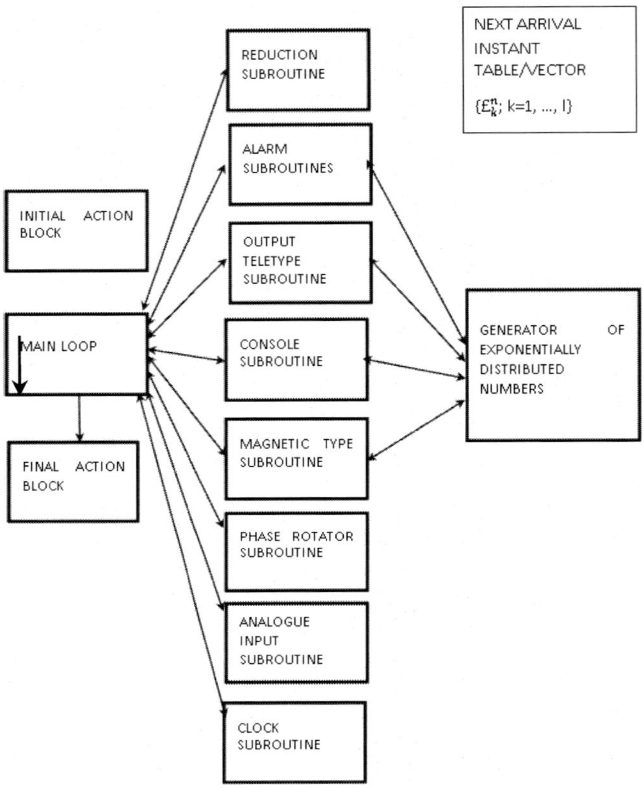

Figure 11. General architecture of the radio-astronomy dish control system modelling program (Simulator 2).

3.5.1. Main Loop of Simulator 2

In the radio-astronomy dish control system, the central processing unit served interrupt requests with use of a pre-emptive resume priority discipline. Thus, it should be kept in mind that service of individual IR-s could be interrupted if an IR of a higher priority arrived. Therefore, waiting times were not sufficient for verification of the conditions for operation in real-time, and it was necessary to determine sojourn time limitations. The basic task of the main loop algorithm for the pre-emptive priority discipline was to compute, on the model, the maximum possible sojourn times of individual IR-s at the basic server. The additional tasks covered assessment of the mean sojourn times for IR-s at the basic server, and the mean occupancy as well as the mean basic server busy period (Ref. Figure 12).

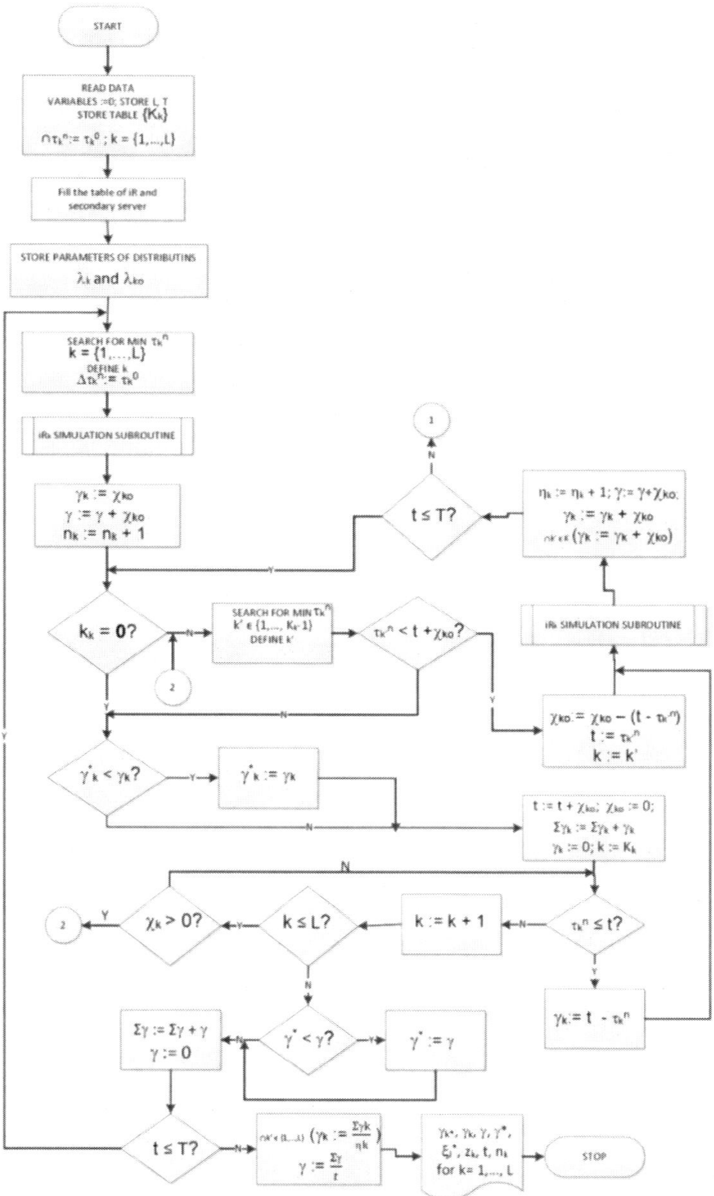

Figure 12. The main loop of Simulator 2.

The initial action block of Simulator 2 was similar to that applied in Simulator 1. The basic simulation data: L (number of IR-s from the process under control and from the secondary servers), T (simulation time), $\{k_k'\}_{k=1,\dots,L}$ and the initial values of the next event instant vector, $\{\tau_k^0\}$ were read. The addresses of subroutines simulating individual IR-s were allocated next where the pre-emptive resume IR priorities were ordered in the decreasing sequence of the IR number, k, defined by the radio-astronomers involved. At the end, the basic parameters of the inter-arrival times or times between dependent IR-s, k and k', and of the service times, χ_k and χ_{ko}, respectively, were stored.

Next, the main loop proper began. The table/vector of the next event instant was searched through for the first occurrence of the minimum value and the number k of that component was taken for further processing. The IR_k simulation subroutine modelled service arrivals of the interrupt request and, possibly, dependent $IR_{k'}$. The k-th *IR* sojourn time, ν_k was substituted by the service time generated in the IR_k simulation subroutine, and the latter value was added to the busy time of the basic server (CPU). For statistical purposes, the number of k-th *IR* passages was incremented.

Next, the main loop checked to see if the least IR number of the pre-emptive resume priority higher than that of IR_k was equal to 0 (there is no such IR). If no, then the set of such IR-s was searched for the first minimum value and the number of the relevant component was assumed as k'. If the component was not lower than the time needed to serve the k-th *IR*, the program skipped to simulation of the k-th *IR* service completion. In the other case, the k-th *IR* service time was decreased by the completed service interval, the k'-the *IR* service was simulated, and the value of the simulation time was set to the next event instant of the k'-*IR* and k' was assumed for simulation as k. In the next step, the number of the k-th *IR* passes was incremented, the CPU busy time and the k-th sojourn time were increased ti the k-th *IR* service time, and the program skipped to looking for possible new interrupts of a higher pre-emptive resume priority.

If there were no IR-s of a higher pre-emptive resume priority, the maximum k-th *IR* sojourn time was updated, the simulation time was increased of the k-th *IR* service time and the latter was zeroed, the total sojourn time was increased of the current value, the latter was zeroed and k was set to the number of IR that caused the interrupt.

If the k-th event arrived earlier, the sojourn time was set to the k-th *IR* waiting time and the program passed to the k-th *IR* simulation subroutine. If not, the next IR was examined. For the end of the k-th number set, the maximum CPU occupied time and the total CPU busy period were updated and, if the simulation time was not reached, the main loop proper was repeated. In the other case, the simulation results were printed, including: the mean and maximum CPU busy time, the maximum queue lengths for all secondary servers, the numbers of lost signals and passages, and the actual time simulated.

3.5.2. IR Simulation Subroutines

3.5.2.1. Clock Subroutine

The clock subroutine is shown in Figure 13.

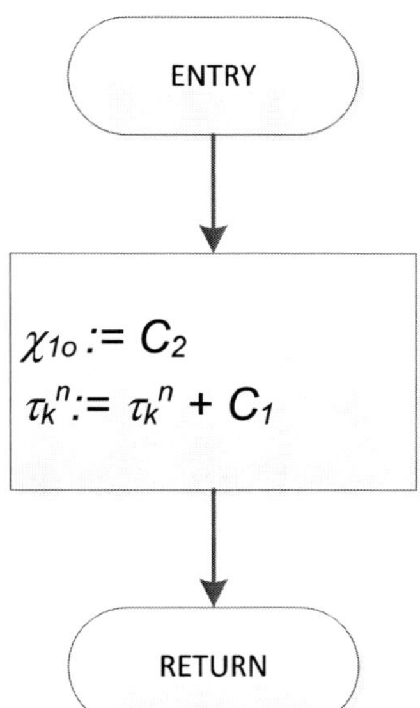

Figure 13. Clock subroutine.

The subroutine generated constant service times and inter arrival times.

3.5.2.2. Analogue Input Subroutine

See Figure 14.

The subroutine set the next instant arrival time to 20 ms for 24 measurements and the service time to the C_3 constant; after the series of 24 subsequent measurements, the buffered next instant arrival time was entered into the *k*-th *IR* service time if a high number signalling that the next *k-IR* had not been loaded into the next instant component; in the other case, the program set the next event instant time of the *k*-th *IR* to the current time value plus the service time.

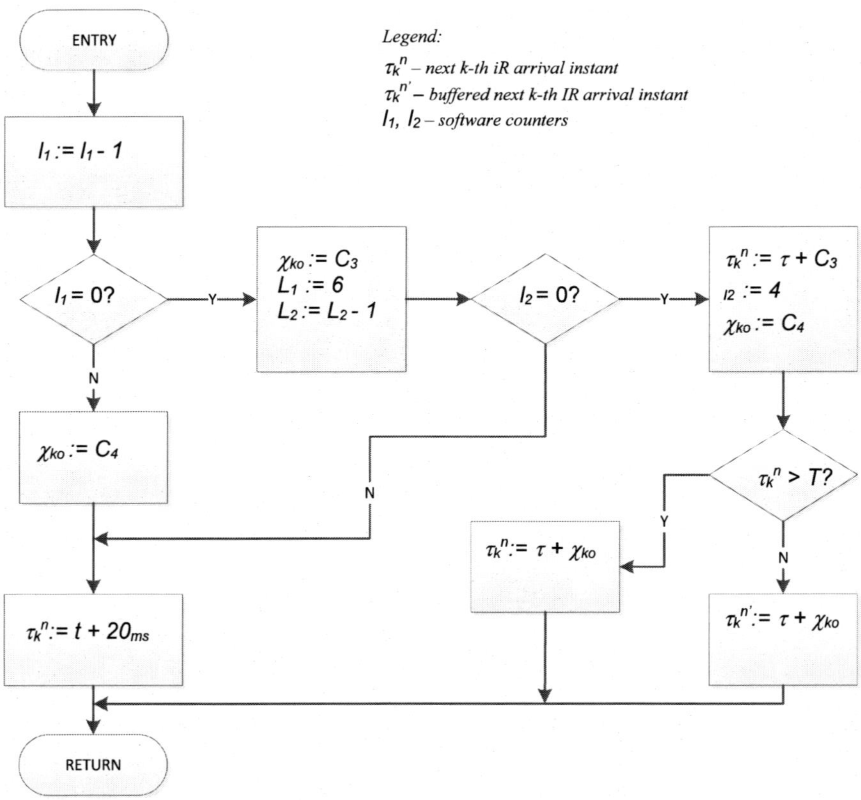

Figure 14. Analogue input subroutine.

3.5.2.3. Phase Rotator Counter

See Figure 15.

After each three phase rotator interrupts, a constant time was loaded into the service time, needed for the calculation of the delays and the phase rotator settings. For the other three of the phase rotator IR, another constant value was loaded into the service time, needed for the phase rotator setting computing only.

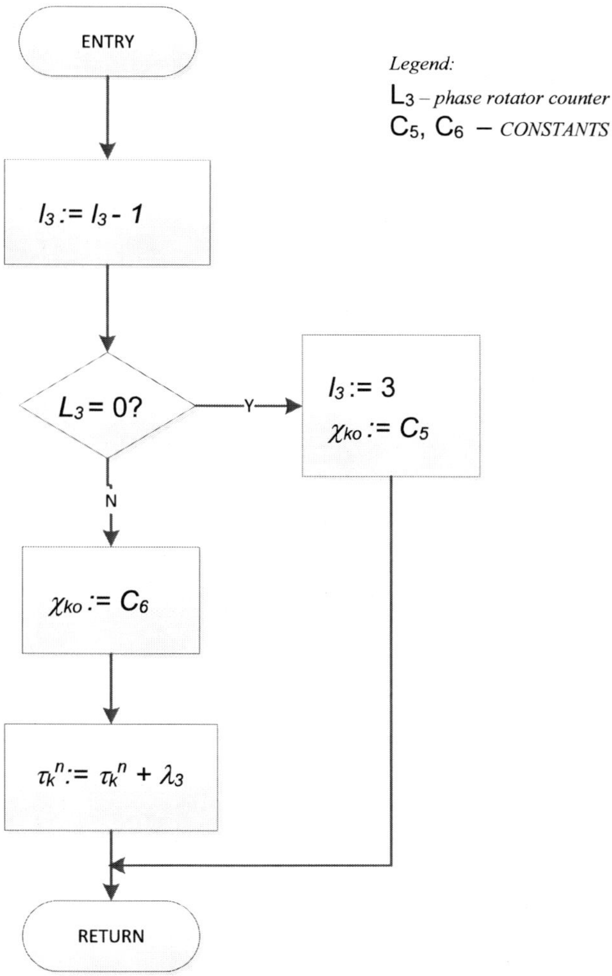

Figure 15. Phase rotator subroutine.

3.5.2.4. Magnetic Tape Subroutine

The next event time for the magnetic tape unit was set to the current time plus a pseudo random number of the parameter $\frac{\lambda}{32}$, and the k-th *IR* service time was set to a constant value.

See Figure 16.

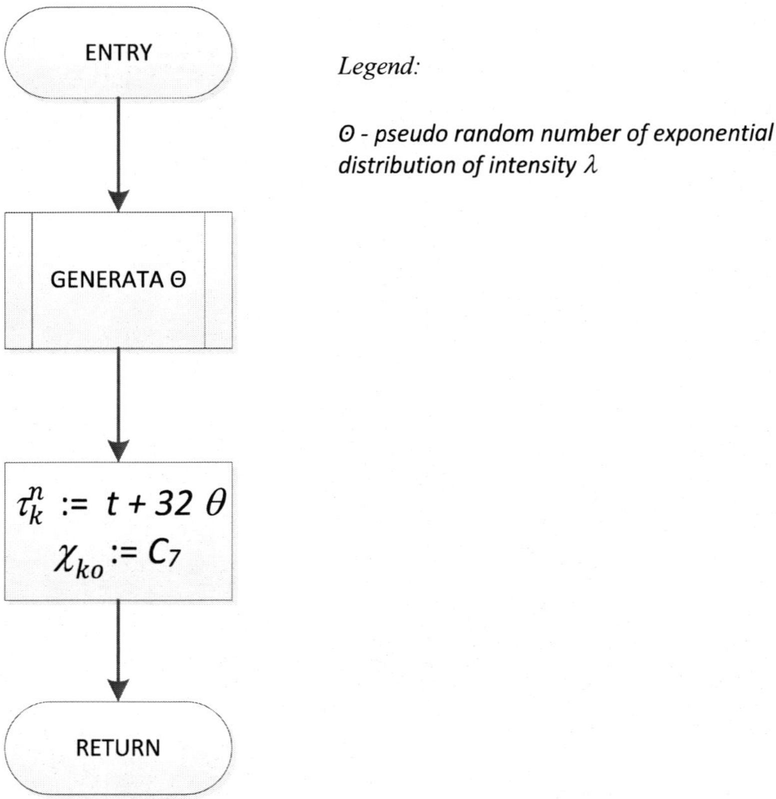

Figure 16. Magnetic tape subroutine distribution, θ, of the parameter λ (modelling the operator's thinking).

3.5.2.5. Console Subroutine

See Figure 17.

The subroutine modelled messages that were 20 characters long. The inter-character time for the IR was set to a constant (the console)

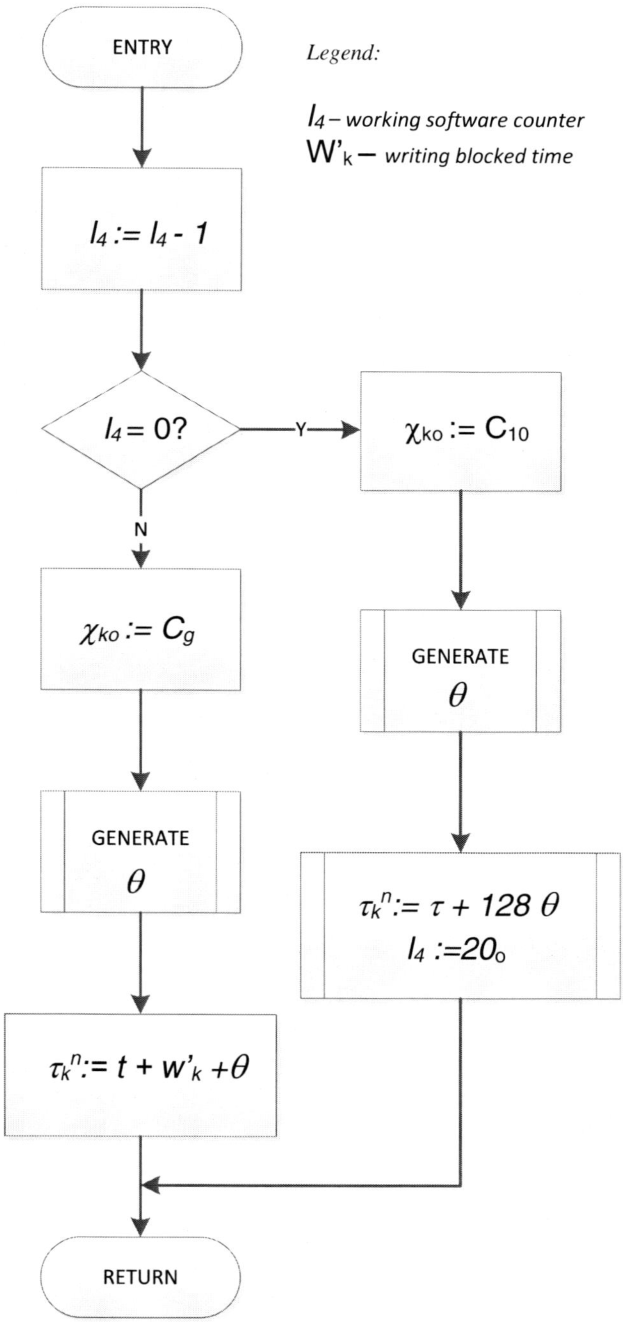

Figure 17. Console subroutine.

3.5.2.6. Teletype Subroutine

See Figure 18.

The current value of the k-th IR next event instant time was set to the teletype blocked value plus a pseudo-random number of the exponential distribution, modelling the operator's thinking time.

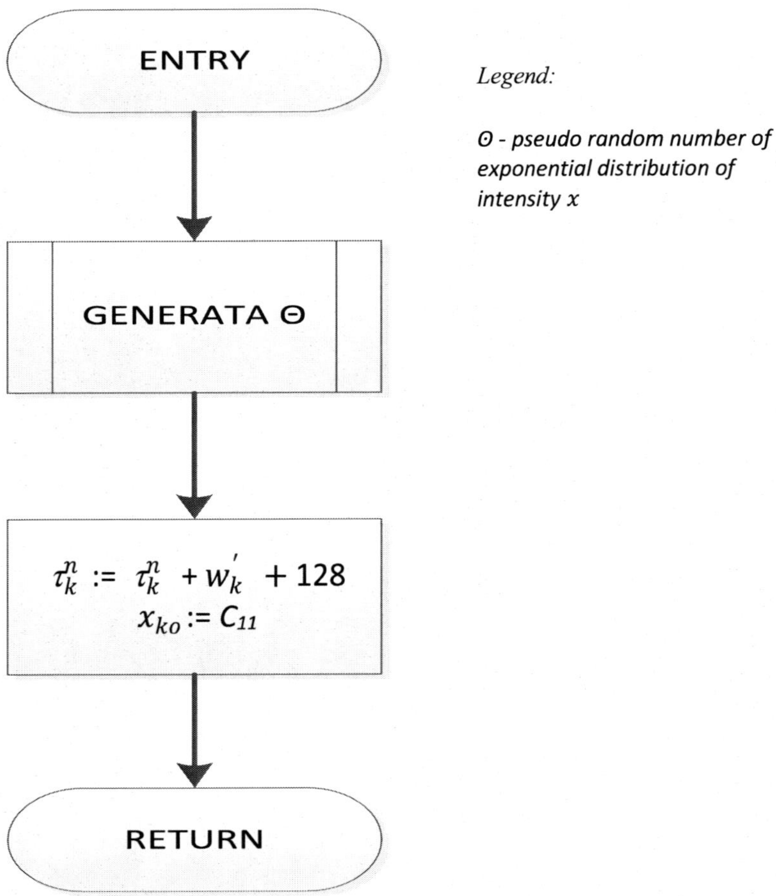

Figure 18. Teletype subroutine.

3.5.2.7. Alarm Subroutine

See Figure 19.

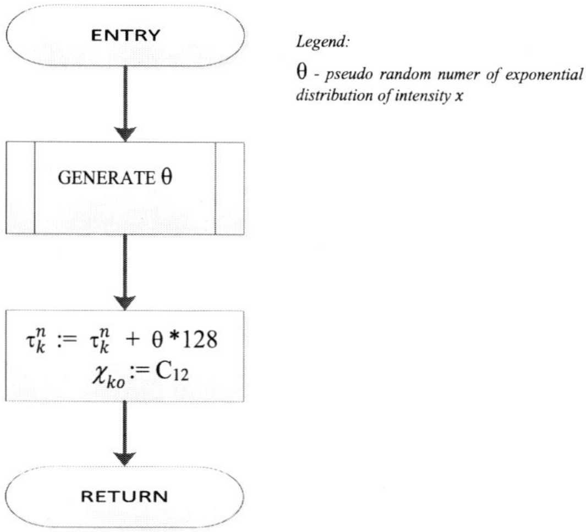

Figure 19. Alarm subroutine.

The inter-arrival time was set to a number of the exponential distribution, and the service time to a constant value.

3.5.2.8. Reduction Subroutine

See Figure 20.

Constant service time was assumed.

The next event instant for the reduction IR was set to a buffered value defined by the analogue input subroutine and a large number was entered into the buffered value.

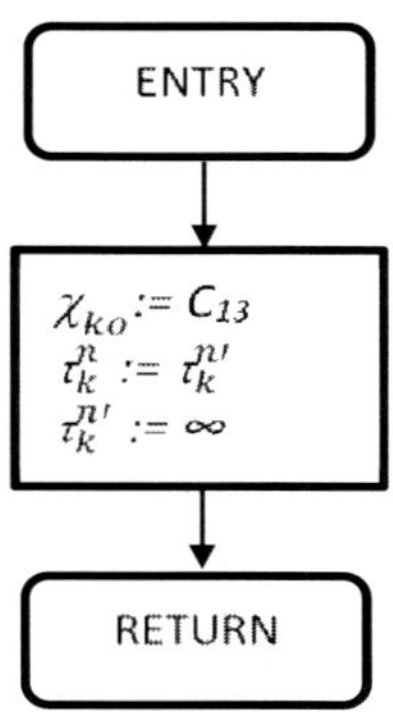

Figure 20. Reduction subroutine.

3.6. The Radio-Astronomy Dish Control System Modelling Experiments

The program discussed above was written in the JAS assembly language (Wikipedia 2012) for the Odra 1204 computer. It was developed at the extended feasibility study of the radio-astronomy project in order to verify that the computer control system would meet the real-time operation requirements for the facility. The program, complete with its data occupied ca. 800 working store cells (24 byte each). The table used by the generator of pseudo-random numbers of the exponential distribution was 256 cells long and its computation time amounted to ca. three minutes.

The project (an extended feasibility study) led by the Team including the Leader, a designer assistant (technician), a drawing person and a typist, proposed a few computers for the system processors and three simulation runs were executed for each version. The recommended version was that realised on the Odra 1204 computer. During the simulation runs, the service time of the phase rotator was set to 10, 20 and 160 ms while that of the reduction program – to 100, 200 and 1600 ms to determine the service time durations not violating the real-time operation conditions.

During the trials, ca. 30 hour system operation period was investigated. At the given interrupt request intensities, the program run time was ca. 50 minutes. The results obtained in the three Simulator 2 runs showed that the task range at the instrument operation as an interferometer could be executed in the real-time. The mean processor busy time was 1.8%, 4.10% and 20.26%, respectively, indicating rather high reserves for complex operations of result-reduction or super-synthesis of aperture, a type of interferometry that mixes signals from a collection of telescopes to produce images having the same diameter as an instrument of the size of the entire collection (Joardar et al, 2010).

The simulation results confirm the opinion of W. Feller, cited in the sub-chapter describing the steel-mill material traffic control system, that reliance upon expected values may be very dangerous. For instance, the mean sojourn time of the console IR for the third run was only some two times higher than that for the first run while the maximum sojourn time was more than fifteen times longer. This could result in that some signals being served too slowly with respect to the facility requirements, while the CPU computing power could be utilised at a limited degree only.

The Leader and his Team developed logical diagrams of the specialized hardware needed to operate the radio-astronomy centre facility, designed and developed Simulator 2, and performed computer trials proving the real-time operation capability of the presented hardware versions. Their work was highly appreciated by the radio-astronomers and the Team won the contest for the technical project, beating representatives of the most famous Polish institutes: PIAP (Industrial Automation and Measurement Institute) and IMM (Mathematical Machine Institute).

The radio-astronomy project was run within the framework of celebrations of the 500-th anniversary of Copernicus birth, together with a project run by a group of optical astronomers. The latter group planned to develop a big optical telescope to be manufactured by Carl Zeiss Jena, DDR, and signed a contract for design and development of a big rotary tower for the telescope. This project proved to be unfeasible and Poland had to pay high fines to DDR. The Copernicus anniversary celebration undertakings were supervised personally by Wladyslaw Gomolka, the First Secretary of the Polish United Workers' Party. When he learned of the fines, he got very angry and cancelled both optical astronomers' and radio-astronomers' projects. It is worth noting that the fines paid due to the optical astronomer behaviour exceeded the total foreign currency demand for the radio-astronomy project.

3.7. Initial Assessment of the Ethical and Human Behaviour Aspects

As in the case of the steel-bar mill material traffic control system, the researchers and practitioners developing the queueing theory-branch of mathematics harmed many designers, developers and users of computer control systems through passing over of the actual *real* problems in their research work. Therefore, their conduct should be assessed as unethical and inappropriate.

On the contrary, computer modelling researchers and practitioners of that time devised and developed useful aids enabling the carrying out of simulation experiments, making it possible to perform performance evaluation of actual real-time computer control systems. Therefore, they did no harm through the omission of actual computer control systems, and their conduct should be assessed as ethical and appropriate.

The first Secretary of the Polish United Workers' Party harmed severely the radio-astronomers of Poland and of the world (all of whom were very interested in development of an instrument in Poland, since diverse data could be collected from radio-astronomy centres in various locations and such a centre, with much less radio-astronomy capabilities, was developed in Poland more than 20 years later. Perhaps his biggest mistake was that he tried to supervise much too many projects in the country (Poland); his decisions must have been dilettantish, and he lost almost all the great popularity in the Polish nation that he had enjoyed at the beginning of his First Secretary period. He harmed many creators and users of the radio-astronomy and of the science in general, and his conduct must be assessed as unethical and inappropriate.

On the other hand, the conduction of the Leader should be assessed as highly ethical and appropriate: he worked harder than other designers, developed the extended feasibility study complete with the simulation project enabling the assessment of the system performance.

4. Regional Power Control Board System

4.1. System Description and Performance Requirements

The architecture of the SAPI ODM (from the Polish *System Automatycznego Przetwarzania Informacji Okregowych Dyspozycji Mocy*: Automatic Information Processing System for Regional Power Distribution

Boards) was designed by the Leader in 1973 and is shown in Figure 21 below (J. Sawicki, A. J. Kowalski and J. B. Lewoc 1974).

The system was based on the Odra 1325 computer under development at that time (Wikipedia 2017a). The computer was a replica of ICL 1902a (Wikipedia 2017b), extended with the industrial peripheral control unit and provided with the control program, EX2P Executive, enabling the servicing of the industrial control peripherals.

The CPU interworked with a set of peripherals, including:

- The Cluster Control Unit (CCU) operating visual displays and *s* Semi-graphic Visual Display Units (SVDU-s), constituting the primary interface between control engineers and CPU.
- The clock and timers synchronising operation of SAPI ODM and determining various time delays.
- Basic peripherals including a paper tape reader/punch and paper card reader.
- A disk unit for data storage and processing.

The industrial peripherals included the following:

- The industrial peripheral control unit enabling interworking of various control interfaces with CPU.
- The digital inputs provided for connection of individual two-state signals (so called relay-type telesignalling) to CPU.
- The analogue inputs (AI) making it possible to read individual measurements to the CPU memory (at that time, the measuring systems were not fully telemechanised and many individual measuring signals were fed to ODM-s).
- *TI* telemechanic interfaces of the single-direction type (for data acquisition only) and bi-directional ones (for data acquisition as well as for transmission of remote commands to the power network region).
- A control engineer keyboard interface in a special version, facilitating the inputting of power industry data.

- A dummy (synoptic) scheme interface enabling data output onto a big wall scheme of the power network region.

The primary system performance requirement defined by the power industry experts was that the data collection and visualisation cycle was not longer than 10 s. A technical requirement was that no IR sojourn times exceeded the values limiting the possible offered interrupt request traffic. Still another requirement was that the fraction of the CPU computing power available for application programs was evaluated.

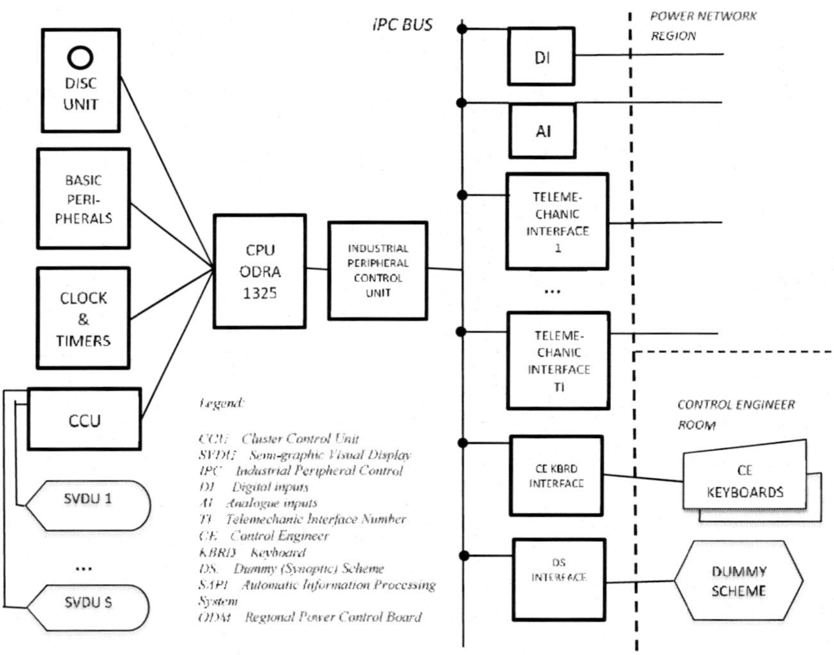

Figure 21. SAPI ODM architecture.

4.2. Available Queuing Systems Aids for SAPI (till 1973)

As in the cases of the steel-mill and the radio-astronomy facility, the queuing theory methods available in 1973, when SAPI ODM was designed, did not allow the system designers to verify whether the sojourn times of all requests to be served by CPU would meet the primary real-time requirement defined by the power industry experts. Though many references (for example, M. Sakata, S. Naguchi and J. Oizumi 1971, P. A. W. Lewis and G. S. Shedler 1971, J. P. Buzen 1973, E. G. Coffman and P. J. Denning 1973, P. B. Hansen 1973, B. Avi-Itzak and D. P. Heyman 1973, D. P. Gaver and G. S. Shedler, 1973) claimed that they were solving actual computer performance problems, they repeated the various basic assumptions of the queuing theory discussed above (e.g., Poisson input stream, exponential service, independent arrivals and service, missed flow control mechanisms) and their results could not be applied to real computer systems.

4.3. Mathematical Model of SAPI ODM

4.3.1. General Notes

Based on the knowledge and experience gained in computer control system performance evaluation through computer simulation, the Leader decided to assess, at the extended feasibility study, if SOSAPI would be capable of meeting the real-time operation requirements for its urgent tasks, and how much of its computing power would be left for the less urgent ones. Since the Odra 1325 computer was under development then, no performance investigations could be conducted, and the CPU and peripheral service characteristics were to be defined based on the declarations of the computer manufacturer (Elwro). To ensure that SOSAPI operation was investigated in the worst operating conditions, service times were approximated upwards while inter-arrival times downwards.

4.3.2. Input Stream and Service Time Assumptions

4.3.2.1. Digital Inputs

Relay-type digital signals were grouped into 8-bit bytes read upon a timer interrupt request (*IR*). The DI interrupt request number was $k = 1$ (IR_1

was generated, in fact, by the real-time clock). The number of digital input bytes was denoted by *d*. The central processing unit, upon a timer signal of the cycle time C_1, read the *d* bytes into the working memory and initiated the clock timer for the next input cycle (the inter-arrival time was constant ($\frac{1}{\lambda_1} = C_1$) and the service time was also constant, χ_{1o}.

4.3.2.2. Analogue Inputs

The analogue inputs were read in a 10s cycle with the use of a selector, and a converter needing a definite time for their operation. It would be a waste of CPU time if it had to wait for selection of the subsequent measuring point and for taking of the measurement. Therefore, after the CPU initiated a measurement (in-cycle constant service time, χ_2^1), the selector selected the measuring point and the converter took the measurement, and generated the next IR_2 (the same constant service time except for the last analogue point where the next cycle was prepared; constant end-of-service time, χ_2^2).

The analogue input IR parameters were the following: $k = 2$, the number of analogue inputs = a, the inter-arrival time = $\frac{1}{\lambda_2}$, the CPU service times were χ_2^1 and χ_2^2.

4.3.2.3. Telemechanic Interfaces

The telemechanic interfaces received cyclically data (tele-measurements or tele-signal groups plus the data point numbers and other control information) from the central telemechanic stations installed in the regional power network utilities close to ODM-s and transferred the data to the CPU memory. For $k = \{3,\ldots,TI+2\}$, θ_k was a constant determined by the baud rate, defined by the data unit length in bits divided by the transmission speed of the corresponding telemechanic station and $\lambda_k = \infty$. In the calculations, the baud rates assumed were higher than those applied currently in the power network regions, taking into account possible modernisation. The service time values at CPU were also constant and equal to χ_{ko}.

Transmission of commands to the remote telemechanic stations needed no corrections of the input data stream and service times: the telemechanic words transmitted in either direction were of the same length, the baud rate was identical and the computer time that was needed to receive a data item from a telemechanic interface was exactly the same as that needed for transmission.

4.3.2.4. Control Engineer Keyboards

There were KB control engineer keyboards facilitating moving across the dummy (synoptic) scheme and the power network oriented dialogue between the computer and control engineers. It was assumed that the inter-character times were random variables of exponential distributions with minimum intervals, of parameters θ_k and λ_k, while, for complete messages, the parameters were θ_k* and λ_k*. The CPU service times for IR-s within the control engineer messages were low (transfer of a character into an input buffer) and those for complete messages were much bigger, reflecting performance of a complex power industry procedure, and were identified by χ_{ko} and χ_{ko}* (the time of the assumed longest path through the message processing program). The distributions reflected constant time device blocking between individual characters and complete messages, and the engineers' thinking times between characters and between messages.

4.3.2.5. Dummy Scheme

The dummy (synoptic) scheme was operated from standard digital outputs connected to the industrial peripheral control unit and produced no IR-s.

4.3.2.6. Disc Unit

The disk unit produced IR_k requests ($k = d = 3 + TI + KB$) after termination of each data block transfer. To investigate the worst-case conditions, it was assumed that the disk unit transmitted data blocks at its maximum speed and the inter-arrival time was constant, θ_d. It was assumed that, in normal operation, the foreground programs organising transfers of information in SAPI ODM did not use disk transfers and the background programs were operating at a lower pre-emptive resume priority; therefore only short actions of the queue updating of constant service time, χ_{ko}, could be taken into consideration.

4.3.2.7. Basic Peripherals

The basic peripherals included a paper tape reader, punch and a card reader, producing the requests IR_{d+1}, IR_{d+2} and IR_{d+3}. In the worst-case condition, the basic peripherals would produce IR-s after transmitting some data blocks, with the constant inter-arrival times, θ_{d+1}, θ_{d+2} and θ_{d+3} (blocked operation of the peripherals) plus exponentially distributed operator thinking times λ_{d+1}, λ_{d+2}, λ_{d+3} and short CPU service times, χ_{ko} (k_o = {d+1, d+2, d+3} (as in the case of the disc, basic peripherals would not be used by the foreground tasks).

4.3.2.8. Clock and Timers

At the stage of the feasibility study it was impossible to define actions initiated by the clock and various timers. For the performance assessment, it was assumed that the clock would produce the IR_{d+4} request initiating the basic data collection and processing cycle of the CPU service time χ_{d+4o}.

4.3.2.9. Cluster Control Unit and Semi-Graphic Visual Displays

The ICL visual display system applied in SAPI ODM-s consisted of the Cluster Control Unit (CCU) and a cluster of s Semi-graphic Visual Display Units (SVDUs).

> **A digression**: At this time, ICL manufactured Alphanumerical Visual Display Units (SVDU-s), and there were horizontal and vertical gaps between character fields, making it impossible to display power network schemes. The company claimed that it was impossible to adapt the displays to present schemes. The Leader attended the ICL visual display training course in Letchworth and, then visited the company's design centre in Kidsgrove. He proposed to the display designer involved a single wire change in the display, enabling entering a few dots (a short linear section) into the horizontal gaps of selected power network characters. The display designer said that the vertical gaps could be

eliminated through a simple increase of the vertical gain and demonstrated that. These minute modifications, plus the power network character patterns added to the display EPROM (Electronically Programmable Read-Only Memory), solved the problem and SVDU-s proved to be a very good control engineer tool during SOSAPI operating life of 15 up to 18 years.

The CCU operated in synchronically with SVDU-s, serving them one after another in their time slots. In the worst-case conditions, all SVDU-s could be active simultaneously (this would be possible, for instance, when long post mortem analyses were run on CPU; of course, such programs would run in the background but transmission signals were served at the highest EX2P control program (Executive) level. In such cases, the CCU would generate IR_k requests for $k = (d+3+1,\ldots,d+3+S)$ needing simple service (SVDU queue control and data transmission).

Some CCU requests connected with SVDU-s, where a control engineer or other SVDU user entered a message to a CPU program, would need an additional service. The IR_k numbers for such requests would be numbered as $k = d+3+S+1 \div d+3+S+S)$ and, for the k number range, the inter arrival time would be equal to the time needed to enter the shortest SVDU keyboard message, θ_k, plus the keyboard operator thinking time of the exponential distribution of intensity λ_k; the CPU service time needed would be χ_{ko} (the assumed longest SVDU service program path time).

4.3.2.10. Hesitation Load

Some SOSAPI ODM peripherals were capable of transmitting data blocks, withholding normal instruction execution for so called hesitations stealing memory accesses. The peripherals included the disc ($k=d$), paper tape reader, paper tape punch and card reader ($k=d+1$, $d+2$ and $d+3$, respectively) and CCU ($k=50$). The set of numbers, k, of the peripherals making use of hesitations was denoted by H.

The mean number of standard CPU instructions for the foreground SAPI ODM programs was denoted by *MIPS* (Million Instructions Per Second).

A good upper assessment of the worst-case intensity of the input stream of hesitations was obtained assuming an uninterrupted transfer of 8-bit bytes (for disks, CCU and basic peripherals) to/from CPU. The high-speed peripherals (disc, CCU) interworked with CPU via so called buffered channels, producing one hesitation per three bytes. The intensities of the stream of hesitations were denoted by λ_k^h, $k \in H$.

4.4. SAPI ODM Performance Assessment Project

Whereas the queuing system methods available in 1973 did not allow the answering of the very basic question as to whether or not SAPI ODM would be capable of real-time operation in the power industry environment (this application was of real importance, since the numbers of analogue and digital variables to be collected and processed by SAPI ODM were higher than a thousand analogue measurements and a thousand 8-bit digital tele-signals comparing with a hundred or so measurements and tele-signals in typical computer system applications in other industries). A simulation performance assessment project was not planned. However, the Leader running the SAPI ODM project at the stage of an extended feasibility study decided to assess the system performance with the use of heuristic approximate calculations.

The earlier experience in the simulation-based performance assessment projects described above and in queuing system projects (the Leader surveyed the results of this branch of mathematics constantly) constituted a basis for this task.

4.5. SAPI ODM Characteristics and Measures Assessed

4.5.1. Basic Assumptions for SAPI ODM Performance Assessment

Several assessments of SAPI ODM performance were taken using various system parameters. The basic assessment was done using the assumptions dictated by the actual power region conditions with ample reserves for possible modernisation. The assumptions are shown in Table 3. The input stream intensities and the minimum intervals were assumed based on the manufacturer's data while the service times were based on the assessed number of foreground instructions divided by the number of such instructions executed by CPU per second, taking the hesitation load into consideration ($MIPS^h$).

The maximum allowable sojourn times, ν_k^*, were determined so that the SAPI ODM offered load was not suppressed in the worst-case situation, i.e., that each IR_k request, $k = 1,\ldots,K$, was served by CPU prior the next one arrived, thus enabling the real-time operation.

Table 3. Basic assumption for SAPI ODM performance assessment

k	**1 DI**	**2 AI**	**3,…,33 Tele-mechanics**	**34,…,44 CE Key-boards**	**45 Disc**	**46 PTR**	**47 PTP**	**48 CR**	**49 CLOCK**	**50 (CCU)**	**51,…,60 SVDU-s**
λ_k	10^{-4}	10^{-4}	∞	$\frac{1}{30000}$	$\frac{1}{51}$	$\frac{1}{422}$	$\frac{1}{853}$	$\frac{1}{422}$	10^{-4}	$\frac{1}{3000}$	$\frac{1}{30000}$
χ_{ko}	0.08	0	0.05	0.08	1	0.8	0.5	0.5	0.2	0.5	0.5
χ_k^1	0	0.05	0	0	0	0	0	0	0	0	0
χ_k^2/χ_{ko}^*	0	0.08	0	10	0	0	0	0	0	0	0
θ_k	0	0	40	20	0	20	20	20	1000	16	16
θ_k^*	0	0	0	1000	0	1000	1000	1000	0	0	0
ν_k^*	10^4	20	40	20	51	20	20	20	1000	16	16

Notes:

1. All time values are given in ms
2. The service times do not include the hesitation delays
3. CCU traffic is connected with updating SVDU screens
4. SVDU traffic is connected with control engineer message reception

4.5.2. Assessment of Odra 1325 Speed Taking Hesitation Load under Consideration

Odra 1325 was a small computer and more complex arithmetic instructions (including fixed point multiplication and division) were micro-programmed, and their execution times were rather high (e.g., 160 μs for fixed point multiplication). Knowing about that, the design and development Team were resigned to using such lengthy instructions in the foreground programs.

The set of peripherals capable of block transfers using hesitations was defined by:

$H = \{45,46,47,48,50\}$, corresponding to {disc, PTR, PTP, CR, CCU}, respectively.

The offered hesitation load intensity (λ^h) was approximated at the maximum possible speed of the peripherals included in H:

$$\lambda^h = \sum_{k \in H} \lambda_k^h = (66700 + 300 + 150 + 300 + 41667)\frac{hesitations}{sec} \leq 109200\frac{hesitations}{sec}$$

Therefore, the time of execution of *MIPS* instructions (1 s) was increased by the hesitations of 0.109 s and the resulting value of $MIPS^h$, taking hesitations into consideration, was approximated by:

$$MIPS^h = \frac{400000}{1.1092} \text{ (foreground instructions per second)} \leq 361000 \text{ (foreground instructions per second)}$$

The value of $MIPS^h$ was taken into consideration when determining the service times specified in Table 3 above. For the initial performance evaluation project, the offered hesitation load was insignificant. However, this became known only after the assessment and, at the same time, the load would not be trivial if e.g., a fast ICL disc were used (more than 10 times faster than the Bulgarian one under investigation).

4.5.3. Assessment of Primary Performance Characteristics and Measures

4.5.3.1. Maximum Possible Sojourn Times

The maximum possible sojourn times were the primary measures determining if the system was capable of real-time operation. Considering that the system did not allow for any request IR_k, $k = 1, \ldots, 60$, to enter the system prior to the previous IR_k one being served, any IR_k could find, at the maximum, one IR_l request, where $l = 1,\ldots,60$ and $l \neq k$. Since the priority discipline for the foreground software was not pre-emptive, a good approximate of the sojourn times, ν_k, was:

$$\nu_k \leq \sum_{l=1}^{60} (\chi_{lo} + Max(\chi_l^1, \chi_l^2 / \chi_{lo}^*)) \tag{6}$$

The dominant value of the sojourn times for the case study was 4.29 ms and it could be concluded that the foreground programs made it possible for SAPI ODM to operate in the real-time mode.

4.5.4. Mean CPU Busy Time

At the SAPI ODM extended feasibility study stage, it was assumed that the user software would operate at the pre-emptive resume priority level, lower than that of the foreground programs. Therefore, the mean computer time fraction available for the user programs could be approximated as follows:

$$\gamma_u = 1 - \bar{\gamma} \geq$$

$$\geq 1 - (\Sigma_1^{60} (\chi_{ko} \frac{1}{\theta_k + \frac{1}{\lambda_{ko}}} + \lambda_2 \left((\chi_2^1 (n_{AI} - 1) + (\chi_2^2 / \chi_{ko}^*) \right) + \frac{n_K (\chi_{34}^2 / \chi_{340}^*)}{\theta_{34} + \frac{1}{\lambda_{34}}}) \tag{7}$$

where:

n_{AI} - number of analogue inputs (assumed number: 400)

n_K - number of CE keyboards (assumed number: 11)

From (7), we have:

$\gamma_u \geq 94\%$.

This meant that even in the worst-case situation, the foreground programs would leave almost all computing power of Odra 1325 at the disposal of the user (application) programs.

The two results of the assessment, that the IR sojourn times could ensure that SAPI ODM would meet the requirements for the real-time operation and that the foreground programs would leave more than 94% of the computing power of Odra 1325 at the disposal of the user (application) software, were clear evidence of the feasibility of the project. This was more than confirmed in practice: SAPI ODM systems were successfully implemented in five power industry control centres, controlled more than half of electric power flowing in the Polish power network and, assuming that the benefits generated by the systems, not exceeding 5% of energy under the control of SAPI ODM. The resultant SAPI ODM benefits exceeded EURO 5 billion (A. J. Kowalski† 2016, Private message). The first big failure (a complete destruction of a 130 MW power generating unit in the second biggest heat and power generating plant in Europe, at Siekierki in 1978), already avoided due to SAPI ODM in Warsaw, paid back not only that project but also all investments in the power industry computer automation in Poland after the World War II.

A digression: The first configuration of SAPI ODM was intended for the Southern Region of the Polish power network. Unfortunately, the delivery of the industrial process control peripherals SMA (See 4.3.1) was delayed considerably and, after the delivery, local PoPs (Power of People) in charge of politically ruling the project, ordered that the system be sent to the Region after it was available for the programmers and hardware people for one week only (this was a typical way of conduct in the Communist times, just to boast that they did something). The actions of debugging and commissioning at the Southern Region premises were, surely, much more difficult and time consuming; in addition, the Region was more interested in a Western system, and so the project failed.

4.6. Initial Assessment of the Ethical and Human Behaviour Aspects

As in the two previous case studies, the researchers of the theory of queues did not provide actual support for computer control system designers. Therefore, they harmed, by negligence, many people involved in the design, development, implementation and operation of computer control systems, and behaved inappropriately and unethically.

On the other hand, Leader and his Team worked harder than they were obliged to and, in spite of the lack of money, ran a manual performance evaluation project. With this project, he assured many people that SOSAPI ODM was feasible, thus increasing their motivation for this work. He did not harm anybody and his behaviour should be considered highly ethical and appropriate.

5. SOSAPI Operating System

5.1. Operating System Description and Performance Requirements

5.1.1. Hardware Architecture

The SOSAPI (from Polish System Operacyjny Systemu Automatycznego Przetwarzania Informacji Okregowych Dyspozycji Mocy = the Operating System for the Automatic Information Processing System of Regional Power Control Boards) project under description was realised for the Central Regional Power Control Board in Warsaw in 1977 when the Odra 1325 computer, complete with the industrial process control system SMA (from Polish System Modulow Automatyki = Automation Module System) and the process control Executive, EX2P, became available in the Polish market. The SAPI ODM system developed for the Central Region of the Polish Electric Power Industry met the general assumptions od SAPI ODM described in the sub-chapter Regional Power Control Board system above. However, there were some significant differences and the hardware architecture presented in Figure 22 is described below.

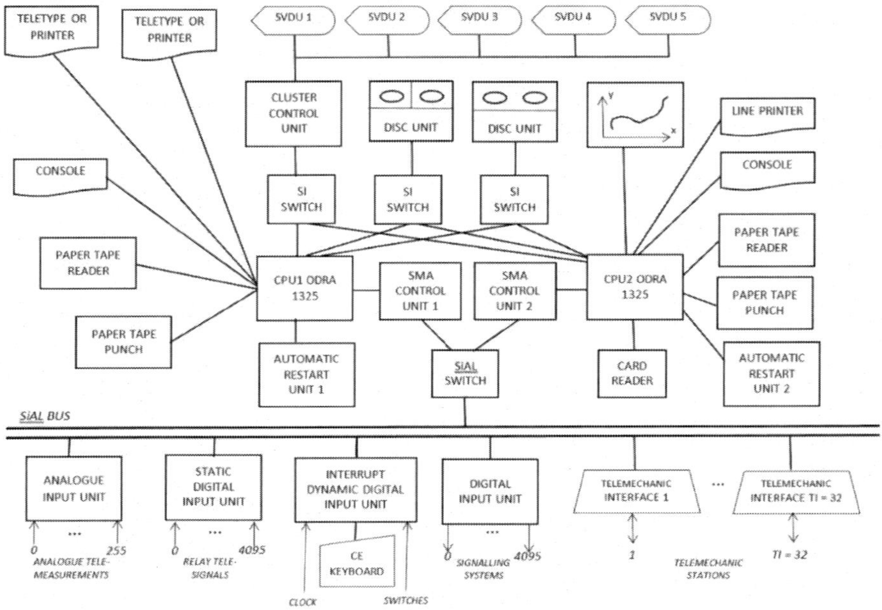

Figure 22. Hardware configuration of SAPI ODM for the Central Region of the Polish Electric Power System.

The ZEOC (from Polish Zaklad Energetyczny Okregu Centralnego = Central Region Electric Power Utility) SAPI ODM was composed of two Odra 1325 computers, CPU 1 and CPU 2. CPU 1 was the central processor intended for online service of the ZEOC Power Control Board while CPU 2 was intended for scientific and technological computation for the utility. The online service of the Power Control Board was very important for the power network operating under ZEOC control; therefore, to ensure maximum possible availability factor of the online service, it was decided that CPU 2 should take over the tasks of CPU 1 when the latter was to be switched off for a longer stoppage period (such as routine maintenance or a serious computer failure). For this purpose, both computers were provided with an SMA control unit, each, and the most important peripherals (cluster control unit, CCU, and the disc units 1 & 2) were connected to both CPU-s via Standard Interface (SI) switches, making it possible to change over them to the other computer manually when needed. There was also used the SIAL switch making it possible to change over the SIAL bus of the industrial process control peripherals to the other SMA control unit.

The SMA industrial process control peripherals included the following:

- An analogue input unit enabling reading of old-type individual tele-measurements (up to 256 measuring points);
- A static digital input unit producing no IR-s and making it possible to read old-type individual tele-signals;
- An interrupt dynamic digital input unit producing IR-s upon information changes and making it possible to receive real-time clock, CE keyboard and switch generated signals;
- A digital output unit intended to operate signalling systems including a big display wall (dummy/synoptic scheme) presenting the current state of the power network region under control;
- Telemechanic interfaces making it possible for the computer in operation to interwork with telemechanic stations installed in the ZEOC utility.

The Automatic Restart Units (ARU) 1 and 2 need a special mention. The early Odra 1325 computers featured a serious fault (most probably, over-controlled memory drivers) and the processor tripped out up to several times a day. This resulted in a theory that Odra 1325 may not be applied in industrial process control (W. Wojsznis 1978, Private message). After some time, the fault was eliminated and the computer could be used successfully even in military applications. But earlier, the Team learned of a solution at the Gdansk Branch of IASE: to generate cyclically a software signal “System alive” and, with the ARU, to check if the signal was transmitted uninterruptedly; if not, to restart CPU automatically. The Team invented a procedure of the periodical dumping of the process image on the disc 1 and of the downloading of the process image after the restart. The SAPI ODM software was written, from the very beginning, as restartable, i.e., such that could be started at any time without any harm to information being collected and processed online. This worked very well and the SAPI ODM availability factor with normal maintenance being considered as a failure exceeded 93%.

5.1.2. SAPI ODM Software (See Figure 22)

When planning the design and development process for SAPI ODM software, it was realised that the application programs, while requiring detailed knowledge of the power industry problems, could not be designed and written by power industry engineers who had poor knowledge of specialised computer problems and assembly language programming. Therefore, it was decided to assemble a team of computer specialists to design and develop a power-system-oriented operating system aimed toward data collection and presentation functions and management of application software. The operating system was called SOSAPI (from Polish System Operacyjny Systemu Automatycznego Przetwarzania Informacji = Operating System of Automatic Data Processing System). SOSAPI is presented below.

Odra 1325, in the computer control applications, operated under the EX2P Executive (control program), managing operation of the computer software. EX2P was derived from the ICL EX2M Executive, fundamental to the ICL 1900 and Odra 1300 range concept. In cooperation with the computer hardware, Executive did the following basic things:

- It managed short-term time sharing between programs and peripherals, and between programs on multiprogramming systems.
- It carried out peripheral transfers for programs, managing the real-time interruptions.
- It controlled program use of store, inter-program protection and switching between programs.
- On Odra 1325 without JAU (from Polish Jednostka AUtonomiczna = Autonomous unit), EX2M even provided some complex instructions such as multiplication and division (Wikipedia 2017c).

- On Odra 1325, EX2P Executive provided programming for so called priority interrupt used for the organisation of the interworking of the CPU and industrial process control peripherals, SMA (from Polish System Modułow Automatyki = Automation module system).

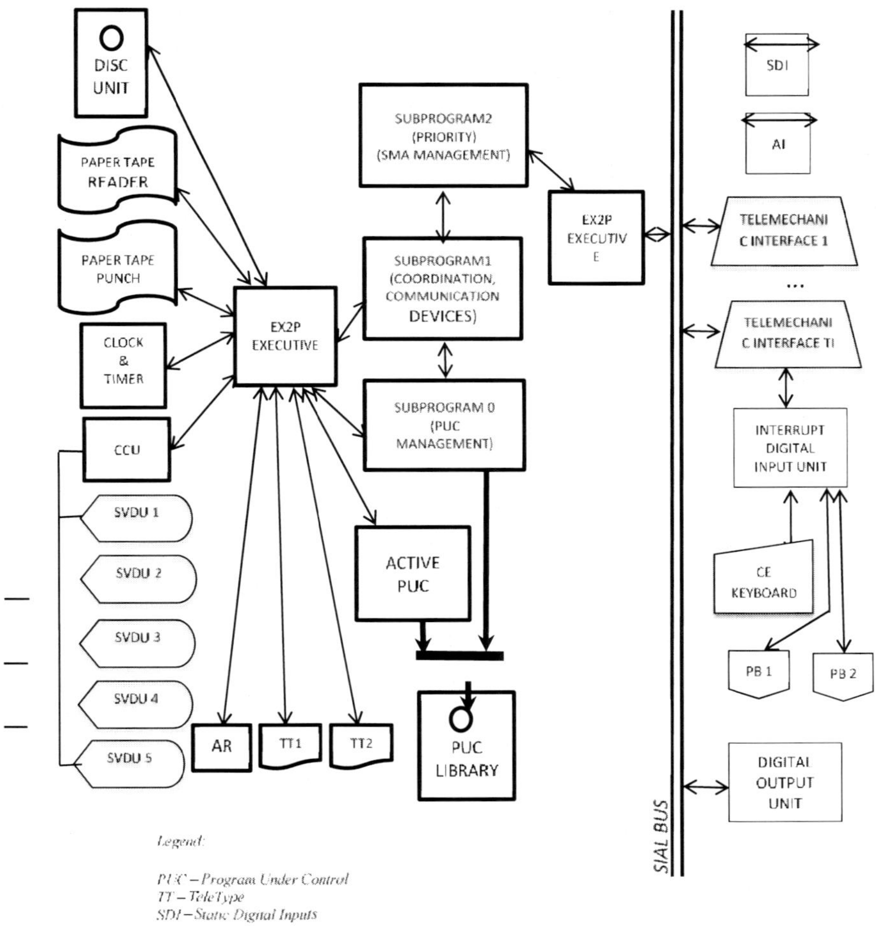

Figure 23. SAPI ODM Architecture – The Central Power Network Region.

Odra 1325 Executive made it possible to run simultaneously two programs in a time-sharing mode. Either program could be composed of up to three subprograms (autonomous program members), subprograms 0, 1 and 2, operating also in the CPU time-sharing mode.

Any Odra 1300 (or ICL 1900) computer could be granted the status of so called 'trusted' program. Such program possessed some capabilities unavailable for standard application (user) programs. The most important one, from the point of view of an operating system creation, was the possibility to allocate, within the trusted program area, a field intended for another program. The latter program was called PUC (Program Under Control). Some Input/Output and organisational instructions of PUC were not executed by Executive but handed over to the trusted program. This made it possible for the trusted program to manage the computing system, covering, principally, any programs intended for the Odra 1300 (ICL 1900) family computers. The power-industry oriented operating system SOSAPI is described below.

5.1.3. SOSAPI Operating System

5.1.3.1. General Information

The operating system SOSAPI for the computers operating on line in ZEOC SAPI ODM (see Figure 23) fulfilled the following basic functions:

- Collection and primary processing (averaging, validation, ordering, logging) of information concerning the electric power system condition;
- Selection, starting up and operation control for application programs;
- Management and servicing of transmissions from/to peripherals;
- Cooperation between the computer and the operating staff;
- Current testing of the computing system operation.

It was found that the best possible way to develop SOSAPI was to build it as a three-subprogram trusted program, where:

Subprogram 2 (the so called *priority subprogram*) fulfilled the basic tasks connected with interworking with the SMA industrial channel.

Subprogram 1 served the control engineer point, performed the primary processing of the telemetry and tele-signalling data; and coordinated the operation of SAPI ODM and distributed primarily the application (user) tasks. In addition, it managed the operation of the communication devices (Semi-graphic Visual Display Units (SVDU-s) and teletypes (TT-s)).

Subprogram 0 selected and operated, under its control, the application programs, and served their contacts with the peripherals and the CE (Control Engineer) point.

Individual subprograms interworked with one another via task arrays and indicating words. Due to effective program tracking and debugging purposes, it was assumed that the subprograms 0 and 2 contacted with each other via the subprogram 1.

5.1.3.2. Subprogram 2

During normal operation, the subprogram 2 performed the industrial channel service functions and some additional tasks implied by the functions, including:

- Signal reception;
- Primary signal processing covering the form conversion, significance and formal correctness control, ordering and distribution into arrays;
- Information outputting into the industrial channel, initiated by the subprogram 2 or on demand of application programs;
- Time computing and synchronising;
- Initiation of the basic system operation cycle (10 second cycle);
- SMA operation diagnostics;
- Setting tasks for the other subprograms and application programs.

The general flow diagram of the subprogram 2 is shown in Figure 24.

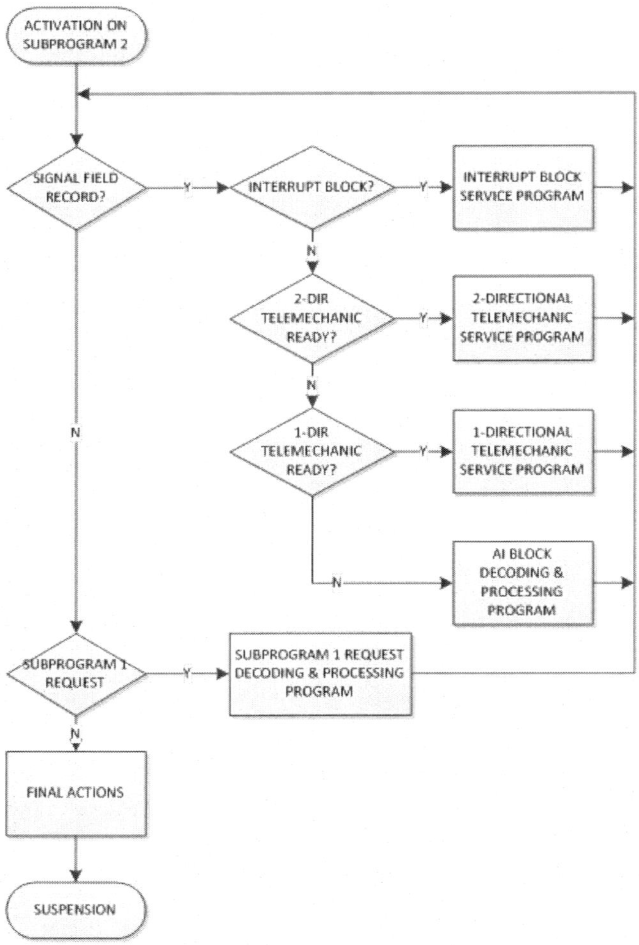

Figure 24. General flow diagram of SOSAPI subprogram 2.

The interrupt block service program provided, primarily, the service of the real-time clock generating interrupts after each 2 seconds, 1 minute and 24 hours, and initiated the primary 10-sec data processing cycle of SAPI ODM. Another function of the program was to receive interrupt requests (IR-s) from power generating units under the synchronisation process. Here, the power system control engineers required that the interrupt input signals were logged by SAPI ODM at the time resolution not longer than 10 ms with not more than some 10 interrupt inputs changing during any 1 minute of any synchronisation periods.

Still another functionality of the interrupt block service program was the handling of signals from the CE keyboard, via which control engineers could request execution of various computational tasks in an easy way. The subprogram 2 logged CE keyboard requests, acknowledged reception of them with appropriate signal lights, operated the subprogram 1 to activate the user program to handle the request and to lock the CE keyboard till the user program acknowledged execution of the function selected.

The telemechanic service programs logged, primarily, the data words received from the telemechanic stations in tele-signal or tele-measurement arrays, to be processed further by the subprogram 1. In addition, the 2-directional telemechanic service program could transmit some information from application programs to remote 2-directional telemechanic stations.

The subprogram 1 request decoding & processing program served the subprogram request recognition and executed the functions required, e.g., data reads and writes from and to SMA units, CE keyboard acknowledgements, etc.

5.1.3.3. Subprogram 1

The basic flow diagram of the subprogram 1 is shown in Figure 25.

The subprogram 0, i.e., the request decoding and processing program, handled application program requests or transferred responses to the requests. Some application programs called the permanent programs were not PUC-es but SOSAPI subprogram 1 subroutines in order that they could be executed very fast and did not suffer delays that were typical for standard PUC-es.

The permanent programs included the following:

- A primary (10-sec) tele-measurement averaging program;
- A tele-signalling change handling program;
- A standard screen displaying program.

The primary PUC-es operating under control of the subprogram 0 included the following:

- Data processing PUC-es (Tele-signalling change reporting program outputting the list of changes onto the alarm SVDU and a hard copy report onto a teletype; Tele-measurement processing program ordering the measuring data validated substantially the data collected and prepared information for offline processing);
- An SVDU keyboard request decoding and handling program;
- Programs performing functions called from the CE keyboard;
- Power flow, short-circuit computing programs and other programs called upon a control engineer demand;
- Subprogram 0 overlays used to serve control engineer requests;
- Diagnostic and auxiliary programs including: SOSAPI array outputting programs, a SAPI free time computing program, an online CPU diagnostic program, a PUC extracode testing program.
- An IR of the subprogram, informing of the beginning of the basic 10-sec data processing cycle, resulted in starting the basic primary averaging program for tele-measurements, uploading the current measuring and signal values onto the disc, and updating the data on the screens. After each 1 minute, a request was sent to activate the long-term averaging program under control of the subprogram 0.
- For tele-signal changes, it was verified whether the signals were under automatic updating or not. The tele-signals verified positively were passed to the relevant PUC program (via the subprogram 0).
- CE keyboard requests were transferred to the SVDU management program or, via the subprogram 0, to a relevant PUC program.
- The subprogram 0 request decoding and processing program transferred the requests or responses of the programs under control of the subprogram 0 for final handling in the subprogram 1 or 2. The display or tele-typing requests from PUC-es were acknowledged by the subprogram 1.
- Possible PUC commands referring to SMA device reads, CE keyboard function acknowledgements and 2-directional

telemechanic commands were transferred to the subprogram 2 via a relevant array.

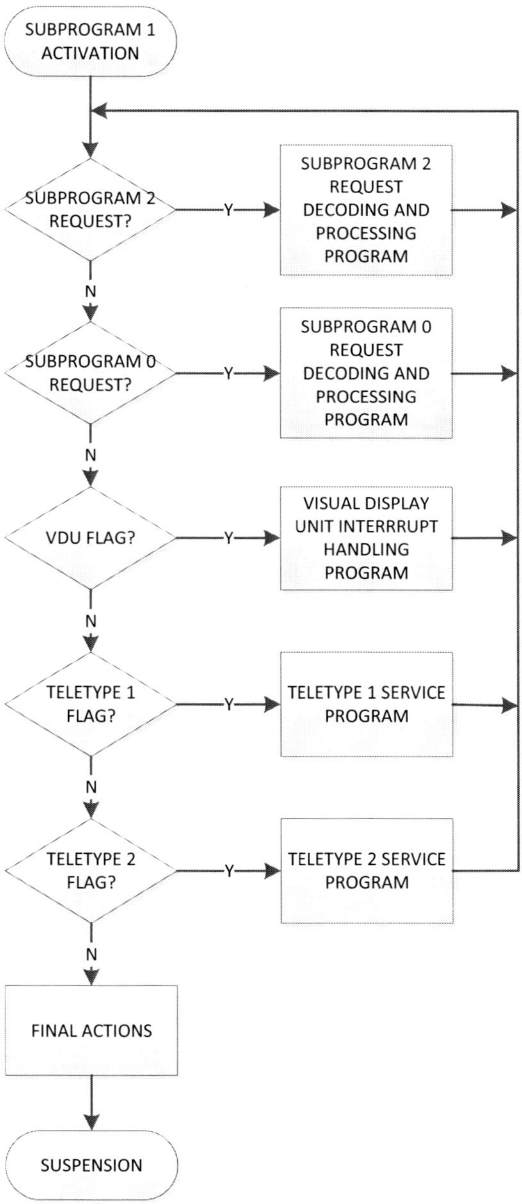

Figure 25. General flow diagram of SOSAPI subprogram 1.

5.1.3.4. Subprogram 0

The subprogram 0 automated the operator activities connected with starting and controlling operation of PUC-es downloaded from the application (user) procedure library. The basic flow diagram of the subprogram 0 is shown in Figure 26.

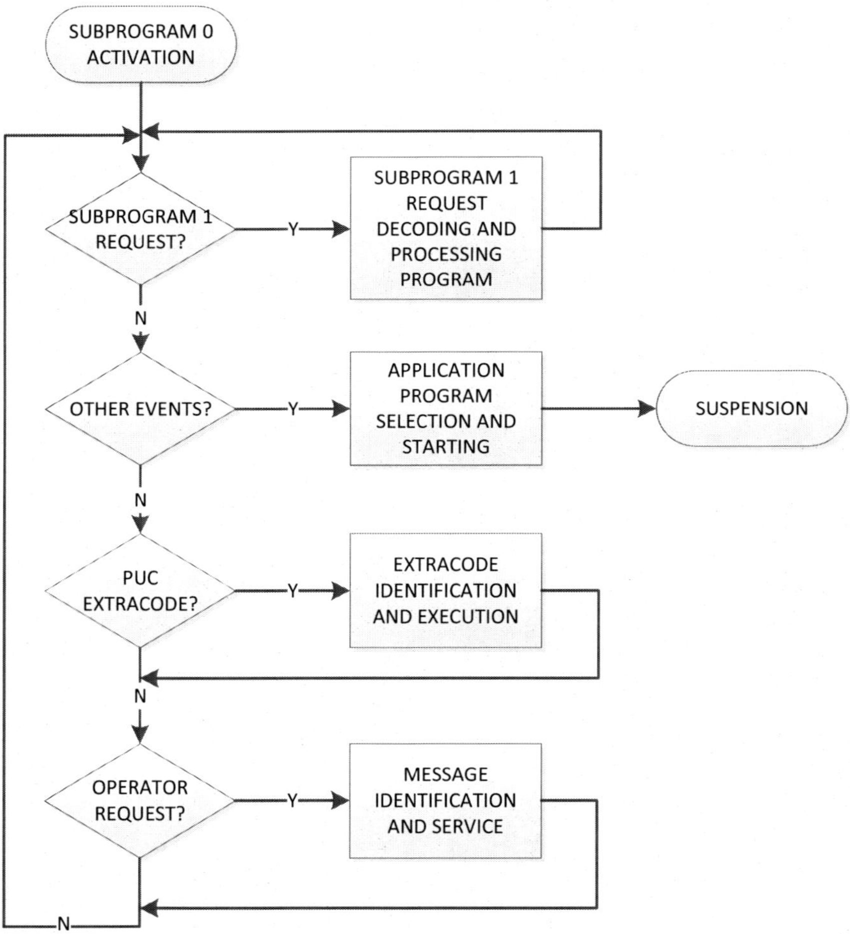

Figure 26. General flow diagram of SOSAPI subprogram 0.

The application program selection and starting routine initiated the needed PUC-es or permanent programs in accordance with other events that had happened.

The extracode identification and execution routine handled extracodes of PUC-es. When an extracode was found in PUC, the program was interrupted and Executive EX2P did not obey the instruction, passing the relevant information to SOSAPI.

For a request to allocate peripherals (ALLOT instruction), SOSAPI presented the standard Executive response to PUC. For a transmission request (PERI instruction), SOSAPI initiated the transfer if the peripheral was free; if not, SOSAPI suspended PUC till the peripheral became free. When PUC requested suspension (SUSTY and SU SWT instructions), the subprogram 0 dumped the program onto the disc and informed the computer operator of the fact.

Some special extracodes were introduced, making it possible to request a standard power network scheme display, to download a PUC overlay (a part of the program downloadable from the disc 0), to acknowledge CE keyboard function execution and to manage interworking of the subprogram 0 and its own overlays operating in the PUC mode.

The message identification and service routine handled various SAPI ODM operator messages, including SOSAPI ones (peripheral errors, an ICT (Information and Communication Technology) system overload, a PUC error, a PUC suspension till an operator action, an operator request execution) and any subprogram or PUC messages. The input messages served by SOSAPI covered cooperation with the online PUC library, decisions concerning suspended PUC-es, disconnection of disc units for disc package removal and SAPI operator communication with PUC-es.

5.2. Available Queuing System Aids for SOSAPI (till 1976)

The two volumes of the book on Queueing Systems (L. Kleinrock, 1975 and 1976) presented some summary of the queuing system applications in computers proposed by the "experts" in the domain.

However, the books used the same assumptions that were inapplicable for properly designed computer systems, in particular computer control systems, which had been applied by earlier researchers working in the theory of queues: the Poisson input stream, sometimes exponential servers, independent inter-arrival and service times, investigations limited to mean values only. Some confirmation of the fact could be the number of the Poisson input stream presented *explicite* for various "computer systems" analysed in L. Kleinrock (1976): 18. The number was, in fact, even higher since some sections of the book were extensions of the previous ones and did not repeat the basic assumptions. And, in properly a designed computer system, the Poisson input stream did not exist: In most cases, the basic flow control mechanism defended the servers (including the basic one, CPU) against a possible congestion by allowing for generation of a new interrupt request only after the previous one was served or, as in the case of the steel rod-mill material traffic control system (See 4.1.3), the inter-arrival time distributions included some minimum intervals, the basic objective of the designers being to ensure that the computer system sojourn times did not violate these intervals. In just one single section, the book mentioned the appropriate actual computer system/network model with thinking time (Page 207, section 4.11.). However, for such verbal descriptions, no calculation formulae were given by the author.

> **A digression**: The Leader was interested very much in the book mentioned above (L. Kleinrock, 1976). He received it just before his annual leave and read it on a Baltic sea beach. He loved the form of the book and, when he finished, his comment was: What a beautiful, useless book.

5.3. Mathematical Model of ZEOC SAPI ODM

5.3.1. General Notes

The SOSAPI operating system could not operate without the input streams generated by the peripherals of SAPI ODM. Therefore, the mathematical model had to include the IR-s produced by all peripherals of ZEOC SAPI ODM. The model was very similar to that of SAPI ODM described above. However, its assumptions covered the final configurations of the system hardware and software, and the service times could be assessed based on the number of instructions needing execution in Executive EX2P and in the subprograms of SOSAPI.

5.3.2. Input Stream and Service Time Assumptions

5.3.2.1. Digital Inputs

Relay type digital signals were grouped in 256 16-bit words being read upon each five 2-second clock interrupt request (*IR*). The DI interrupt request number was $k = 1$ (IR_1 was generated, in fact, by the real-time clock after each five 2-second cycles). The central processing unit read the $d = 256$ words into the working memory (the inter-arrival time was constant: ($\frac{1}{\lambda_1} = 0\ s;\ \theta_1 = C_1 = 10\ s$)) and the service time was also constant $\chi_{1o} = 3.2$ ms.

5.3.2.2. Analogue Inputs

The analogue inputs were read cyclically after each 10 seconds with the use of a selector and a converter, needing a definite time for their operation. Thus, it would be a waste of CPU time if it had to wait for the selection of the subsequent measuring point and for the taking of the measurement. Therefore, after the CPU initiated a measurement (of the in-cycle constant service time, χ_2^1), the selector selected the measuring point and the converter took the measurement, and generated the next IR_2 (the same constant service time except for the last analogue point where the next cycle was prepared; of the constant end-of-service time, χ_2^2).

The analogue input IR_k parameters were the following: $k = 2$, the number of analogue inputs = 256, the inter-arrival time, $\frac{1}{\lambda_2} = 0$; the minimum interval length, $\theta_2 = 20$ ms, the CPU service times were $\chi_2^1 = 0.15$ ms and $\chi_2^2 = 0.2$ ms.

5.3.2.3. Telemechanic Interfaces

The telemechanic interfaces received cyclically the data (tele-measurements or tele-signal groups plus the data point numbers and other control information) from the central telemechanic stations installed in the regional power network utilities close to ODM-s, and transferred the data to the CPU memory. For $k = 3,\ldots,TI+2$ ($TI = 34$), θ_k was a constant determined by the baud rate, defined by the data unit length in bits divided by the transmission speed of the corresponding telemechanic station (200 baud) and $\lambda_k = \infty$. The service time values at the CPU were also constant and equal to $\chi_{ko} = 0.025$ ms.

Transmission of commands to the remote telemechanic stations needed no corrections of the input data stream and service times: the telemechanic words transmitted in either direction were of the same length, the baud rate was identical and the computer time needed to receive a data item from a telemechanic interface was exactly the same as that needed for transmission.

5.3.2.4. Control Engineer Keyboard

There was one control engineer keyboard including $k = 35,\ldots,98$ pushbuttons facilitating moving across the dummy (synoptic) scheme and power network -oriented dialogue between the computer and control engineers. It was assumed that the inter-depression times were random variables of exponential distributions with minimum intervals of parameters $\theta_{35} = \ldots = \theta_{97} = 20$ ms and $\lambda_{35} = \ldots = \lambda_{97} = \frac{1}{0.5\ s}$ while, for complete messages ($k = 98$), the parameters were $\theta_{98}{*} = 1$ s and $\lambda_{98}{*} = \frac{1}{30\ s}$. The CPU service times for *IR*-s within the control engineer messages were low (transfer of a character into an input buffer) while those for complete messages were much bigger, reflecting performance of a complex power industry procedure, and were identified by $\chi_{98o} = 0.04$ ms and $\chi_{98o}{*} = 0.5$ ms (the time of the longest path through the message processing program). The distributions reflected constant time device blocking between individual depressions within a message and between complete messages, and the engineers' thinking times between depressions within messages and between complete messages ($k = 98$).

5.3.2.5. Real-Time Clock

The real-time clock generated IR_{99} after each 2 seconds, 1 minute and 24 hours. The clock signals were used by the subprogram 2 to update time and to initiate various processing cycles (including the basic 10-second data collection and processing cycle).

5.3.2.6. Switches

The switches generated, among others, the signals making it possible to follow the power generating unit synchronisation process in so-called post-mortem data processing programs. The power industry engineers required that ZEOC SAPI ODM included 256 such switches (k = 100,…,355) and that switch state changes were logged (at CPU service time, χ_{ko} = 0.1 ms) with 10 ms resolution, where not more than 10 state changes could happen in 1 minute. This implied that the state changes were recorded online and processed post-mortem, and the logging time resolution, i.e., the maximum permissible sojourn time of IR_k for k = 100,…,355, v_k^* = 10 ms.

5.3.2.7. Dummy Scheme

The dummy (synoptic) scheme was operated from standard digital outputs connected to the industrial peripheral control unit and produced no *IR*-s.

5.3.2.8. Disc Unit

The disk unit produced IR_k requests (k = 356) after termination of each data block transfer. To investigate the worst-case conditions, it was assumed that the disk unit transmitted data blocks at its maximum speed and that the inter-arrival time was constant, θ_{356} = 20 ms (somewhat below half of the mean disc head positioning time).

Note: In ZEOC SAPI ODM, two disc drives were used in comparison with one drive in the general version of SAPI ODM analysed above.

However, the two drives of ZEOC SAPI ODM operated alternatingly and produced, actually, the same input stream.

It was assumed that in, normal operation, the foreground programs organising transfers of information in SAPI ODM would not use disk transfers and the background programs would be run at a lower pre-emptive resume priority; therefore, short actions of the queue updating, of a constant service time, by Executive EX2P and SOSAPI subprogram 0, χ_{356o}, should be taken into consideration only.

5.3.2.9. Basic Peripherals

The basic peripherals included a paper tape reader and punch, producing the requests IR_{357} and IR_{358}. In the worst-case condition, the basic peripherals would produce *IR*-s after transmitting some data blocks, with constant inter-arrival times, θ_{357} = 5 s and θ_{358} = 10 s (blocked operation of the peripherals) plus exponentially distributed operator thinking times of intensities $\lambda_{357} = \lambda_{358} = \frac{1}{30\ s}$ and Executive + subprogram 0 service times, χ_{ko} = 0.125 ms (k_o = {357o and 358o. As in the case of the disk, basic peripherals would not be used by the foreground tasks.

5.3.2.10. Clock and Timers

For the performance assessment, it was assumed that the clock would produce the IR_{359} request initiating execution of simple diagnostic actions after each second (constant service time, χ_{359} = 0.05 ms).

5.3.2.11. Cluster Control Unit and Semi-Graphic Visual Displays

The ICL visual display system applied in ZEOC SAPI ODM consisted of the Cluster Control Unit (CCU) and a cluster of 5 Semi-graphic Visual Display Units (SVDU-s).

The CCU operated in synchronisation with the SVDU-s, transmitting data at the constant speed of 1,000,000 bits per second and serving the SVDU-s one after another in their time slots. In the worst-case conditions, all SVDU-s could be active simultaneously (this would be possible, for instance, when long post mortem analyses were run on CPU; of course, such programs would run in the background but transmission signals were served at the highest EX2P control program (Executive) level. In such cases, the CCU would generate IR_{360} requests when the CPU was to transmit new screen content, i.e., after transmitting 2000 bytes x 8 bits/byte : 1000000 bits/second = 16 ms, needing simple CPU service (SVDU queue control and data transmission).

Some CCU requests connected with the SVDU-s occurred when a control engineer or other SVDU user entered a message to a CPU program, needing an additional service. The IR_k numbers for such requests would be numbered as $k = (361,\ldots,365)$ and, for this k number range, the inter arrival time would be equal to the time needed to enter the shortest SVDU keyboard message, i.e., the screen full data due to the transmission synchronism, θ_k, plus the keyboard operator thinking time of the exponential distribution of intensity $\lambda_k = \frac{1}{30000}$; the CPU service time needed would be constant and equal to $\chi_{ko} = 0.25$ (the assumed longest SVDU service program path time).

5.3.2.12. Teletypes

In ZEOC SAPI DM, the teletypes TT1 and TT2 were used for outputting various reports concerning the electric power system state. The reports were prepared by various application programs (PUC-es) at constant intensities dominated by $\lambda_{366} = \lambda_{367} = \frac{1}{60\ s}$. It was assumed that the reports would be outputted in parts not exceeding 40 character in length. After a part of any report was outputted, the teletypes produced IR_{368} and IR_{369} shifting the teletype queues.

5.3.2.13. Automatic Restart Unit

The Automatic Restart Unit (ARU) was initiated by IR_{366} after each 2 seconds (θ_{370}) measured by the CPU timers, to reset the hardware switch of ARU. If the switch remained set at the end of the ARU cycle (10 s), the unit initiated the CPU hardware restart. In the other case, it set the switch, waiting for the next software resets (a constant service time $\chi_{370o} = 0.05$ ms).

5.3.2.14. Hesitation Load

Some ZEOC SOSAPI ODM peripherals were capable of transmitting data blocks, withholding normal instruction execution for so called hesitations stealing memory accesses. The peripherals included the disc (k = 356), paper tape reader (k = 357), paper tape punch (k = 358), CCU (k = 360) and teletypes (k = 366 and k = 367). The set of numbers, k, of the peripherals making use of hesitations was denoted by H = {356,357,358,360,366,367}.

As for the SAPI ODM case study, the mean number of standard CPU instructions for the foreground SAPI ODM programs was denoted by *MIPS* (Million Instructions Per second).

A good majorant of the worst-case intensity of the input stream of hesitations was obtained by assuming uninterrupted transfer of 8-bit bytes (for disks and basic peripherals) or 6-bit characters (for CCU) to/from the CPU. The high-speed peripherals (disk, CCU) interworked with the CPU via so called buffered channels, producing one hesitation per three bytes. The intensities of the stream of hesitations were denoted by λ_k^h, $k \in H$ = {356,357,358,360,366,367}.

5.4. Basic ZEOC SAPI ODM Characteristics and Measures Assessed

5.4.1. Basic Assumptions for ZEOC SAPI ODM Performance Assessment

The ZEOC SAPI ODM performance assessment was done at the system parameters that were planned for the end of the first year of system operation. The assumptions taken are shown in Table 4. The input stream intensities and the minimum intervals were majorised based on the manufacturer's data while the service times - based on the assessed number of foreground (SOSAPI and EX2P) instructions divided by the CPU speed in $MIPS^h$.

The maximum allowable sojourn times, v_k^*, were determined so that the SAPI ODM offered load was not suppressed in the worst-case situation, i.e., that each IR_k request, $k = 1,\ldots K$, was served by CPU prior to the arrival of the next one, thus enabling real-time operation.

Table 4. Basic assumptions for ZEOC SAPI ODM performance assessment

K	λ_k	χ_{ko}	χ_k^1	χ_k^2/χ_{ko}^*	θ_k	θ_k^*	ν_k^*
1 DI	∞	3.2	0	0	10^4	0	10^4
2 AI	∞	0	0.15	0.2	10^4	20	20
3,…,34 Telemecha-nics	∞	0.025	0	0	40	0	40
35,…,98 CE keyboard	$\frac{1}{30000}$	0.04	0	0.5	20	1000	20
99 Real time clock	∞	0.25	0	0	2000	0	10^4
100,…,355 Switches	$\frac{10}{60000}$	0.1	0	0	0	0	10
356 Disc	$\frac{1}{45}$	0.125	0	0	20	0	20
357 Paper tape reader	$\frac{1}{422}$	0.125	0	0	20	1000	20
358 Paper tape punch	$\frac{1}{853}$	0.125	0	0	20	1000	20
359 CPU clock	$\frac{1}{1000}$	0.05	0	0	1000	0	1000
360 Cluster control unit	$\frac{1}{6000}$	0.25	0	0	16	0	16
361,…,365 SVDU-s	$\frac{1}{30000}$	0.25	0	0	16	0	16
366,367 Teletypes	$\frac{1}{10000}$	0.125	0	0	1000	0	1000
370 Automatic restart unit	∞	0.05	0	0	2000	0	2000

Notes

1. All time values are given in ms
2. The service times do not include the hesitation delays
3. CCU traffic is connected with updating SVDU screens
4. SVDU traffic is connected with control engineer message reception

5.4.2. Assessment of Odra 1325 Speed Taking Hesitation Load under Consideration

The hesitation load of CPU in ZEOC SAPI ODM was almost the same as that for SAPI ODM, assessed above. The only difference was that, in ZEOC, two teletypes were used and the card reader was not used, and the set of peripherals capable of block transfers using hesitations was defined by: $H = \{356,357,358,360,366,367\}$, corresponding to {disc, PTR, PTP, CCU, TT1, TT2}, respectively.

The offered hesitation load intensity (λ^h) was approximated at the maximum possible speed of the peripherals included in H:

$$\lambda^h = \sum_{k \in H} \lambda_k^h = (66700 + 300 + 150 + 41667 + 3 + 3)\frac{1}{sec} \leq 109000\frac{1}{sec}$$

Therefore, the resulting value of $MIPS^h$, taking hesitations into consideration, was the same as for the SAPI ODM case study, being approximated by the same value as for SAPI ODM above:

$$MIPS^h = \frac{400000}{1.109}$$

The value of $MIPS^h$ was taken into consideration when determining the service time dominants specified in Table 4 above.

5.4.3. Assessment of Primary Performance Characteristics and Measures

5.4.3.1. Maximum Possible Sojourn Times

The maximum possible sojourn times were the primary measures determining if the system was capable of real-time operation. Considering that the system did not allow for any request IR_k, $k = 1, \ldots, 370$, to enter the system prior to the previous IR_k one being served, any IR_k could find at the maximum one IR_l request, where $l = 1, \ldots, 370$ and $l \neq k$. Since the priority discipline for the foreground software was not pre-emptive, a good approximate of the sojourn times, ν_k, was:

$$\nu_k \leq \sum_{l=1}^{370}(\chi_{lo}+Max(\chi_l^1,\chi_l^2/\chi_{lo}^*)) \tag{8}$$

The dominating value of the sojourn times for the case study was 5.125 ms and it could be concluded that the foreground programs made it possible for SAPI ODM to operate in the real-time mode even for the most severe demand implied by the 10 ms resolution for changes of the switches.

5.4.4. CPU Computing Power Available for User Programs (PUC-es)

In ZEOC SAPI ODM, the user programs (PUC-es) operated at the pre-emptive resume priority level lower than that of the foreground programs (SOSAPI and EX2P). Therefore, the computing power available for the user programs could be approximated as follows:

$$\gamma u = 1 - \bar{\gamma} \geq 1 - \left(\sum_1^{370}(\chi_{ko}\,\frac{1}{\theta_k+\frac{1}{\lambda_k}} + \frac{1}{\theta_2}\left(\chi_2^1\,(n_{AI} - 1) + \left(\frac{\chi_2^2}{\chi_{2o}^*}\right)\right) + \frac{1}{\theta_{98}+\frac{1}{\lambda_{98}}}\frac{\chi_{35}^1}{}\chi_{35o}^*\right) \geq 1 - 0.03 = 0.97 \tag{9}$$

where:

n_{AI} - number of analogue inputs (256),

$n_{CE} = 64$ - number of control engineer keyboard pushbuttons.

From (9), we have:

$\gamma_u \geq 90\%$.

This meant that, even in the worst-case situation, the foreground programs would leave 90% remaining, i.e., most of the computing power of Odra 1325 was at the disposal of the user (application) programs.

5.5. Initial Assessment of the Ethical and Human Behaviour Aspects

The researchers specialised in the queuing theory, in particular the author of the monograph (L. Kleinrock 1975 and 1976) harmed many computer system designers, developers, operators and users by proliferating inadequate performance evaluation models based on assumptions far from computer systems reality; even more so when the monograph mentioned above was a very nice book attracting numerous readers and citations.

Recommending performance evaluation methods and procedures based on inadequate models should be assessed as a very inappropriate human behaviour.

On the other hand, the Leader and his team, who developed and used voluntarily (as a work for the society) their own performance evaluation approximations based on the true assumptions for real-life computer systems exhibited a high ethical level and very appropriate behaviour.

6. Power Industry VDU Project

This Section describes the project aimed towards designing a low-cost VDU system intended for power industry applications.

6.1. VDU System Description and Performance Requirements

6.1.1. Description of the Solution

The set including the ICL Cluster Control Unit (CCU) and the Semi-graphic Visual Display Units (SVDU-s), discussed in the Chapters Regional Power Control Board system and SOSAPI operating system, above, proved to be devices well adapted to the requirements of the Polish electric power industry. The only deficiency in this solution was its rather high price. For the regional power hierarchy level, where the benefits generated by the SAPI systems were high, this price was recognised as reasonable; however, in other applications, it would be seen to be too high. Therefore, a project was set up to design a solution similar to ICL display system but cheaper. The Leader was appointed as the leading designer of this project.

For the project realisation technology, it was chosen to emulate the ICL system on a Polish minicomputer Momik 8b (MERA 300). In the 1970s, such an approach was most often used in the teleprocessing systems, leading to creation of so called distributed processing domain (R. G. Matteson 1974; California Data Processors 1974; S. N. Saslow 1975; J. Bailey 1974; J. M. Steele and R. C. Mattson 1973; S. Davies 1974; R. M. Holt and M. R. Lemas 1974).

The hardware architecture of the visualisation set designed and developed for the Odra 1325 computers in the power industry applications is shown in Figure 27.

Note: The Odra 1325 visualisation set could operate with any computer of the Polish Odra 1300 family (or ICL 1900 Series computers). However, only the Odra 1325 was provided with the industrial process control automation system, SMA, and Executive EX2P making it possible to interwork with SMA and the visualisation set under discussion was implemented, exclusively, for Odra-s 1325.

Odra 1325 was the central processing unit (CPU) of the computer automation systems implemented in the Polish power industry in the late 1970s. The low-cost visualisation system was designed and developed with use of the Momik 8b small minicomputer (byte-oriented architecture, small (8KB) memory). The minicomputer operated under the CCU emulator, designed and developed for the project. To enable operation with Odra 1325, a special-purpose 1300/8a inter-processor buffer, visible for the host computer as the standard inter-processor buffer of the Elwro Odra 1300 family and ICL 1900 Series computers, was designed and developed by the design team (the Team).

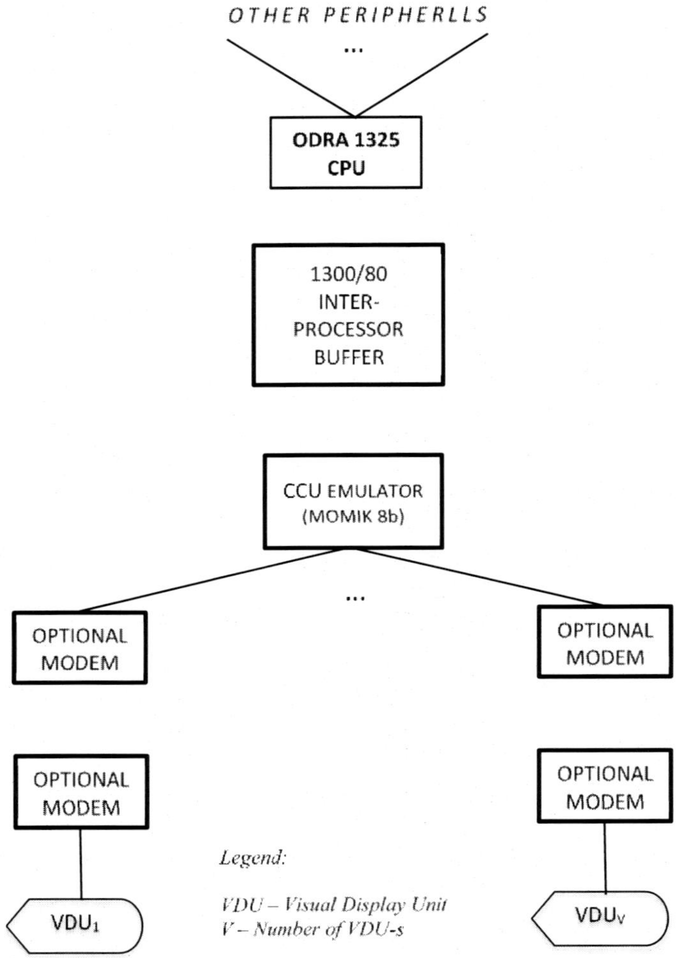

Figure 27. Odra 1325 visualisation set.

The CCU emulator served V home-made Visual Display Units (via optional modems enabling remote interworking) which could be either semi-graphic (S9607 type), manufactured by IASE (from Polish Instytut Automatyki Systemów Energetycznych = Institute for Power System Automation) or alphanumeric (ALFA 311/M type, manufactured by the Minicomputer System Works MERA ZSM).

The flow diagram of the CCU 7180 cluster control unit is presented in Figures 4.28. a (the initial part) and b (the final part).

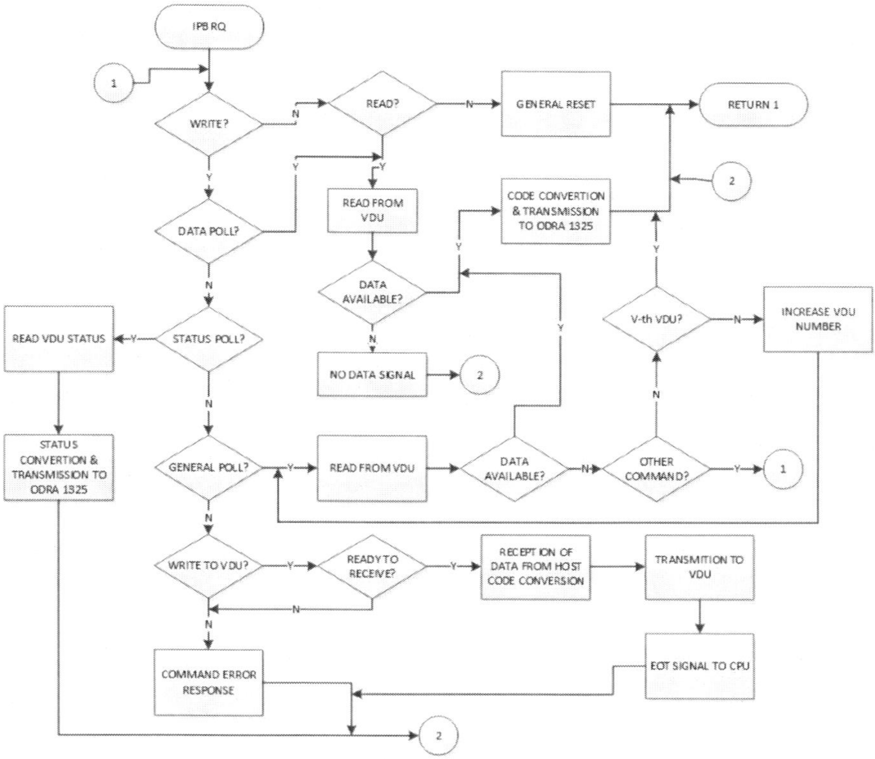

Figure 28a. CCU 7180 emulator flow diagram (the initial part).

The emulator could recognise two types of Odra 1325 commands: the READ and WRITE ones.

The READ command resulted in an attempt to read from a specific VDU; if it was successful, the data was read from the VDU, the data code was converted (the visual displays operated with the ISO7 byte code while Odra 1325 operated with a 6-bit character code) and the transmission buffer was sent to the host. If not, the NO data message was sent to Odra 1325.

The WRITE command could include some polling sequences: DATA POLL (or UNSOLICITED READ) – reading data from a specific VDU selected by the host, STATUS POLL – reading the status of a specific VDU selected by the host, GENERAL POLL – reading data from the first VDU of V units connected to the emulator, that has data available.

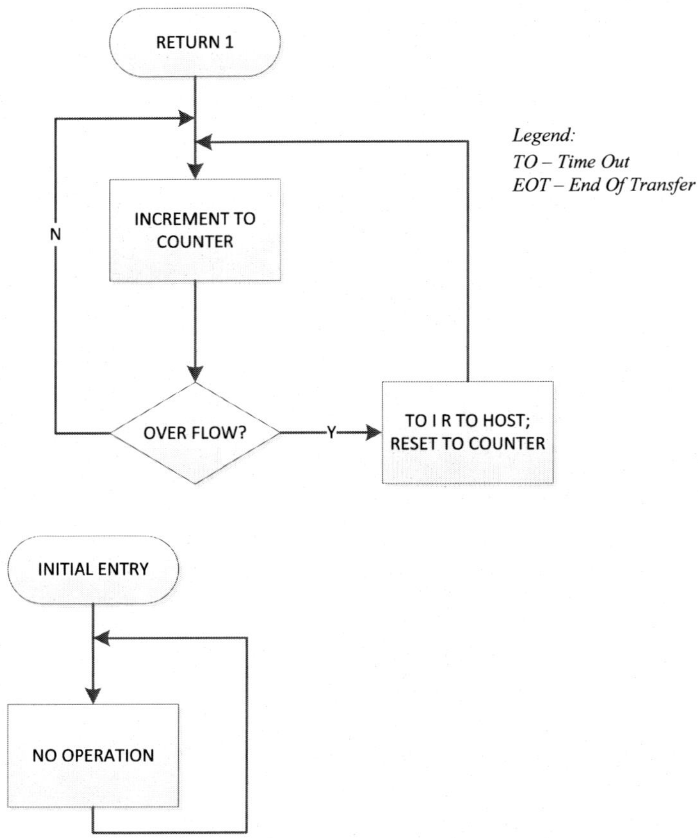

Figure 28b. CCU 7180 emulator flow diagram (the final part).

If the WRITE command requested to actually write data to a VDU that was ready to receive data, the CPU message was read and transmitted to the VDU.

On the background level, the emulator generated the Time-Out signal producing an Interrupt Request to Odra 1325.

Momik 8b proved to be very well matched to the needs of the application: the emulator program and data used almost all 8 KB memory of the minicomputer, leaving only a hundred bytes free in the maximum configuration of V = 8 VDUs.

6.1.2. Performance Requirements

The basic real-time operation requirement for the CCU emulator was that, in worst-case situations (uninterrupted transmission in both directions to/from V (8) VDU-s), the data update cycle did not exceed 10 seconds established for the power industry applications described hereinabove.

6.2. Queuing System Aids for CCU Emulator Available till 1978

The publications on queuing computer systems, available till 1978 (A. G. Konheim and M. Reiser 1978; G. Scott 1978; A. O. Allen 1978, C. Griffin 1978; H. Kobayashi 1978; M. Reiser 1978; J. P. Buzen 1978; H. Kobayashi and A. Konheim 1977, S. S. Lam 1977) repeated, in general, the assumptions of (L. Kleinrock 1975 and 1976) that were inappropriate for actual, well designed computer systems. A glaring example was that of exponential service-times, while the service time of well-designed programs should be as constant as possible and thinking time of people should be exponential, reflecting their freedom in thinking. Thus, the investigations assuming Poisson input stream and/or exponential servers were some examples of theoretical studies on models of objects that didn't exist. And, what was much, much worse, the conclusions drawn from such investigations could be used by the biggest world computer manufacturers who developed systems that responded exponentially; and the users who wanted to get relatively good service had to ensure as short as possible and deterministic thinking times. Such results are to be expected from making up real systems in accordance with the possibilities of a theoretical science.

The available queuing system aids did not enable verification if the visualisation system would meet the requirements for the real-time operation.

6.3. Problem Solution

To evaluate performance of Odra 1325 in configurations similar to SAPI ODM (Ref. Regional Power Control Board above), the Team designed a transmission speed test located in the host and in the CCU emulator. The test part located in Odra 1325 transmitted a block of 8 characters, via the Inter-processor buffer, to the CCU emulator which converted the characters into the ISO7 code and set the resulting transmission status (EOT IR). Then the program in the host initiated reading of an 8-character block from the emulator which re-converted the bytes into 6-bit characters and transmitted the latter. The data received by the host was compared with that transmitted earlier and, if the result was OK, the cycle was repeated the number of times defined by the computer operator.

During many tests, the mean character/byte transmission speed in one direction, taking the Odra 1325 and emulator program times (code conversions included) into consideration, determined by the test, was equal to $v \geq 52$ KB/characters per second. Thus, in the worst-case situation, the time needed to send and receive the full-screen data to and from V VDU-s could be approximated by:

$$t_{VDU} \cong 2\,\frac{V \bullet FS}{v_{EMU}} + 2\,\frac{V \bullet FS}{v_{VDU}} + 2 \bullet V \bullet v_k \tag{10}$$

where:

t_{VDU} - time needed to send FS data to/from V VDU-s;

V - maximum number of VDU-s per the CCU emulator ($V = 8$);

FS - full screen byte number (1000 for S9607 SVDU-s and for ALFA311 SVDU-s);

v_{EMU}- transmission speed Odra1325 – CCU emulator ($v_{EMU} \cong 52$ KB/sec);

v_{VDU} - transmission speed CCU emulator – VDU ($v_{EMU} \cong 14$ KB/sec);

v_k - sojourn time of the *k*-th *IR* for the SOSAPI operating system (k = 360, CCU).

From 10, we have:

$t_{VDU} \cong 1.524$ s

The visual display system for the Odra 1325 computer would be capable of real-time operation in configurations similar to those applied in ZEOC SAPI ODM.

The above assessment was confirmed in reality: the visualisation system discussed above was applied in, among others: the power industry training simulators (see hereinafter), an experimental computer monitor for a 200 MW thermal power generating unit, an area level electric power control centre and a power industry computer system testing centre. Everywhere, the visualisation system worked well and there were no negative remarks concerning its performance. Without the low-cost visualisation system solution, the projects of very high research importance for the overall power industry in Poland could not have been realised.

6.4. Initial Assessment of the Ethical and Human Behaviour Aspects

The researchers claiming that their queuing theory solutions were intended for real computer applications were wrong and, thus, harmed many people involved in design, development and operation of computer systems. In addition, through making up actual computer systems to the capabilities of theoretical science, they harmed even more such people through drawing wrong conclusions of their research work.

On the other hand, the Leader and his Team harmed nobody with their useful work and his behaviour should be recognised appropriate and highly ethical.

7. Power Industry Training Simulator

7.1. Simulator Description and Performance Requirements

Irrespectively of the power industry hierarchy level, the power network parts subordinated to power grid control engineers were very complex objects and the engineers needed adequate training to run them in an efficient manner. In the 1970s, the problem was recognised for big objects in many industries, the common solution proposed being a development of computer training simulators of such objects. Some references discussing the problems for the electric power industry, available at that time, included D. L. Alderman (1972; A. B. Bolopion and J. C. Sabonnadiere (1975); and Ph. Masse and J. C. Sabbonadiere (1975).

Such a commission was granted to IASE (from Polish Instytut Automatyki Systemow Energetycznych = The Institute for Power System Automation) and the Leader was appointed to the leading designer position for the power network training simulator project on the extended feasibility stage.

Due to the earlier experience with Odra 1325 systems in the power industry applications (Ref. Regional Power Control Board system, SOSAPI operating system and Power industry VDU project), it was decided to develop the simulator using the hardware architecture presented in Figure 29 (M. Rozent, 2017; J. B. Lewoc, M. Rozent and E. Weksej, 1992).

The computer hardware located in the computer room of the Polish Power Industry Training Centre in Bielsko-Biala was a limited single-computer version of ZEOC SAPI ODM (Ref. SOSAPI operating system) and included a disc unit, a paper tape punch, a CCU emulator (ref. Power industry VDU project above), a teletype and the Automatic Restart Unit (as per IASE standard), as well as the industrial peripheral control unit (SMA).

The specific training hardware located in the training room included the following devices:

- The dummy scheme (synoptic board) similar to the wall-mounted dummy schemes in power network control boards;
- The power network control engineer console simulating the control engineer keyboard used in power network control boards;
- The trainer console, the Semi-graphic Visual Display Unit and the teletype (or mosaic printer provided with a keyboard) serving for

the easy running of the training process and for calling the programs needed.

The software architecture of the power network simulator (see Figure 30) was designed and developed based on well proven software intended for the power industry applications, consisting of Executive EX2P (supplied by the Polish computer manufacturer, Elwro), derived from ICL Executive EX2M but provided with the Polish software for so-called priority interrupt, making it possible to apply the Odra 1325 computer in industrial control systems. It was decided also to use the operating system SOSAPI developed by IASE for power industry applications.

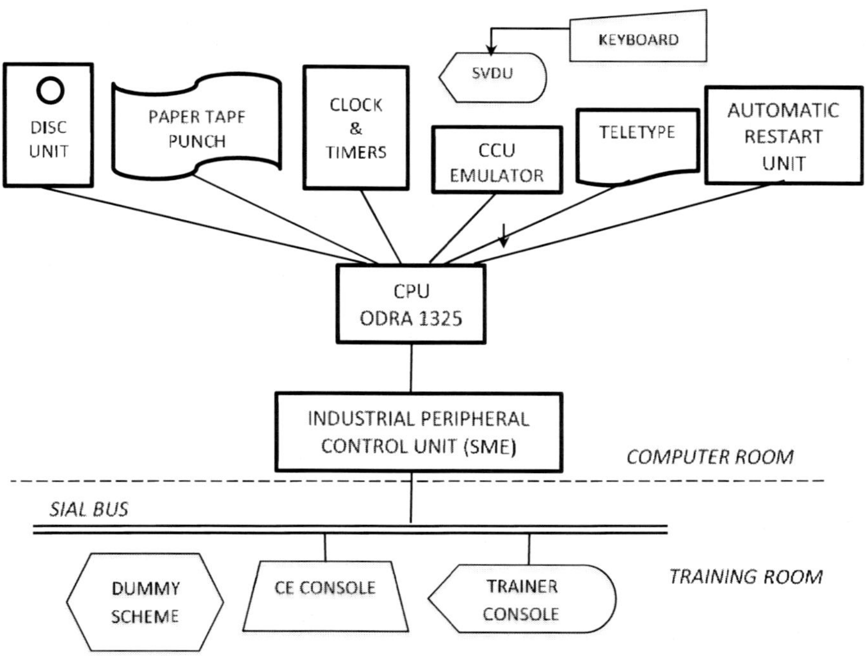

Figure 29. Hardware architecture of the power network training simulator.

However, the power industry engineers developing the power systems proper requested that the operating system should make it possible to run two types of programs:

- PUC (Program Under Control) models operating at the low pre-emptive priority level and mapping various parts of the power network being simulated;
- PUC coordinators operating at the high pre-emptive priority level, managing the training simulation process.

The Team decided to modify to a large extent the subprogram 0 of the operating system SOSAPI (Ref. SOSAPI operating system above) responsible for the PUC management, thus developing the operating system SOSYM (from Polish System Operacyjny dla SYMulacji = The operating system for simulation applications).

The software architecture of the power network simulator is shown in Figure 30.

Generally speaking, similar to SOSAPI, the subprogram 0 of SOSYM defined a working memory area, within its own area, wherein various programs under control, stored in a disc PUC library, could be run. The basic difference with regard to SOSAPI was that SOSYM, within its area, defined another area for coordinator PUC-es which were memory resident to ensure the possible high simulation speed. When needed, the subprogram 0 generated START or SUSPEND COORDINATOR signals changing the type of PUC-es being run.

The hardware and software architectures of the power network simulator were similar but smaller to that of SAPI ODM (Ref. Regional Power Control Board system and SOSAPI operating system above) and the real-time operation considerations for the foreground software were the same. From this point of view, there was no doubt that the simulator would be capable of operation in real-time. However, there was another problem for this case study.

The models used in training simulators of complex objects were also complex and time consuming. At that time, very many computer simulator projects for various domains failed due to too the low computing power of the computers applied. There was a common opinion that a training simulator computer should have the computing power above 1 MIPS (E.

Weksej 1995, Private message) to operate in real-time. Such fast computers were not available for training simulators at end of the 1970s.

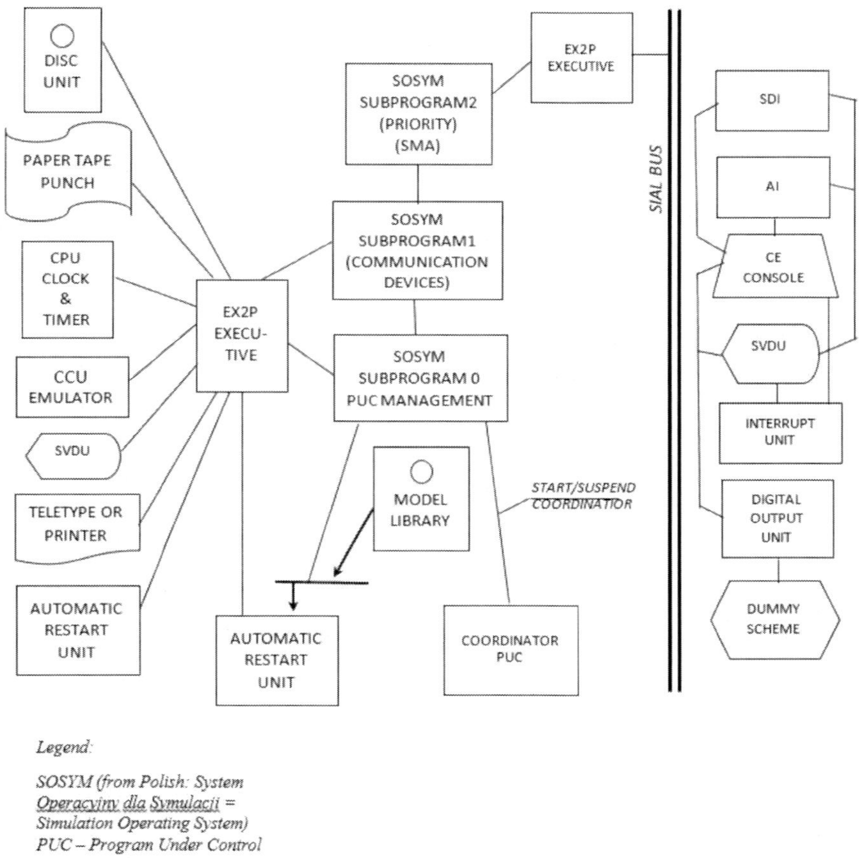

Figure 30. Software architecture of the power network training simulator.

For the Polish case study and the Odra 1325 computer, the situation was much, much worse. The Odra 1325 computing power was assessed above at some 0.4 MIPS but for foreground programs only (floating point instructions excluded). The Odra 1325 was a small computer and the floating point instructions were realised as extracodes, and were executed by standard programs. For the Odra 1300 family, there were so called JAU-s (from Polish Jednostka Autonomiczna = Autonomous Unit), highly accelerating floating point instruction execution time. Unfortunately, JAU for the Odra 1325 was never launched. This resulted in a dramatically high execution time of floating point instructions on that computer: roughly 1 millisecond for a floating point multiplication and roughly 10 millisecond for division.

And most simulator models had to be written using floating points, and the computing power requirements for the electric power network were really severe: For instance, the test on-line power flow computing program run on the Odra 1305 computer, much bigger than the Odra 1325 and provided with a hardware realisation of the floating point instructions, would need roughly the computing power 3 times bigger than actually available, in order that the power flow computing program could work in real-time.

Therefore, the Team did not start to debug standard network model programs and began to program network responses to trainee actions on the CE console, under the direction of a trainer, a former very experienced power network control engineer.

7.1.1. The Basic Real-Time Operation Requirement

To ensure smooth operation of the simulator, it was required that it responded within 1 second for any command entered by the trainee via the CE console.

7.2. Available Queuing System Aids for the Power Network Simulator

The queuing system aids available until 1980 repeated the earlier assumptions inadequate for the power system simulator under discussion. See e.g., K. M. Chandy and C. H. Sauer (1980); K. Bharath-Kumar (1980); Y. Takahashi, H. Mijahara and T. Hasegawa (1980); V. Ramaswami, (1980); and S. S. Lavenberg and M. Reiser (1980).

7.3. Mathematical Model of the Power Network Simulator

To verify if the power network simulator could meet the real-time operation requirement, it should be checked whether the full sojourn time, N_k, of an IR_k generated by any CE console pushbutton, i.e., $k \in K_{CE}$, where K_{CE} was the set of all CE console pushbutton numbers, could not be higher than 1 s. We have:

$$\prod_{k \in K_{CE}} \left(N_k \leq (Max_{\,k \in K_{CE}} (\nu_k + \nu_k^{COO} + \nu_k^{MOD}\right)) \tag{11}$$

where:

ν_k - IR_k request sojourn time, the foreground fraction;
ν_k^{COO} - IR_k request coordinator sojourn time;
ν_k^{MOD} - IR_k request model sojourn time.

Since the ZEOC case study was more complex than the simulator, we had $\nu_k \leq 5.125$ ms.

To ensure efficient management of the simulation process, the coordinators were to be core resident and fast; therefore we had: $\nu_k^{COO} \leq$ 0.5 ms.

To execute the simulator model, it was needed to download it from the disc and to read the network response to the trainee action. This needed just two disc transfers without any need to wait in any queues (during the simulation process, there were no competitors to discs). Thus, the IR_k request model sojourn time could be majorised by two maximum possible disc head positioning times, the transmission times needed to read the maximum possible model PUC and so-called simulation process status array that, in total, were lower than 0.32 s.

The PUC programs operating on pre-programmed network responses instead of modelling network states could be fast (in addition to much lower work burden, no floating point instructions were needed). Thus, the total IR_k request sojourn time could be majorised by 0.5 s and the simulator could operate in real-time.

This was confirmed in reality: during its roughly 10 year operating life, the power network simulator made it possible to train more than 90% of Polish power network engineers.

7.4. Initial Assessment of the Ethical and Human Behaviour Aspects

At the turn of the 1980s, many researchers working in the theory of queues, a section of mathematics, presented their studies, claiming that they could be applied to computers while their assumptions made such applications impossible. In this way, they harmed many people involved in design, development and operation of computer systems. Therefore, their behaviour should be recognised inappropriate and unethical.

On the other hand, the Leader and the Team harmed nobody. On the contrary, due to their hard work, a great majority of Polish power network control engineers passed adequate training resulting in a higher quality of their power network control work and, consequently, in significant benefits to the overall society of the Country. Therefore, their behaviour should be recognised appropriate and ethical.

The fact that the CCU simulator design and development team did not harm anybody and, on the contrary, made it possible to train almost all power network control engineers in use of the simulator was appreciated by the Power Industry Ministry that granted a monetary award to the team.

8. Microprocessor-Based Power Control Board System

This Section describes the project intended to design and develop a simplified, microprocessor based version of SAPI ODM for the lower hierarchy levels of the power industry.

8.1. System Description and Performance Requirements

8.1.1. Technical Description

In spite of the spectacular success of SAPI ODM on the regional power network control level in Poland (Ref. Regional Power Control Board system and SOSAPI operating system above), the problem of data acquisition, processing and presentation to power network control engineers on the lower hierarchy levels still needed a good solution. First of all, on the lower hierarchy level, control engineers controlled smaller parts of the network and a system as complex as SAPI ODM would produce much lower benefits than on the regional level and it would be doubtful if it would pay for itself. This referred not only to the computer hardware proper: For instance, SAPI ODM used discs that necessitated the installation of the system in air-conditioned rooms. Such rooms, usually, were not available in lower hierarchy level control boards. Therefore, robust (capable of operation in presence of external disturbances) low cost solutions were looked for.

The first idea was to design and develop a device making it possible for control engineers to choose selected power network analogue variables for legible local display (usually, control engineers read such information from big dummy schemes; however, this mode was not too good in dramatic alarm conditions like those mentioned in the SAPI ODM characteristics and measures assessed, para. D, above). A project was granted to IASE (the Institute for Power System Automation in Wroclaw) and the Leader was appointed for the position of the leading designer during the technical design phase.

It was decided to develop the device called the power control engineer display (the Display) on the basis of the Intel 8080 processor. The hardware architecture of the display is shown in Figure 31 (T. Lorenc 2017, Private message).

The structural units of the Display were interconnected via the Intel 8080 data and address buses. The general-purpose structural units included a single-PC board Intel 8080 microprocessor, the program and fixed data store (EPROM - Erasable Programmable Read Only Memory) and the working store (RAM - Random Access Memory).

The power network Display specific structural units included the following:

- Telemechanic interface units, comprising up to 8 telemechanic interfaces serving one central telemechanic station each. The telemechanic stations delivered the power network data cyclically, 64 8-bit data items in each cycle. The telemechanic interface units transmitted the data into the RAM memory in the block transfer mode, i.e., using so called hesitations and not interrupts after each data unit (byte). After the end of each cycle, the *k-th* telemechanic station involved produced the Process signal changed into the IR_k interrupt request, calling the analogue data processing (validation, averaging) routine, thus enabling the processing of the variables collected within one data acquisition cycle.

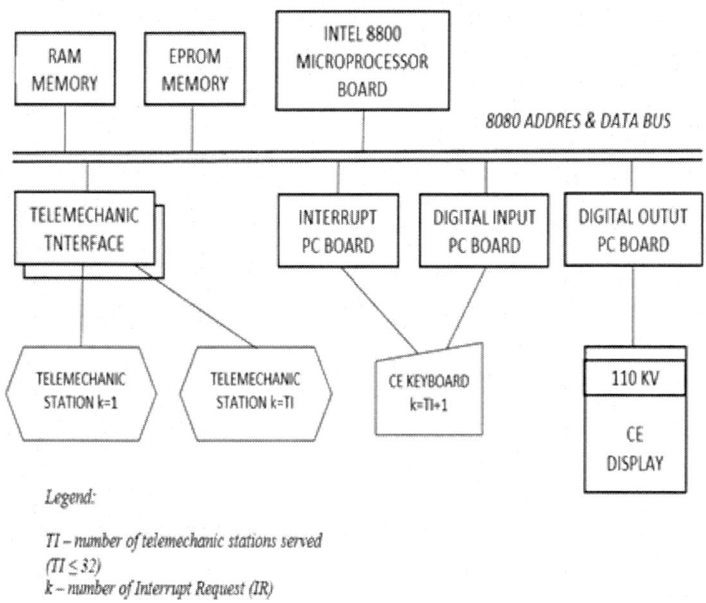

Figure 31. Hardware architecture of Intel 8080-based power control engineer display.

- The interrupt PC board producing IR_k requests to the microprocessor in order to process a power network data segment transmitted by a telemechanic station or to read (via the digital input PV board) the message (measuring point selection) input by the control engineer via the CE keyboard.
- The digital output PC board operating the CE display.

The power network Display electronics was located in a standard 19-inch rack and did not need any air-conditioned room.

The power network Display flow diagram is shown in Figure 32.

The routines operate on two pre-emptive repeat priority levels.

The low priority routine fetched (from the EPROM memory) the Display parameters, computed the presentation-form value and sent it to the display. The pre-emptive repeat priority discipline had to be applied in order to avoid erroneous displays if the low priority program was interrupted by high priority interrupts.

The high priority level program used the interrupt request number, *k*, to identify the interrupt reason. For the Process signal from a telemechanic station, the routine pre-processed the k-th store of the input data in a way similar to that used by the subprogram 1 of the SOSAPI operating system in the 10 second cycle for all analogue variables (validity checks, averaging).

For a CE keyboard message, the routine read the message input by the control engineers into the digital input PC board and set the new Display parameters for the low priority level routine. Until that instant, the CE keyboard was blocked and no subsequent IR-s could be generated.

8.1.2. Real Time Operation Requirements

To ensure that no telemechanic data was lost, the Process signal from any *k*-th telemechanic station should be accepted and served before the next data item was sent to the Display.

In addition, to ensure easy operation, any IR_k request from the CE keyboard should be accepted and served within 1 second.

8.2. Queuing System Aids Available for the Display

The references available till 1981 (M. L. Chaudhry, 1981; S. Halfin and W. Whitt, 1981; L. Kleinrock and A. Nilson, 1981) repeated the same inadequate assumptions and did not make it possible to investigate the power network control engineer Display.

8.3. Mathematical Model and Basic Characteristics Assessed

8.3.1. Basic Assumptions

The basic assumptions concerning the power network Display case study are given in Table 5.

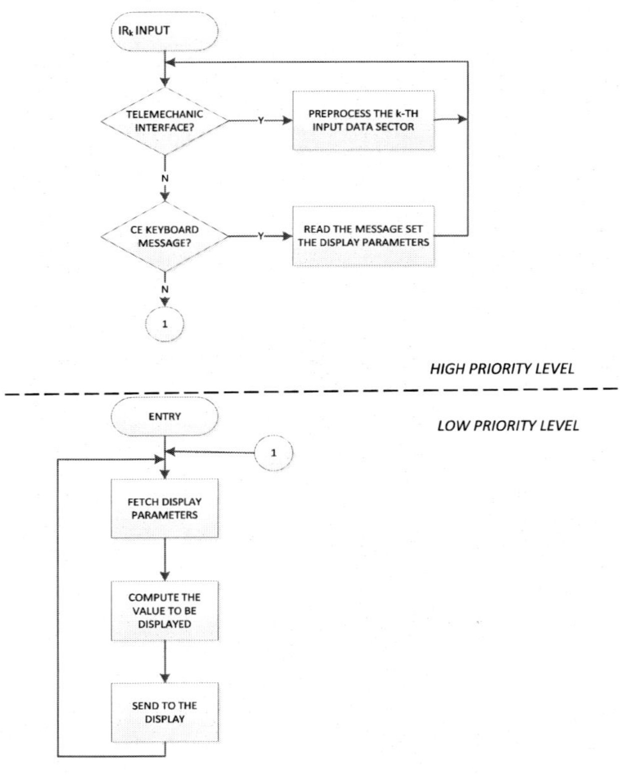

Figure 32. Power Network Display flow diagram.

Table 5. Basic assumptions concerning the power network Display case study

k	λ_k	χ_{ko}	θ_k	ν_k^*
1,…,32 Telemechanics	∞	0,15	2560	40
33 CE keyboard	$\frac{1}{10000}$	0.1	1000	1000

Notes: 1. All values are in ms.

8.3.2. Evaluation of the Hesitation Load

In the power network CE display, the telemechanic interfaces were connected to the RAM memory via the DMA (Direct Memory Access) channel. For 32 telemechanic stations operating at the speed of 200 baud, this produced the hesitation traffic of the intensity:

$$h = \frac{32}{40\ msec} = 80\frac{1}{sec},$$

extending the period of execution of MIPS instruction, i.e., 1 second, of 160 μsec only. Therefore, it could be assumed that the hesitation load in the case study of the power network CE Display did not decrease the value of MIPS.

8.3.3. Assessment if the Real-Time Operation Requirements Were Observed

To answer the questions, it was needed to assess the maximum possible value of the sojourn time of the relevant IR_k request, ν_k^{Max}. In the worst-case situation, IR_k could find all other requests waiting for service or in service.

Therefore, we had:

$$\prod_{k=1,\dots,33}(\nu_k^{Max} \leq \sum_{k=1,\dots,33} \chi_{ko}) \tag{12}$$

From 12, we have:

$$\prod_{k=1,\dots,33} (v_k^{Max} \leq \sum_{k=1,\dots,33} \chi_{ko} \leq 5\, msec)$$

This meant that both requirements for the real-time operation were observed by the power network CE display.

This was confirmed in an actual application in an area-level Power Control Board.

The success was possible primarily because of the approach adopted when developing the power network CE Display design: all the design Team including the hardware and software specialists worked together, solving, under direction of the Leader, the design problems one after another. In this way, the Leader educated and upgraded the Team of designers to adequate knowledge levels in the hardware and software domains, capable of continuing his work after he was transferred to another job.

Unfortunately, in December 1981, Martial Law was introduced in Poland which resulted in a severe recession in the country. The demand for electric power decreased dramatically and many projects for the power industry were abandoned, including the power network CE engineer Display.

8.4. Initial Assessment of the Ethical and Human Behaviour Aspects

The researchers of the branch of mathematics, the theory of queues, made light of the actual assumptions valid for computer systems and often claimed that their work could be applied in the ICT domain. In this way, they harmed many people involved in the area of computers. Therefore, their conduct should be considered inappropriate and unethical.

On the other hand, the Leader and his Team did not harm anybody; in particular, this refers to his way to leading the project, educating and upgrading his younger colleagues in the domain of adequate designing microcomputer systems. Thus, his conduct should be assessed as appropriate and highly ethical.

9. Interuniversity Communication Network

This Section describes the project intended to design, develop, commission, use and investigate the communication network of the first Polish wide-area public computer network.

9.1. Communication Network Description and Performance Requirements

In the 1970s and 80s, there was visible a strong movement of computer users who were opposed to the position of the world's biggest computer hardware manufacturers, who tried to design, develop and implement so-called homogeneous computer networks, being built on the basis of a single manufacturer's computer hardware. The computer users (primarily in Academia) designed and developed their own heterogeneous network solutions in the form of public computer networks (Techopedia, 2017).

The Wroclaw Technical University joined this movement and opened a research and technical project of MSK (from Polish Miedzyuczelniania Siec Komputerowa = Interuniversity Computer Network)- see E. Bilski, Ed. (1987). The Leader was drafted in to the lead of the project of the MSK communication network.

The architecture of the MSK network, phase 1, is shown in Figure 33.

The MSK network was to interconnect three big Polish academic centres: Warsaw (the Computing Centre of the Polish Academy of Sciences (PAN) Informatics Bases Institute), Wroclaw (the Computing Centre of the Wroclaw University of Technology) and Gliwice (the Electronic Computing Technique Centre of the Silesian University of Technology).

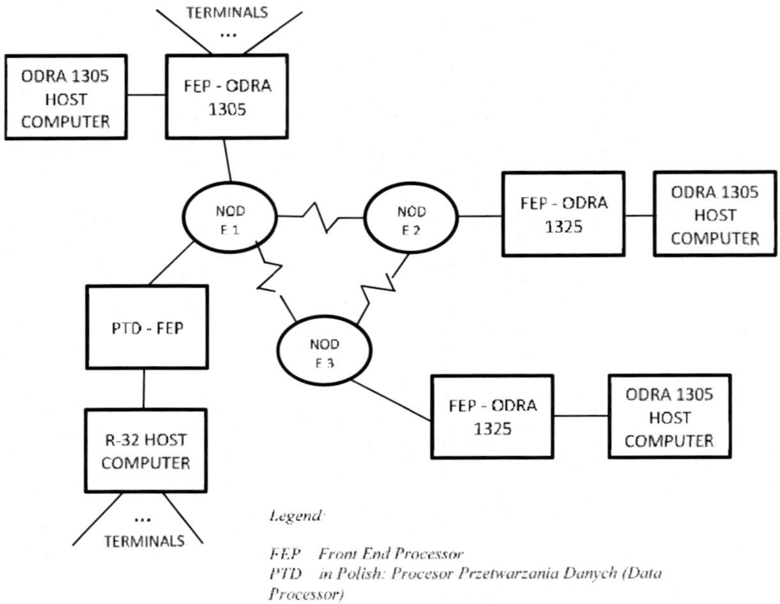

Figure 33. MSK network architecture, phase 1.

A project assumption was that the communication network was to be composed of almost identical nodes (switches) built on Russian SM-3 minicomputers compatible with Digital Equipment Corporation's PDP-11/20 (Wikipedia, 2017e). The node/switch hardware is shown in Figure 34. All hardware units were interconnected via the computer bus and included the following:

- SM-3 processor,
- Working memory,
- Disc,
- Paper tape reader/punch,
- Visual Display Unit (VDU),
- A set of communication adapters with optional modems.

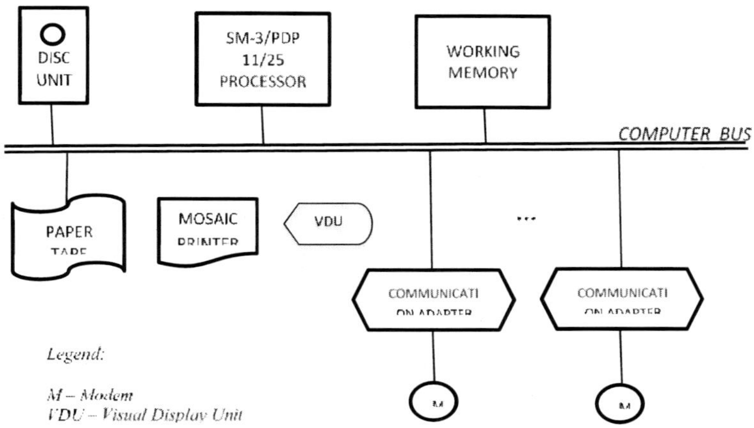

Figure 34. Communication network node/switch hardware.

To facilitate programming of individual node/switch functions, it was decided to design and develop a communications-oriented operating system Sonet (from Polish/English System operacyjny (Operating system) for networking applications) (Ref. Figure 35). Under Sonet, programs could be run on the pre-emptive resume priority levels: level 1 (of the lowest priority) to level 5 (of the highest priority).

The highest priority level 5 (actually, in accordance with the DEC's terminology, this was the priority 6) was devoted to the communication drivers serving the communication adapters. The adapters used in MSK were not provided with DMA (Direct Memory Access) and, for the data transfer rate of 9600 bits per second and 4 adapters per node/switch, any byte should be served within 3 milliseconds, roughly, so the drivers had to have been rather fast.

Level 4 was used for the local disc. There was no need to use the disk for normal node/switch operation but the project was of a research character and the disk was used for storing and swapping measuring data.

Level 3 was used to serve the basic peripherals destined to input and output possible measuring data.

On Level 2, there were run the basic node/switch jobs fulfilling the networking functions.

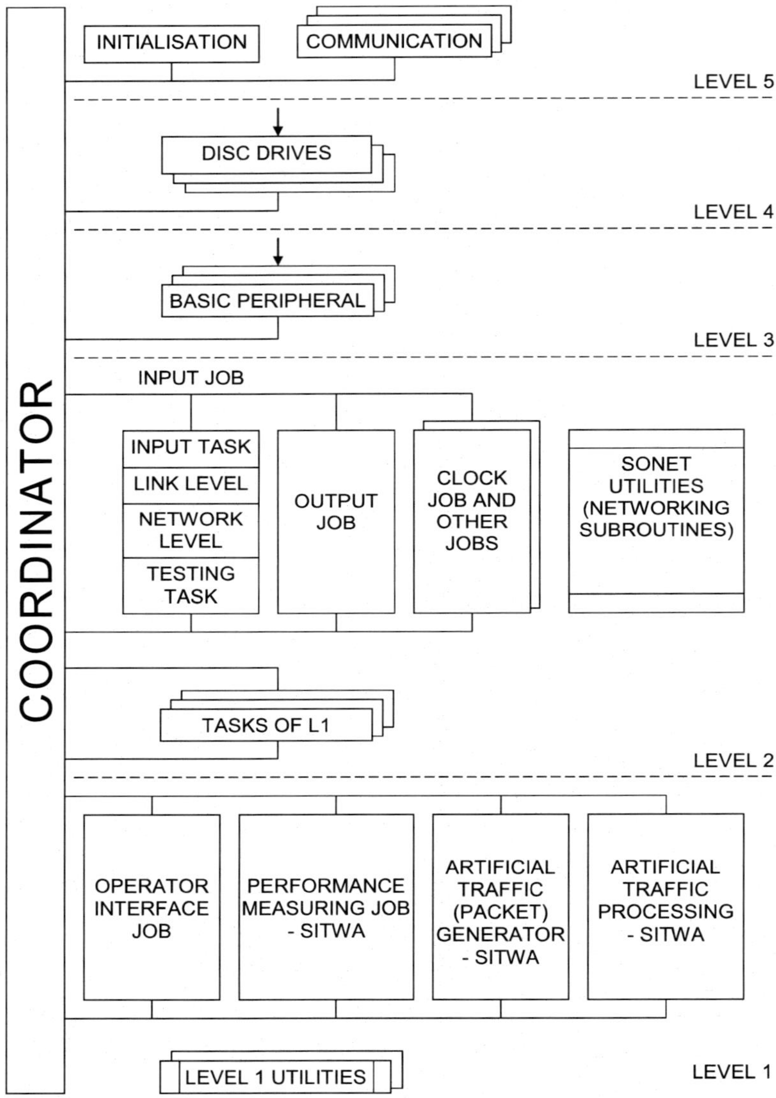

Figure 35. Node/switch software (Sonet) architecture.

The input job was composed of four tasks:

- the input task pre-processing data received from the communication adapters,

- the link level serving the physical layer protocol,
- the network level serving the network layer protocol,
- the testing task serving the network measuring system.

The output job managed outputting Sonet data buffers to individual communication adapters.

There were also some other jobs run on the level 2, devoted for fulfilling auxiliary node/switch functions.

- The set of Sonet utilities serving for execution of common functions on level 2.
- The tasks of level 1 that were enabled to protect level 1 jobs against interruption by level 2 programs when they were to operate on data common with level 3.

Level 1 was the lowest priority level under Sonet. On this level, the following jobs could be run:

- the operator interface job enabling control of the node/switch operation,
- the performance measuring job Sitwa (from Polish System intensywnego testowania wezla = intensive node/switch testing system), i.e., the internal network measuring tool (see below),
- the artificial traffic generator for the Sitwa tool;
- the artificial traffic processing job for Sitwa.

Level 1 utilities performed the common functions on the level 1.

The coordinator was the Sonet kernel managing operation of the node/switch software.

The MSK network under discussion belonged to actual computer networks by which it was understood as a WAN (Wide Area Network) network (ref. Figure 36) with packet switching and end-to-end acknowledgement, defined by the following quadruple (13):

$$\text{WAN} = \{\text{DTE, DCE, IN, SUB}\} \tag{13}$$

Where:

DTE was the set of network subscribers, $d_1,\ldots,d_u$;

DCE was the set of communication network switches (nodes, routers, gateways, etc.), $w_1, \ldots, w_c$;

IN was the set of communication network input links;

SUB was the set of links (hops) within the communication network.

On *IN* and *SUB* were stretched a set of closed routes (14). An exemplary network route is presented in Figure 37.

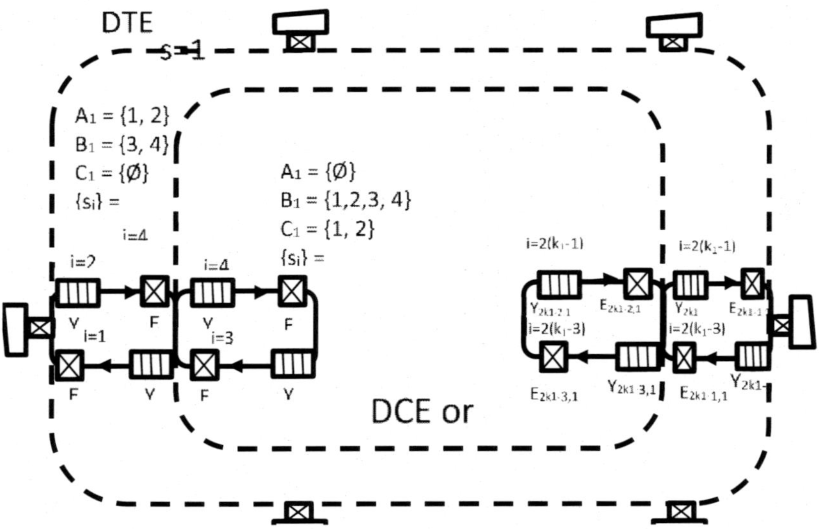

Figure 36. Illustrative diagram of a wide area network.

Note:

MSK observed the assumption that no computer network component was allowed to transmit an arbitrary number of entities (packets) into any link but it had to obey some flow control rule and defer from transmitting more entities (packets) than the credit allowed, informed of by the last acknowledgement received. This assumption was true for all communication and computer networks known to the Authors.

When the expected values of the random variables presented in Figures 4.36 and 4.37 were denoted by corresponding lower case letters, the obvious balance equations for each s=1,…,n could be described by the formula (15):

$$\bigcap_{s\in S}(t_s = m_s + \sum_{i\in I_s}(y_{i,s} + e_{i,s})); \qquad (15)$$

Where:

S is the set of all closed routes, $\overline{S} = v$; and

I_s is the set of links through which the s-the route passes.

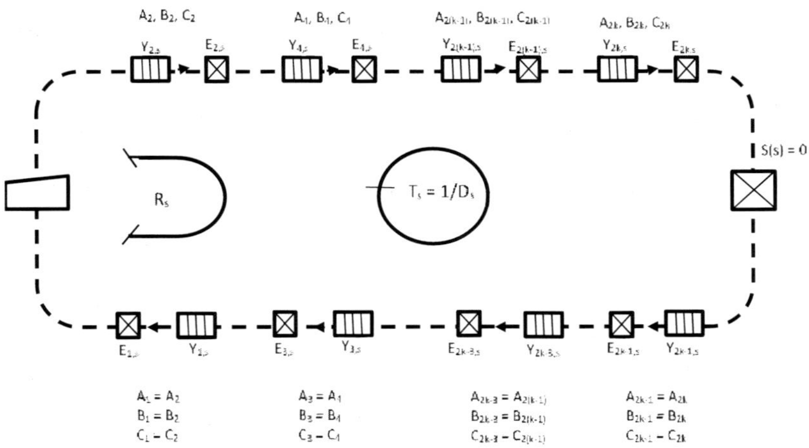

Figure 37. Exemplary route for the s-th network subscriber.

$$LOOP = \left\{\left(i_{1,s}, i_{2,s}, \ldots, i_{k_s,s}\right)\right\}_{s=1}^{n}. \qquad (14)$$

In (15), the known values were m_s and $e_{i,s}$. It was needed to find $y_{i,s}$ and t_s values. To summarise, an actual network was described as a superposition of the closed routes (calls, connections, virtual calls, etc.) passing via the set of links available in *IN* and *SUB*. In accordance with a real practice, the links passiing by individual closed routes were predefined (at least, in normal operating conditions), where *S* was the set of all closed routes and I_s was the set of links through which the s-th route passes.

Another important job undertaken by the Leader was that of the R-32 computer, compatible with the IBM/360 mainframes, that would be included in the MSK network. A common opinion of computer user, was that the performance of R-32 was very poor. The Computing Centre in designing the MSK project used the multi-access systems built on R-32 and run under the IBM operating system OS/MVT (Wikipedia, 2017e) and the Telecommunication Access Method, TCAM (Wikipedia, 2017g), and on a small Polish computer Odra 1325 (ICL 1902a compatible (Wikipedia, 2017i)), run under the operating system Executive (Wikipedia, 2017i) and the multi-access system MINIMOP (Wikipedia, 2017h). The Leader made use of that and took comparative performance measurements for the two systems using similar operation types: debugging and running programs written in high level languages. The results were amazing: the computing costs for R-32 were some 100 times higher than those for Odra 1325.

Three University of Cambridge (UC) Computer Laboratory (CL) researchers visited the Leader and delivered, among other things, the Parrot program substituting the TCAM method on R-32 and the technical descriptions of the Phoenix system programs eliminating many serious errors in OS/MVT (University of Cambridge, 1980). Responsibility for the errors was blamed on inappropriate performance evaluation methods or missed performance investigations for such big computer projects.

The Leader supported voluntarily the team responsible for design and development of the R-32 Front End Processor (FEP), drawing the program flowcharts in front of them. The Parrot program was implemented on R-32 and its counterpart, originally run on the CL PDP-11/20, was transformed onto the MSK R-32 FEP (Front End Processor).

This solution proved to be successful (Ref. Figure 38).

A very big fault of the IBM/System 360 and IBM/System 370 (or the Polish replicas R-32 and R-34, respectively) was that the processors were not provided with registers equivalent to ICL 1900 (Odra 1300) Datum and Limit making it possible to reload the downloaded programs. Due to this, the programs in the IBM computers had to be executed in the memory area into which they were downloaded, which resulted in memory fragmentation and unused areas in the memory (Unknown author, 2017). The UC researchers made some use of the unused areas by loading some interrogating-mode sessions therein.

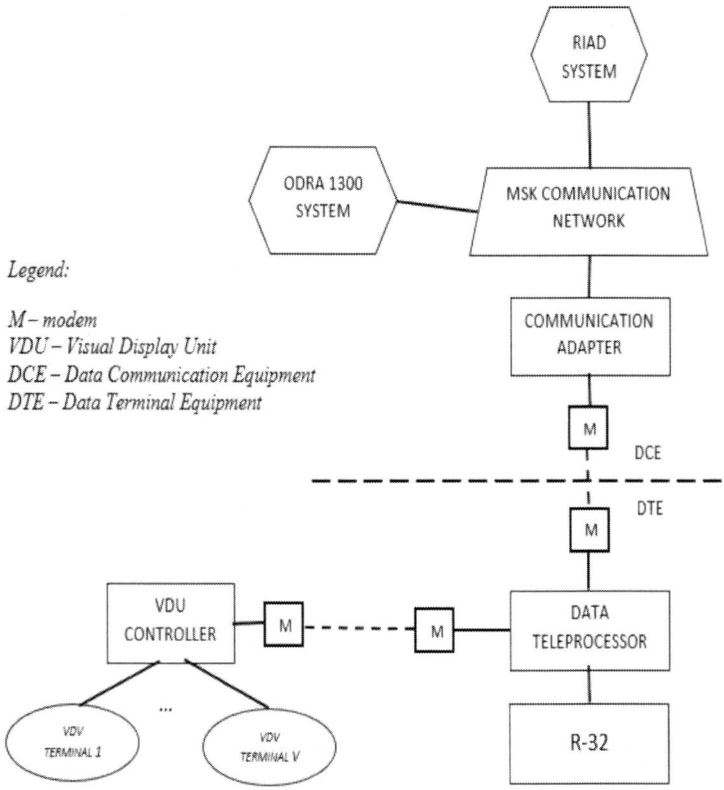

Figure 38. R-32 system of the Wroclaw MSK node/switch.

The Leader devised an idea of the complete elimination of the fragmentation problem. He proposed to add the hardware Datum and Limit registers similar to those used in ICL 1900 Series (or Odra 1300 family) computers to the R-34 (OS/370) CPUs and to modify the OS/VS operating system basically at a very limited number of the operating system points entered when some user programs were completed. He discussed the idea with the leading designer (constructor) of the R-34 computer and they agreed that the project would be feasible. Unfortunately, the PoPs (Power of People) in charge of the R-34 development were scared to even think of such big modifications in the Big Brother's (Soviet Union's) computer and the project was never commissioned.

A digression: When delivering the CL software, the UC researchers told the Leader that he could give it to anybody he wanted, provided that he did not sell it.

During a Phoenix presentation, the researcher talked about frequent IBM/360 computer crashes. The Leader asked: what about an automatic restart? The violent negative reaction was really amazing to the Leader since he was always happy when his subordinates (usually called his students) devised a solution competitive to that of his own, and such a solution was always accepted, provided that it was feasible, in order that the students acquired the motivation and self-assurance that would be much-needed when they were to substitute him as the leading designer. The ultimate argument of the CL researcher was: Bogdan, if it were so simple, we, in Cambridge, would have devised it.

After some time, the Leader was involved in a project commissioned by the Solidarity underground, TV Solidarity (A. Kuberska, J. B. Lewoc and L. Misiura, 1986). The objective was to add Solidarity texts to the programs displayed by the governmental TV. He had problems with a TV signal processing since he believed that all good TV engineers were being watched by the political police (SB). But he got a chance to go to the United Kingdom for a 3 month practice (most probably due to some action by his Solidarity principals). He was very happy, the CL researchers claimed to be after him, after Solidarity. He visited the UC Cavendish Laboratory where they were designing the Radio-astronomy centre control system (See 4.2 above) and he knew they had radio signal processing experts of the highest expertise and believed that they could improve the TV signal processing part, the TV Solidarity unit could be assembled and, perhaps, even some field trials could be done.

Unfortunately, the CL Head refused to accept him and added that the Leader distributed CL programs illegally.

It was a too strong blow at the Leader and hospital treatment was needed. When he recovered, he thought over the case: He agreed that, in spite of claiming to be after him, the researchers could be scared of joining his project, of getting involved in a political affair but, he thought, nobody, unpunished, should dare to call him a program thief in an official letter. So he asked for the technical description of the Cambridge Ring LAN and compared its performance with the performance of Ethernet LAN. He wrote a paper: (J. B. Lewoc and R. Sibilski, 1985), concluding: We do not suffer the well-known illness: English is the best, and Cambridge is the best of English. On the contrary, what really makes me sick is a way of arguing: "Bogdan, if it were so simple, we, in Cambridge, should have devised it." And this sickness was the actual not virtual reason for not approving my visit in the Computer Laboratory of the University of Cambridge. This had been written to give some evidence that if we tried to cheat, we would do it against not for the Computer Laboratory.

The paper must have been red by UC CL since, sometime later, a UC researcher told the Leader that he had an entry-ban to UC (perhaps as the only human being of the World?) and added: But you will be there, I tell you this. And the Leader wished to be there, indeed, to tell them what he thought about them, looking straight at their eyes.

In a month or so, the Leader found a call for papers on his desk: a conference on robustness in the UC Pembroke College. He knew nothing about robust control systems and even never heard the word robustness. But he found soon the Polish university active in the domain, visited them and got the very basic reference on the μ function, a robustness measure (Doyle, 1982), and applied it to the power industry. The paper (A. Izworski and J. B. Lewoc, 1991) was accepted and the Leader invited the CL researchers for a meeting during the conference.

Of course, no member of the conference committees had ever heard of him and he was allotted the presentation slot reserved for such men of nowhere; the last slot of the session, roughly at 9 PM. When he entered the stage, he felt somewhat uneasy: an auditorium of some 300 robustness experts, the Chairman – a Dutch Professor, No. 2 in the European robustness domain and the very useful book (J. M. Maciejowski, 1989) reached him much too late since the parcel was opened in a big German airport by somebody looking for possible money. So he began: "I am happy to speak here and now, since I believe that the conference organisers know the Bible rule that the best wine should be served last." There was a few seconds of silence and a roar of laughter, and, during the presentation, the Leader could hear even a housefly. The presentation was assessed as a real success by the conference committees and by J. M. Maciejowski.

After the session finished, the Leader looked for the CL researchers; nobody came. He felt uneasy again but, next, he thought: It seemed that they, the researchers of one of the most recognisable computer laboratories in the World were scared and ashamed of meeting him, a stupid engineer (he loved this nickname of him since an engineer was someone who could do useful things and stupid, in the spheres of science, meant someone who did not use a heavy cannon to shoot a housefly), from a poorly developed Country. He became very proud and finished the Cambridge incident.

A CL researcher informed the Leader that he had been appointed by the Laboratory as their representative responsible for implementation of the Phoenix system in the Country. But they refused such a person without a due respect to the CL researchers and selected another Polish programmer. Unfortunately, the latter was not successful and the Phoenix system was not implemented in Poland.

The results were very severe for Poland. The R-32 and R-34 computers were not accepted for professional computing due to their high computing costs. In addition, due to an unpardonable deed of some PoPs, the Odra 1300 family computers were not registered as Comecon computers and their production was abandoned by Elwro (the biggest Polish computer manufacturer) which was the basic reason for the crash of the company and of the large-scale computing in the overall Country.

The questions to be answered for the communication network were:

1) What were the maximum possible values of the round trip delay random variable (R_s) for various distributions of the thinking times (M_s) and the service times (S_s); s=1,..,v.
2) What were the maximum possible and mean values of the closed route cycle times (T_s) (and the minimum possible and mean values of the throughput variables ($D_s = \frac{1}{T_s}$)) for various distributions of the thinking times (M_s) and the service times (S_s); s=1,..,v.

The questions would only be answered when the communication network was handed over to useful operation, i.e., 1984.

9.2. Available Queuing Network and Network Measuring Aids

9.2.1. Closed Queuing Networks

In the early eighties of the previous century, the researchers of the theory of queues began to investigate closed queuing networks of the product form which had a simple form expression of the stationary state distribution that allowed to define efficient algorithms to evaluate average performance measures. The Authors of the publications (M. Reiser, 1981; M. Reiser and S. S. Lavenberg, 1980) proposed two algorithms:

- MVA (Mean Value Analysis) based on the arrival theorem which stated: In a closed queuing network, the (stationary) state probabilities at customer arrival epochs were identical with those of the same network in long-term equilibrium with one customer removed.
- NCA (Normalised Convolution Algorithm), i.e., a new formulation of the of the convolution algorithm based on mean-value formulae, working entirely with marginal probabilities and throughputs thus eliminating floating-point overflow problems encountered in previous convolution algorithms.

The objectives of the Authors were the following:

- To give an efficient algorithmic formulation of the mean-value analysis for the class of queue-dependent servers.
- To eliminate a numerical instability of the mean-value algorithm for queue-dependent servers, arising from subtraction of nearly equal numbers.
- To give a new formulation of the convolution algorithm based on the mean-value formulae.

- To show how the MVA and NCA methods could be combined.

The Author claimed that the closed queuing-network models with product form solutions had found widespread applications in the performance analysis of computer systems and data communication networks.

However, it is obvious from the objectives of the Authors, cited above, that the methods proposed touched the computational problems only and did not change the description of the previous queuing networks. In particular, the offered load or input stream of the queuing networks was determined by the random variables being the inter-arrival times, and the flow control mechanisms implemented in all actual computer systems and networks, were not taken into account. Thus, between the closed queuing networks that could be investigated with the MVA and NCA methods and the actual computer networks there was no isomorphism necessary for application of the methods in investigation of actual computer networks like MSK. Considering the fact that the determination of the offered load had a severe impact on the results, possible results obtained from the closed queuing networks would be decidedly different from the performance characteristics and measures valid for actual computer networks.

In addition, the Authors claimed that they showed that the mean values only could be computed with the MVA and NCA methods. Therefore, even if the offered load description were changed, the maximum possible values of the actual network measures could not be computed.

9.2.2. Network Measurements

The inadequacy of the analytical technique (closed queuing networks) for the investigation of actual computer networks resulted in the development of the measuring methods and systems (P. F. Polwita, 1981; J. F. Schoch and J. A. Hupp, 1980; D. N. Murray and P. H. Enslow, 1984; F. A. Tobagi, 1978). However, the overwhelming majority of the measuring systems and methods, for both LANs (Local Area Networks) and WANs (Wide Area Networks), were located in the Data Terminal

Equipment (DTE) component of the WAN network (13) and it was rather difficult to perform complex measuring projects. Most probably, the basic reasons for that was that the communication network designers and developers were not seriously interested in measurements, and were afraid of allowing measuring system specialists to make any changes in the communication network interior, which would be necessary in the case of an internal measuring system development.

However, in the MSK case, the Leader led the communication network project and the measuring system project, and there was a chance to develop an internal network measuring tool of capabilities much bigger that those of standard external measuring tools.

9.3. Mathematical Models

9.3.1. Introduction

In the early period of wide area network development, when researchers were extensively employed in the network design teams, the problems of performance tests or measurements could be tackled rather easily. The detailed solutions applied in computer and communication networks held no secrets for the researchers.

Some network researchers underestimated the basic difference between the internal and external measuring tool, claiming that it was not important where the tool was to be implemented. This is evidence that many of them did not know the networks to be investigated.

For the purposes of this book, an *internal* measuring/testing tool was a program located in a TCP/IP network switch (node, router, gateway, etc.) and serving to generate artificial traffic and modelling/testing of the network performance while an *external* one was a hardware and/or software system connected to the communications network and simulating a network subscriber or a group of subscribers, and serving similar purposes. Actually, most external testing/measuring tools were realisations (models) of network subscribers, and were limited to single subscriber interfaces. They could generate, therefore, only local Internet traffic. Of course, they could be very useful e.g., for the network protocol testing purposes. But in no way could they generate network traffic and measure performance on the overall scale of the communication network involved.

Considering the facts specified above, it seemed to be worthwhile to propose the general structure and feasible functionality of an internal network performance testing/measuring tool intended especially for networks operating under the TCP/IP protocol suite (Techtarget Network, 2017). The proposal was based on the experience in development and applications of the internal network performance measuring tool Sitwa (from Polish System intensywnego testowania wezła =_intensive node testing system). Some results obtained with Sitwa are presented hereinafter in order to show some possible benefits of an internal performance evaluation measuring tool.

9.3.2. Measuring/Testing Tool

9.3.2.1. Initial Assumptions

It was planned to investigate the overall structure of an Internet network and, therefore, Sitwa was to be located within the critical communication network switches (nodes, routes, gateways) operating under some Specialised operating system for network purposes (Sonet), i.e., a collection of possible tasks and jobs (task sequences) operating on several pre-emptive resume priority levels available in any computers up-to-date in the 1980s (ref. Figure 35). Sitwa was designed and developed by a three-student Team supervised by the Leader and presented in Czajkowski et al., (1984 and 1985).

Prior to discussing the basic solutions adapted in Sitwa, the general assumptions adopted should be briefly presented. The basic idea assumed in the testing/measuring tool consisted of establishing “measuring calls” between two Sitwa (virtual) subscribers or between one virtual and one actual subscriber, called the Sender and the Addressee, respectively, and in recording the following:

- mean and maximum possible network delay time between the Sender and the Addressee,
- mean and maximum possible network response delay time between the Addressee and the Sender,
- mean and maximum possible round-trip delay time between the Sender and the Sender.

The expected values of the delay times enabled the calculation also of some secondary characteristics such as:

- mean throughput in any measuring call (in packets per a time unit),
- rough transit and round-trip delay distributions (histograms).

Performance measurements were taken for the superposition of an artificial load generated by virtual subscribers operating within the communication network, and current load produced by actual network users. This policy was in conformity with the philosophy adopted from the very beginning in the queuing theory (T. G. Robertazzi, 2000) - that any queuing system was to be investigated by adding additional customers to the normal configuration of the system and by evaluating the service quality experienced by the additional customers.

To ensure that the traffic generated by virtual subscribers was similar to the actual traffic that would be generated by equivalent actual users, Sitwa computed the time instants that the next packet/frame was to be transmitted, making use of predefined density function tables and the standard switch software used in valid flow control mechanisms. Thus, the virtual traffic was generated in a way similar to generation of the actual traffic and not by forcing some predefined offered load for the network.

The performance testing/measuring process within the whole communication network was conducted as follows (Figures 4.39 and 4.40): the artificial traffic generator read in the run control parameters (including the run time, the scenario and the default values of the Sitwa line descriptions). Sitwa, in all nodes except one, started to establish connections transmitting initial sequence packets, while the station where

Sitwas started, as the last one in the communication network (Master Sitwa), produced acknowledgement packets, thus enabling operating of Sitwas initiated before (Slave Sitwas). There was no other major difference between Master Sitwa and Slave Sitwas.

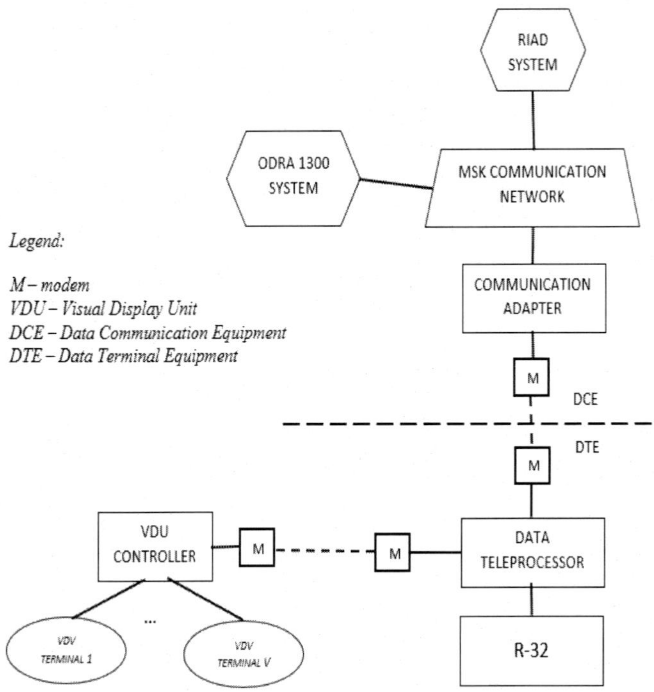

Figure 39. Functional block diagram of Sitwa in Sonet.

The artificial traffic generator produced supervisory frames or information frames with data packets in accordance with some predefined distribution of the virtual user thinking time. The credit control rules were applied next. In this way, traffic in the network was generated from the offered load of the virtual subscriber, that was defined as the distribution of the time from the instant that a frame was received to the instant that the subscriber was ready to send a response frame. The round-robin service for individual connections and Sitwa lines ensured a fair service.

The receiving, testing, measuring and control process is presented in Figure 41.

When the process was woken up, it scanned the Sitwa lines looking for those with the transfer completed condition. For the lines in such conditions, Sitwa updated the performance testing/measuring values and logged the traffic measured.

When reception was completed, the control process woke the Rx process (Artificial traffic generation, operating at level 1 of Sonet).

LINK FLOW CONTROL		
INCOMING FRAME COUNT		
FRAME TRANSMISSION / RECEPTION TIME		FLOW CONTROL VARIABLES, GENERATOR No.
CURRENT CONNECTION DESCRIPTION ADDRESS		CONNECTION GROUP; CONNECTION No.; CALLING NODE No.; CALLED NODE No.
INITIAL CONNECTION DESCRIPTION ADDRESS		PACKET TRANSMISSION / RECEPTION INSTANT
CURRENT CONNECTION NUMBER		PACKETS RECEIVED COUNT
...		SPARE
CONNECTION DESCRIPTION		
...		
k-th SITWA LINE DESCRIPTION		*CONNECTION DESCRIPTION*

Figure 40. Sitwa line description table.

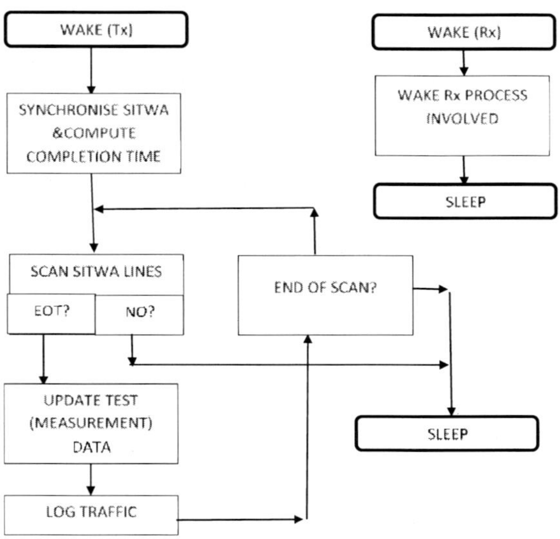

Figure 41. Receiving/testing (measuring) and control process.

9.3.3. Exemplary Performance Tests/Measurements

The basic notion used in the performance tests/measurements conducted with use of the Sitwa tool was that of the "closed route" (circuit, connection) within a computer network. The computer network loop (Figure 41) consisted of the *k*-th subscriber exchanging data with the s-th one (possibly a process within some host). The *k*-th subscriber thought (received and analysed the response, and generated a subsequent data packet/packets or automatically delivered a control packet/frame) for M_k (a random variable). The *k*-th subscriber transmitted a packet/frame which, after the random variable, T_k, was delivered to the *s*-th subscriber that served the request for the random variable, S_s and transmitted a reply. This one was queued, transmitted by the network and reached the *k*-th subscriber after a random variable, T_s.

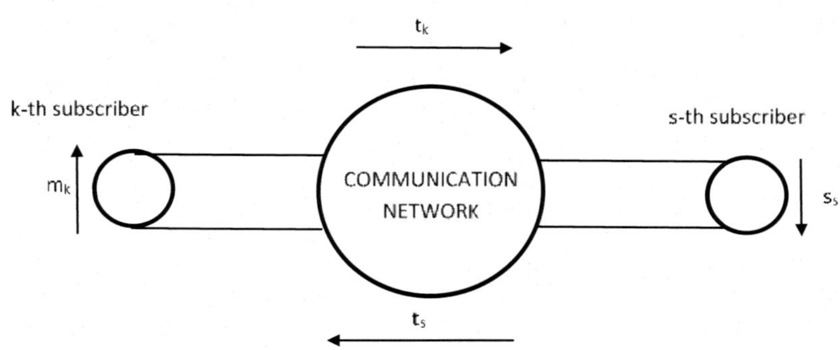

Figure 42. Computer network loop diagram.

In accordance with the testing/measuring scenario applied, M_k and S_s could include the application (or a human being) time only or the operating system service time and transmission time also, e.g., when a remote scientific information retrieval or a foreign communication network were modelled.

The random variables presented in Figure 42 are denoted here by the upper-case letters while their mean values (used in the text) – by the corresponding lower case letters.

Thus we have:

- Mean transit delay: t_k (from the k-th user) or t_s (from the s-th server)
- Mean round trip delay (from the k-th user): $r_k = t_k + s_s + t_s$
- Throughput (for the k-th user): $q_k = (m_k + t_k + s_s + t_s)^{-1}$

The throughput value in packets per second should be multiplied by the mean data field length to obtain the throughput value in bytes per second. In this way, the artificial traffic processing job (Figure 35) could obey fast fixed-point instructions (additions) only in the performance evaluation computations, thus increasing the experiment quality.

Typical results presenting the mean values specified above for a typical case of connections established in earlier networks are shown in Figures 43, and 44, respectively.

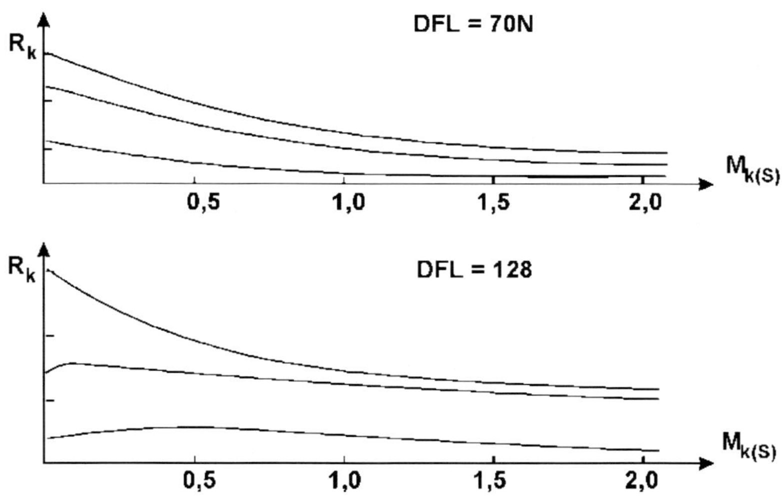

Figure 43. Round trip delay R_k versus mean thinking time $M_{k(S)}$.

The control variable for all experiments described above was the mean thinking time m, assumed the same for all subscribers simulated in order that the experiments could be controlled and analysed more easily. The plots of Figure 43 show the phenomenon of congestion (saturation): for the Data Field Length (DFL) of 128 bytes, the mean round-trip delay in the connection under investigation decreased when *M* decreased (the low *M* region). For the same testing/measuring scenario, no congestion (saturation) can be observed (the upper plots in Figure 43) when the DFL equals to 70N (approximate normal distribution of the mean value equal to 70 octets).

The plots of the mean throughput, shown in Figure 44, exhibit slight congestion (saturation) even at DFL = 70N, while the plots of the transit delay – for the DFL = 128 octets only.

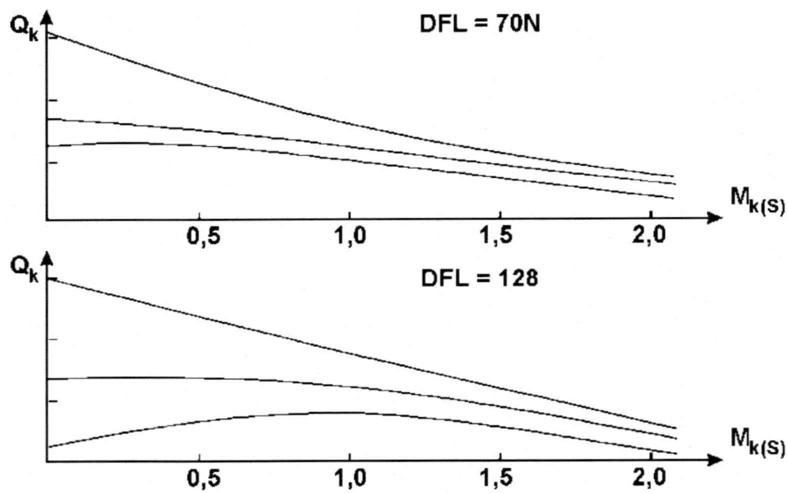

Figure 44. Throughput (Q_k) versus mean thinking time $M_{k(S)}$.

The phenomenon of congestion (saturation) was not an obvious thing for communication networks, where packets may not be lost. However, it was proved by testing/measurements with Sitwa for the case that some subscriber tried to increase its throughput (by decreasing his or her thinking time) when other subscribers do the same. The testing/ measurement results confirmed the results of simulation investigations carried out for earlier networks.

The congestion phenomenon was one of the interesting findings for data communication networks, obtained through using the internal network performance testing/measuring tool.

However, perhaps the most important result of developing and running Sitwa was the detailed understanding achieved in the things that actually happened in the communication and/or computer network, at least the ones with end-to-end acknowledgement. It was possible to propose and investigate some feasible proposals for network optimisation (e.g., small credit value 1 for connections operating in the interrogating mode, high credit values for file transfers).

This understanding could possibly help some researchers to avoid theoretical investigations on models of non-existing networks: the very basic assumption in the classic analytical performance evaluation method (mean-value analysis) was that the packet (entity) routing probabilities were known (Riser, 1981; Robertazzi, 2000). When one thinks in the categories of the closed routes, as those tested/investigated with Sitwa, he or she learns quickly that the whole queuing problem must be solved before it is possible to evaluate the "known" routing probabilities for any actual computer/communication network.

On the other hand, using the notion of the network closed route (call, connection), it is possible to develop useful approximate analytical performance evaluation methods, that may be of value to actual network designers (J. B. Lewoc, A. Izworski and S. Skowronski, 2003; A. Izworski and J. B. Lewoc, 2003). Thus, the understanding of the phenomena occurring in actual networks, obtained due to development and applications of Sitwa, helped to a great extent in developing an approximate analytical method of network performance evaluation and in conducting optimisation work in networking. Of course, the network performance testing and measuring tool Sitwa was also very useful for tuning the analytical method and for validation of the results, providing more credible though more expensive results than simulation.

9.3.4. Conclusion

To summarise, the solutions of the internal network performance testing/measuring tool Sitwa proved to be correct and very useful for investigation of the actual computer networks. The solution is applicable in the present-day networks (especially those operating under the TCP/IP protocol suite) of much higher transmission rates and computing powers for the basic network components. This is consistent with the reasonable rule that the design solutions, that are as simple as possible, are useful for a rather long time.

9.4. Basic Characteristics Assessed

The basic MSK network characteristics assessed with the internal network measuring tool included the typical network characteristics, namely the mean and maximum possible values of the transit delay, of the round-trip delay and of the throughput, of various data field length and variable thinking times.

9.5. Initial Assessment of the Ethical and Human Behaviour Aspects

The creators of the MVA and NCA methods, claiming that the methods may be applied to computers and communication networks though the assumptions of the methods could not be observed by well-designed computers and computer networks harmed a lot of people involved in computer system and communication network design, development and operation. Therefore, their conduct should be assessed as unethical and inappropriate.

On the other hand, the Leader harmed nobody, developing a novel solution of the internal network measuring tool, allowing the student team to make changes in the node operating system Sonet and performing the MSK network investigations resulting in interesting and important scientific results. Therefore, his conduct should be considered highly appropriate and ethical.

Referring to the conduct of the University of Cambridge Computer Laboratory, it should be noted that conceit may be equally unethical and inappropriate as dilettantism.

10. Approximate Network Performance Assessment Tool (Anapaest)

10.1. Description of a General Network with End-to-End Acknowledgment and Performance Requirements

10.1.1. General Description

In this section, the case of actual wide-area networks is considered. A similar approach may be used for local-area networks, metropolitan networks or star networks (e.g., centralised computer control systems). However, to maintain the clarity of description, the latter cases will not be analysed in this book.

By an actual wide-area network (*WAN*) with packet switching and end-to-end acknowledgment, is meant the quadruple (13) (See 4.8.1). The illustrative diagram of *WAN* is shown in Figure 36.

Note:

Anapaest is based on the assumption (fulfilled by any reasonably designed communication networks) that no computer network component is allowed to transmit an arbitrary number of entities (packets) into any link but it has to obey some flow control rule and defer from transmitting more entities (packets) than the credit allowed, informed by the last acknowledgement received. This assumption is true for all communication and computer networks known to the authors.

On *IN* and *SUB,* there is stretched a set of closed routes (14).

An illustrative diagram of *WAN* is shown in Figure 36 and an exemplary closed route is depicted in Figure 37.

When the expected values of the random variables presented in Figures 4.36 and 4.37 are denoted by corresponding lower case letters, the obvious balance equations for each s=1,…,n may be described by the formula (15).

In (15), the known values are m_s and e_s. It is needed to find $y_{i,s}$ and t_s values.

To summarise, an actual *WAN* is described as a superposition of the closed routes (calls, connections, virtual calls, etc.) passing via the set of links available in *IN* and *SUB*. In accordance with real practice, the links passed by individual closed routes are predefined (at least, in normal operating conditions).

10.1.2. The Anapaest Method

J. B. Lewoc (Lewoc, 1990) proposed a performance evaluation method for actual computer networks, i.e., those with end-to-end acknowledgement and composed of some set of closed network routes. The method was described for those three basic cases of actual computer networks: the star-topology networks (multi-access systems), wide-area networks and local-area networks. The reference (J. B. Lewoc, 1990) is not widely available now. In addition, some other network topologies are to be considered at present (e.g., the authors are interested in the CIMM - Computer Integrated Manufacturing and Management- networks, being, in fact, networks of the metropolitan character). Therefore, the method was thought over and applied for investigation of this interesting case. It was also adjusted and validated again to a limited extent. The present section is a proposal for application of the method in a general case of actual computer and communication networks with end-to-end acknowledgement.

In addition to the denotations defined in Figures 36 and 37, the following will be used in the present section:

A_i is the set of closed routes beginning at the i-th link, such that the $s(i)$-th user is connected directly to the i-th link (17):

$$A_i = \{s_{i,1}, s_{i,2}, \ldots, s_{i,a_i}\} \tag{17}$$

B_i is the set of closed routes passing via the i-th link but not beginning at that link (18):

$$B_i = \{z_{i,1}, z_{i,2}, \ldots, z_{i,b_i}\} \tag{18}$$

The link preceding the i-th link in the s-th closed route is denoted by $h = h_s(i)$, provided that $s \in B_i$.

The set of closed routes parallel to the s-th closed route in the i-th link is defined as (19):

$$C_i = B_i \cap (A_h \cup B_h) \tag{19}$$

The power of C_i is given by:

$$\overline{C_i} = c_i \tag{20}$$

The mean cycle time of the closed routes encountered by the s-th route at the i-th link (21):

$$\bar{t}_{i,s} = \frac{a_i + b_i - 1}{\sum\limits_{l \in \{A_i \cup B_i\}/\{s\}} \frac{1}{t_i}}; \frac{0}{0} = 0; \tag{21}$$

The mean waiting time of the closed routes encountered by the s-th route at the i-th link is given by (22):

$$\bar{y}_{i,s} = \frac{\bar{t}_{i,s}}{(a_i + b_i - 1)} \left(\sum_{l \in \{A_i \cup B_i\} \setminus \{s\}} \frac{y_{i,l}}{t_i} \right); \tag{22}$$

The mean service time for the closed routes encountered by the s-th route at the i-th link is given by (23):

$$\bar{e}_{i,s} = \frac{\bar{t}_{i,s}}{(a_i + b_i - 1)} \left(\sum_{l \in \{A_i \cup B_i\} \setminus \{s\}} \frac{e_{i,l}}{t_l} \right); \tag{23}$$

The mean thinking time for the closed routes encountered by the *s*-th route at the i-th link is given by (24):

$$\overline{m}_{i,s} = \frac{\overline{t}_{i,s}}{(a_i + b_i - 1)} \left(\sum_{l \in \{A_i \cup B_i\} \setminus \{s\}} \frac{e_{i,l}}{t_l} \right); \tag{24}$$

The definitions of the mean values defined above for the set of closed routes that are not parallel to the *s*-th route are as follows (25÷28):

$$\overline{t}'_{i,s} = \frac{a_i + b_i - c_i}{\sum\limits_{l \in \{A_i \cup B_i\} \setminus C_i} \frac{1}{t_i}}; \tag{25}$$

$$\overline{y}'_{i,s} = \frac{\overline{t}'_{i,s}}{a_i + b_i - c_i} \sum_{l \in \{A_i \cup B_i\} \setminus C_i} \frac{y_{i,l}}{t_i}; \tag{26}$$

$$\overline{e}'_{i,s} = \frac{\overline{t}'_{i,s}}{a_i + b_i - c_i} \sum_{l \in \{A_i \cup B_i\} \setminus C_i} \frac{e_{i,l}}{t_l}; \tag{27}$$

$$\overline{m}'_{i,s} = \frac{\overline{t}'_{i,s}}{a_i + b_i - c_i} \sum_{l \in \{A_i \cup B_i\} \setminus C_i} \frac{m_{i,l}}{t_l}; \tag{28}$$

For all closed routes, the balance equations (15, 28) are valid. The basic reasons for the balance equations are as follows:

The first set of equations (15) is obvious: the cycle time, t_s, for any closed route is a sum of the thinking time, m_s, all waiting times, $y_{i,s}$, and all transmission times, $e_{i,s}$, for that closed route (ref. the example in Figure 37).

$$\bigcap_{s\in A_i}(y_{i,s} = \frac{(a_i+b_i-1)\bar{e}_{i,s}^{2}}{\bar{t}_{i,s}(1-\frac{e_{i,s}}{t_s})}(\frac{1}{2}+$$

$$+(a_i+b_i-2)(1-\frac{\bar{m}_{i,s}}{\bar{t}_{i,s}-\bar{e}_{i,s}})\frac{\bar{y}_{i,s}}{\bar{t}_s-\bar{e}_{i,s}}+(a_i+b_i-1)(1-\frac{\bar{m}_{i,s}}{\bar{t}_{i,s}-\bar{\bar{e}}_{i,s}})\frac{\frac{\bar{e}_{i,s}}{2}}{\bar{t}_{i,s}-\bar{e}_{i,s}});$$

$$\bigcap_{s\in B_i}(y_{i,s} = \frac{(a_i+b_i-c_i)\bar{e}'^{2}_{i,s}}{\bar{t}'_{i,s}(1-\frac{e_{i,s}}{t_s})}(\frac{1}{2}+(a_i+b_i-c_i-1)(1-\frac{\bar{m}'_{i,s}}{\bar{t}'_{i,s}-\bar{e}'_{i,s}})\frac{\bar{y}'_{i,s}}{\bar{t}'_{i,s}-\bar{e}'_{i,s}}+$$

$$+(a_i+b_i-c_i)(1-\frac{\bar{m}'_{i,s}}{\bar{t}'_{i,s}-\bar{e}'_{e,s}})\frac{\frac{\bar{e}'_{i,s}}{2}}{\bar{t}'_{i,s}-\bar{e}'_{i,s}});(28)$$

(29)

For the two other balance equation sets (29), the unknown mean values are approximated by the mean values of uniformly distributed variables and the probabilities that any entity (packet) is in any specific state (thinking, waiting for transmission, transmission) is approximated by the mean duration for that state divided by the mean cycle time for the variable under consideration, provided that it is not in any excluded state. Another assumption is that there may exist one and only one entity (packet) in any closed route of the network.

The first equation set in (29) refers to the case of an entity (packet) of the *s*-th closed route beginning at the *i*-th link. This entity may find there an entity of any closed route passing via the *i*-link with the probability $(a_i+b_i-1)\frac{\bar{e}_{i,s}}{\bar{t}_{i,s}(1-\frac{e_{i,s}}{t_s})}$ (the latter dividend describes the condition that the entity (packet) under consideration is not in the state of transmission).

The expression in the parenthesis in the first equation set of (29) is a sum of three terms, denoted here by $e_{i,s}(A+B+C)$. After multiplying, the first term is the mean value of the time from the instant that the entity of the *s*-th closed route finds the entity in transfer till the instant that the latter transmission is completed, i.e., $\frac{\bar{e}_{i,s}}{2}$, in accordance with the assumptions accepted.

The second term approximates the queue that may have been gathered during the time interval that the entity (packet) encountered in transfer by the entity (packet) of the s-th closed route waited for transfer via the i-th link ((a_i+b_i-2) eligible candidates), provided that the eligible candidate is not in the thinking state (the probability value $(1-\frac{\bar{m}_{i,s}}{t_{i,s}-e_{i,s}})$).

The third term approximates the queue of the entities (packets) that may have gathered during the time interval from the instant that the entity encountered is in transfer until the instant that the entity of the s-th closed route appears at the i-th link (note that the previous entity (packet) of the s-th closed route is an eligible candidate).

The second equation set in (29) describes the routes passing via the i-th link but not beginning there. It is approximated that any route parallel to the s-th one is of no impact on the waiting time spent by any entity of the s-th closed route at the i-th link (the complete share of the parallel routes in the waiting time of the route under consideration is included at the beginning link). Therefore, the averaging in this equation set is done only for the closed routes that are not-parallel to the one under consideration. Excepting that, this set of equations is analogous to the second one (note that in this case, the minimum value of c_i equals to 1.

The set of equations (15) and (29) enables one to compute iteratively the basic unknown mean values of the network performance, i.e., the closed route cycle time, t_s, the throughput in the s-th closed route, $d_s = \frac{1}{t_s}$, and the mean round-trip delay, $r_s = t_s - m_s$.

The approximations were adopted on the basis of the earlier experience in design and investigation (especially in performance evaluation) of real-time computer systems and networks, and they were somewhat heuristic, but the method operated well for star networks (multi-access systems), local area networks of various types and WANs.

10.1.3. Validation of Anapaest

The approximate analytical method was validated extensively.

At the very beginning, the method was tuned on the basis of available results for cyclic closed networks. The latter networks are quite accurate approximations for star-topology networks. Therefore, a considerable effort was done to compare the results given by Anapaest and those found in the available bibliography (this is not cited here, since the sources are as old as thirty or more years). Finally, after many dozen comparison runs and several adjustments of Anapaest, the relative error did not exceed 2%. At that stage, it was considered that the Anapaest approximations were good enough to be employed for wide-area networks and local-area networks. This needed some generalisation of the approximating formulae and led to formulae (3) and (15) for WANs.

Secondly, the simulation model of WANs was used for validation of Anapaest. Most of the simulation runs were performed for the current (at that time) and planned future configurations of the MSK network but, where some detailed data on performance of foreign networks was available, specific comparisons were carried out. Even presently, network simulators are developed individually; therefore, a well proven simulator developed earlier for investigation of real-time computer control systems and intended for running on computers of rather low computing power (therefore, a highly efficient simulator) was adapted to network performance evaluation tasks.

More than five hundred comparison runs were carried out. The results exceeded the expectation: validation with simulation showed no relative error exceeding 3.5%. In addition, the approximations tended to the accurate ones for the numbers of lines and closed routes tending to 0 or tending to infinity, and the relative error took some maximum values at some intermediate numbers. This may be evidence that the Anapaest method may be further tuned, but this was not done.

Simulation models for performance evaluation of specific WANs usually required some simplifications. For instance, in the validation of Anapaest, the problem of the link pass-band needed for flow control packets and frames was neglected. To validate the simulation model itself, especially the possible impact of omitting the flow control entities in simulation, an internal measuring tool Sitwa was developed. The test runs of Sitwa (more than a hundred of test runs) proved that the simulation results did not differ from the measurements by more than 2%.

The results are more than good for actual network designers and operators. Therefore, validation and tuning of the method were finished at that stage and the method was successfully applied for investigation (performance evaluation) of many configurations of various actual networks.

10.1.4. Exemplary Application of Anapaest

10.1.4.1. Introduction

The Computer-Integrated Manufacturing and Management (CIMM) systems have been greatly needed by prospective users, especially big and medium manufacturing enterprises. In spite of that, big manufacturers and vendors of Integrated Management (IM) systems, having at their disposal financial resources sufficient to develop and implement at least pilot CIMM systems, were not quick to enter the manufacturing domain. The basic reason for that seemed to be the fact that the large IM system manufacturers and vendors did not possess at their disposal the designers and implementers educated and experienced enough to cope with both manufacturing and management issues. Such persons were available, paradoxically many of them are available in less-developed countries where the designers had to possess a wide scope of experience in order that they are successful, but they were dispersed in various industrial and/or research organisations and they did not have, at their disposal, the financial resources needed to develop novel IT systems of the CIMM type.

In such circumstances, a reasonable duty of research and development workers seemed to be to carry out the initial work on the prospective project of CIMM systems, even if no financing were available for such work. This work could be considered a volunteer work or a work for the society that had financed their earlier research and development work.

A team of IT experts and process technologists was established and worked out an approach to development of CIMM systems that seemed to be feasible, rather fast and inexpensive (L. Franasik et al., 2001; A. Izworski, J. B. Lewoc and S. Skowroński, 2006; J. B. Lewoc, A. Izworski and S. Skowroński, 2006). The next step that could and should be made by the research and development team, even before the CIMM project was established, was that of performance evaluation of probable hardware structures. The task of performance evaluation was particularly important in the case of CIMM, since the project concerned a novel (emerging) ICT system for which nobody possessed a sense of performance, and no rules of thumb concerning performance could have been developed earlier. The performance evaluation issues connected with the development of CIMM systems is the subject matter of this Section.

The authors believe that a specific in-depth example is more educational than a general study, this is particularly so in the context described above, and, therefore, the form of a case study was adopted for the present section.

The following section presents the architecture of the CIMM system under investigation.

10.1.4.2. Exemplary CIMM Architecture

The pilot Polish CIMM system was designed several years ago for the biggest then Polish manufacturer of household appliances, Polar, Wroclaw (the Enterprise), employing several thousand people. The CIMM issues have been analysed for the Enterprise already, but the project was abandoned because of the severe turndown in the Polish economy in the nineties. In conformity with the early design work, it was assumed that the target organisational structure of the Enterprise was that depicted in Figure 45.

For the general Enterprise organisation presented in Figure 45, the hardware architecture of the CIMM system, depicted in Figure 46, was proposed.

10.1.4.3. The Network under Investigation

It was assumed that the time needed for transfer of data via any switch (server, gateway, node or router) was insignificant in comparison with the time needed to transfer the data via a co-operating data link. This was in conformity with the specifications of actual hardware proposed for the CIMM system since the data was transferred via network switches as 8-bit byte blocks transmitted via fast direct memory access (DMA) channels and internal processing of the data was usually connected with the message headers only.

However, the method proposed enabled to consider the delays in network switches though the calculations could be somewhat more complicated.

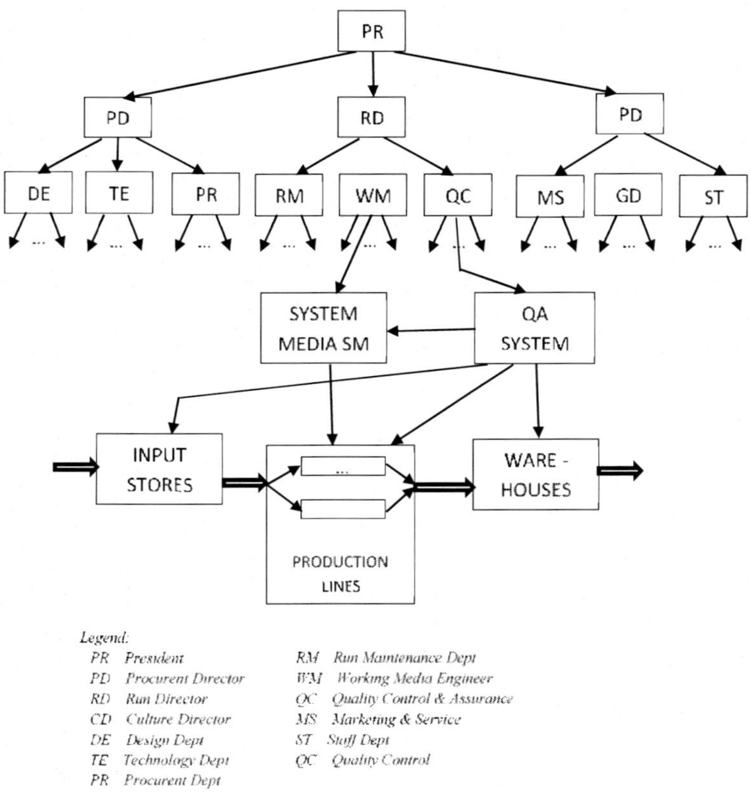

Figure 45. General organisational diagram of the enterprise.

With the assumption that the delays in transmission links were insignificant, the hardware structure of the CIMM system could be presented as in Figure 46. The network depicted in this figure was composed of 30 switches (15 routers and 15 servers). Let the individual switches and data links be numbered as shown in Figure 46 (server Nos: 1÷15, router Nos: 16÷30, link pairs (for both transmission directions): (1,2) ÷ (85,86)).

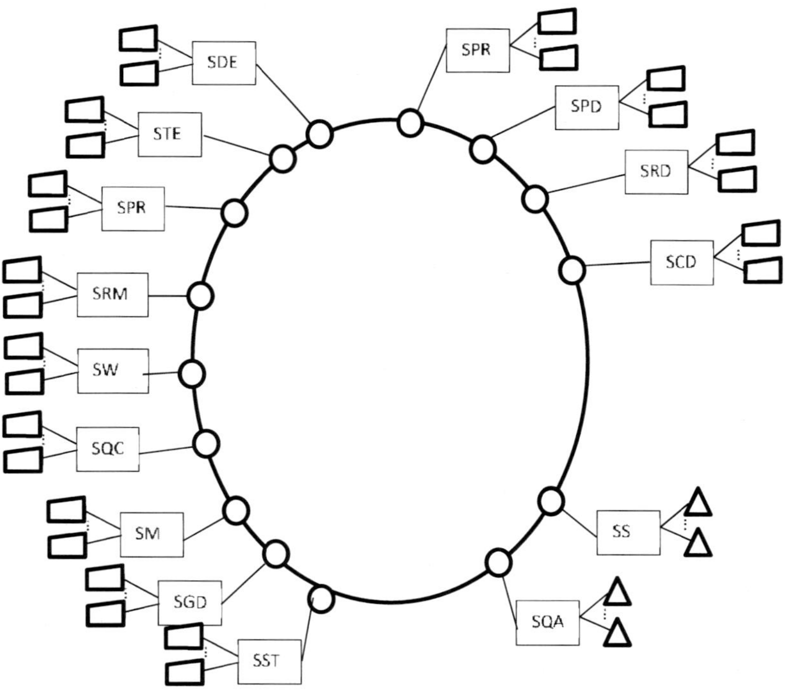

Legend:

SXY – Server of the XY unit
O – Router, RXY
Δ - Controller

Figure 46. Hardware architecture of the CIMM system.

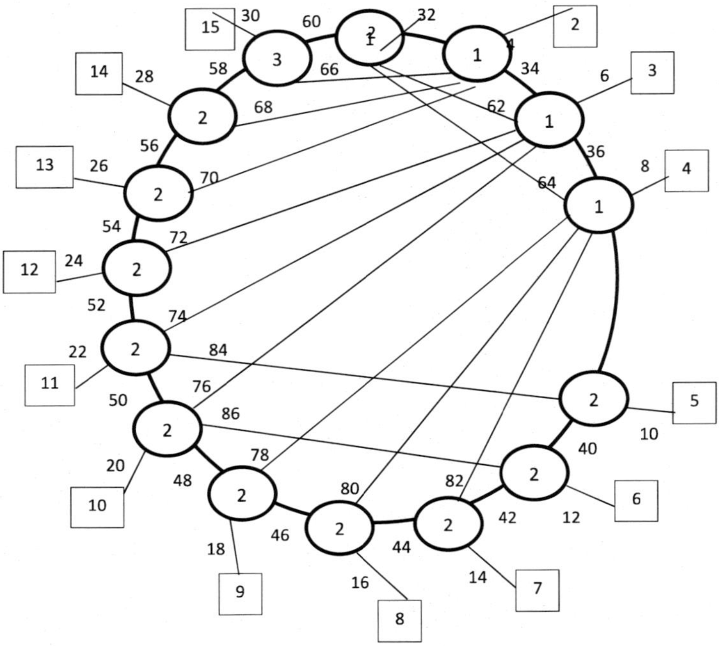

Note:

Link number, i=2k, k=1,2,...,43 is, in fact, a pair of numbers, 2k and 2k-1; the first one is the number of the line directed from the node of the lower number to that of the higher one and the other in the opposite direction.

Figure 47. Numbering of links and nodes – switches.

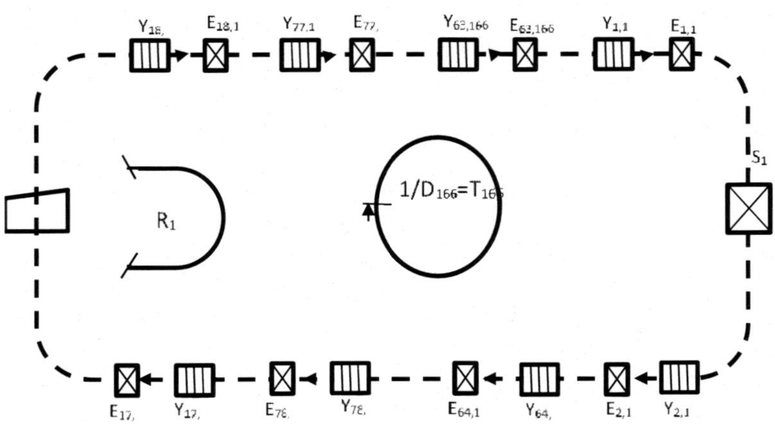

Figure 47a. Exemplary closed route of a Marketing & service employee using the general corporate database.

Exemplary closed routes of Marketing & Service employees using the general corporate database are shown in Figures 4.47 a and b.

Note:

It was assumed that any *p*-th server, $p \in 1,\ldots,15$ (ref. Figure 46), was able to support 20 closed routes of numbers $s = (p\text{-}1)\ 20, \ldots, (p\text{-}1)\ 20 + 19$.

To avoid the problems connected with the closed queuing network, described in the present Chapter, it was decided to adapt the approximate performance evaluation method presented in this section, hereinabove, developed and validated earlier for computer and communication networks with the end-to-end acknowledgement, to the cases of the CIMM system and to apply this method for performance evaluation for the case study under discussion.

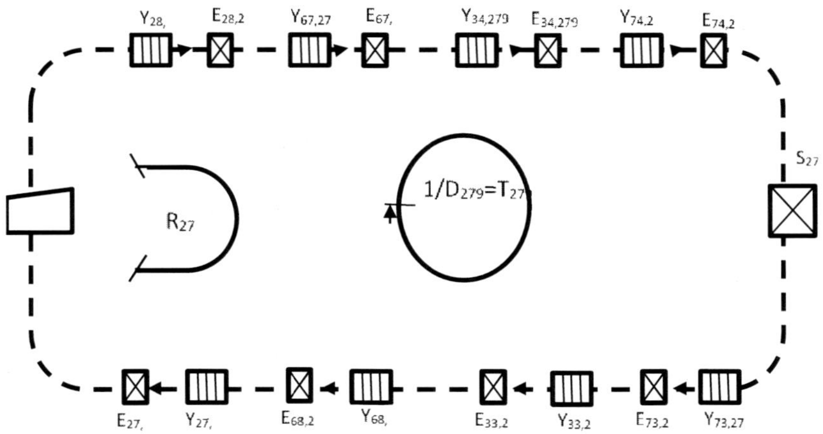

Key: $s \in S = 1,\ldots,299$; $i \in I = 1,\ldots,86$; R_s = round route – trip - delay for the s-th closed route; T_s = the s-th closed route cycle time; D_s = the s-th closed route throughput; $Y_{i,s}$ = waiting time of the s-th closed route to the i-th link

$E_{i,s}$ = service time of the s-th closed route to the i-th link

M_s = the s-th closed route thinking time

S_s = the s-th closed route ultimate service time

Note: Upper case letters denote random variables while the lower case ones – the relevant expectances.

Figure 47b. Exemplary closed route of a Marketing & service employee using the general corporate database.

10.1.4.4. The Approximations

Ref. 9.1.

10.1.4.5. Validation of the Approximations

10.1.4.5.1. Validation with Accurate Results for Cyclic Queuing Systems

The problem of performance evaluation of homogeneous star-topology networks is the same as that investigated for cyclic queuing networks. The accurate solutions in the form of limit probabilities of the entity (packet, request) numbers have been known since the early nineteen-seventies. These results, for exponential thinking time, were employed to validate the approximations presented above.

Several hundred comparisons were done for the number of the customers (closed routes), v, changing between 2 and several dozens. The relative error of the mean cycle time, t_s, calculated for the set of comparison, reached the maximum value less than 3% at $v \approx 14$ and decreased for v tending to zero or to infinity.

10.1.4.5.2. Validation with Simulation

In order that the approximations could be validated, a fast WAN simulator was developed on the basis of earlier simulation studies for real-time computer control systems. This simulator was used, primarily, for the Polish pilot wide area network MSK. However, both actual and planned network configurations (including those that were to operate at much higher transmission rates) were investigated. In addition, available foreign simulation results for local and wide area networks were also used for validation.

The number of validation experiments was higher than 500, with the number of closed routes and links equal up to 500 and 100, respectively. In the case of results obtained for MSK, where the fair conditions of comparison could be ensured (this, obviously, was not true for foreign simulation investigation), the maximum relative error of the mean cycle time (and throughput) was lower than 3.5%.

10.1.4.5.3. Validation with Measurements

To investigate MSK and the approximations presented above, the internal communication network measuring tool Sitwa was developed and implemented (Ref. 4.8). It was used, primarily, to validate the simulation results on the existing possible configurations of MSK. The investigations showed that the simplifying assumptions in simulation (e.g., omission of the flow control packets and/or frames) did not result in significant simulation errors. The maximum relative error of the approximations under discussion did not exceed 5%.

10.1.4.5.4. Exemplary Results

The set of equations (20) ÷ (28) was solved iteratively. The basic user characteristics, the mean round-trip delay, r_s, and the mean throughput, d_s, for the exemplary closed routes, s = 166 and s = 279, are presented in Figures 4.47 ÷ 4.50.

The closed route, s = 166, passed via the most severely loaded links, i = 1 and i = 2. This resulted in that r_{166} reached more than 4 s at m_s values close to 0 (ref. Figure 48). If it were assumed that an annoying value (i.e., the value that could not be accepted by the Enterprise employees) of r_s was higher than 2 s, then the m_s values below some 0.5 s should be avoided.

The d_{166} values (the mean throughput values depicted in Figure 49.) show a definite saturation (congestion) at m_s values below ca. 0.5 s. If the mean offered load for the 166-th closed route is defined by (30):

$$t_{166}^{off} = \sum_{i \in 166} (e_{i,s} + m_s) \tag{30}$$

then the increased offered load resulted in the decreased mean throughput, d_{166}, for the given scenario and for $m_s < 0 .5$ s, s=1,…,300.

The closed route, s = 279 (Figure 50.), showed only the acceptable r_s values (below 1 s) while the values not greater than 2 s were acceptable as not annoying ones and the d_s value was decreasing monotonically with increasing offered load ($m_s \rightarrow 0$, s = 1,…,300) (Figure 51.). The reason was that the 279-th closed route did not pass via any link under heavy traffic. Therefore, even when the mean thinking time was decreased towards zero, no saturation (congestion) occurred in the links passed by the 279-th closed route.

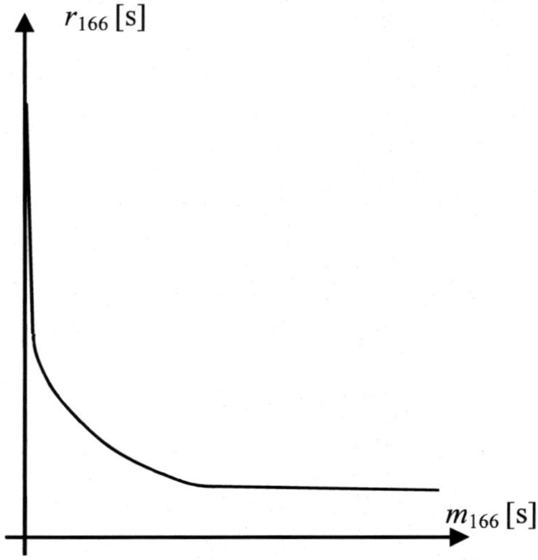

Figure 48. r_{166} versus m_{166}.

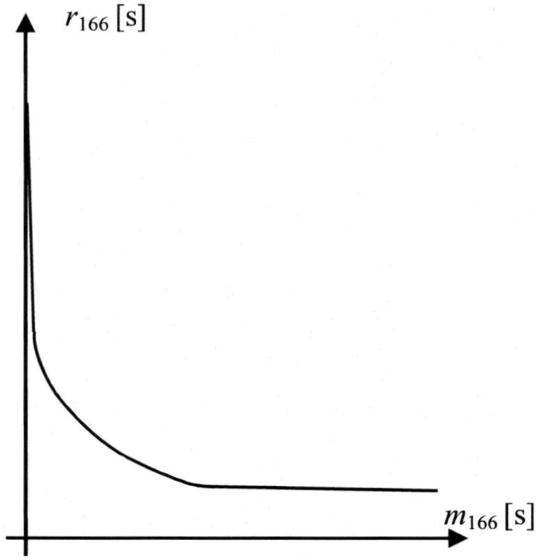

Figure 49. d_{166} versus m_{166}.

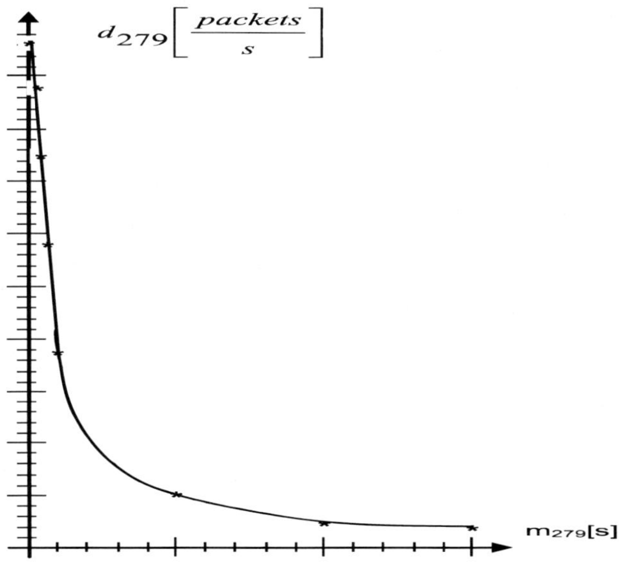

Figure 50. r_{279} versus m_{279}.

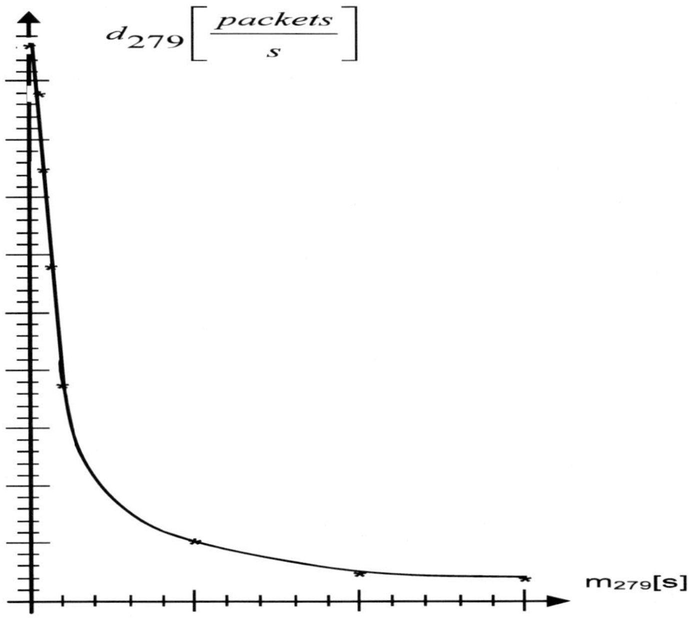

Figure 51. d_{279} versus m_{279}.

10.1.4.5.5. Final Remarks

The authors do not claim that the method devised and verified some thirty years ago needs no further work. On the contrary, they do realise that the method validated primarily on the pilot Polish Interuniversity Computer Network MSK, operating at rather low transmission rates and in a limited configuration, needs further validation and possible tuning. In addition, the method may and should be upgraded: thanks to the rapid growth of the computing power that has happened during the last decade, more accurate approximations may be done for the balance equations (e.g., the simplifying assumption that an entity (packets) may find only one entity of one closed loop in the queue to some link) may be discarded. Then the balance equations become more complicated but they may be still solved by the iterative method. And the networks with sliding windows or credit-based flow control may be modelled directly, instead of modelling several loops for credits bigger than 1, as it has been done earlier.

However, the authors believe that the method may and should be published in its original form now. Any protest against it, raised by the queuing theory experts pointing at some possible formal deficiencies of the method, would sound rather false: in the general case, the classic queuing theory methods have failed and have not produced any useful tools for performance evaluation of actual computer and communication networks, greatly needed by network designers, developers and operators. The authors are designers and/or consultants for actual computer systems and networks. To do their jobs in a proper way, they had to get involved in research work in the domain of performance evaluation. Any further work is, however, within the duty range of the queuing theory people.

During Anapaest program iterations, the maximum possible values and rough distributions (histograms) of the of the selected random variables R_s (round-trip delay) could be recorded.

10.1.5. Final Remarks

It could be stated that Anapaest was a successful method of performance evaluation for the purposes of network designers and operators of the eighties of the previous century. The authors do believe that this method may be successfully applied for performance evaluation of actual computer and communication networks even now. However, it must be noted here, that most of the validation work was done for limited configurations of networks operating usually at medium data transmission rates.

In addition, it should be noted here that the approximations applied in Anapaest assumed that one and only one entity (packet) could exist, at one time, in any closed route. This means, that the closed routes were modelled with the flow control measures (sliding window, credit) set to 1. To investigate networks with higher values of the window size or credit value, the relevant closed routes were modelled as n (n = window size or credit value) independent closed routes passing via the same link set. This approach was validated successfully for several dozen test runs.

However, due to the enormous increase in the computing power available in PC-s, it is possible now to propose better approximations for actual networks operating with the TCP/IP protocol suite and to model directly some closed routs operation with the window size or credit value greater than 1. Since the authors are consultants and designers for computer systems and networks, it is rather unlikely that they will continue the work on Anapaest for much longer. The only promise they can make is that they will provide any reasonable help to anybody who will be involved in such work if she or he contacts with the authors.

10.1.6. Conclusion

The method proposed eliminates the basic assumption of definition of the input stream by the inter-arrival times, omitting the flow control mechanisms implemented in all actual computer systems and networks. It could be and was applied for performance evaluation of present-day networks, though the most validation work was done for networks of limited configurations, operating at medium transmission rates. The simplified approximations (20) ÷ (28) proved to be rather useful (low approximation error, limited computational complexity) for star-topology networks (centralised control systems), various local-area networks and wide-area networks. More accurate and direct approximations proposed in the present section seem to be promising for investigation of actual networks, though they may require more computational complexity.

10.2. Available Queuing Networks and Simulation Aids

The references that were available until 1986 included S. Agraval and J. Buzen (1983); J. Agre and S. Tripathi (1982); I. Akyildiz and G. Bolch (1983); S. Bruell, G. Balbao and P. Afshari, 1984; A. E. Conway and N. D. Georganas (1986); and J. G. Shanthikumar and d. D. Yao, (1986). These repeated the erroneous assumptions for MVA and NCR methods of closed queuing network investigation, consisting in omission of the flow control mechanisms implemented in all actual computer systems and networks and, therefore, could not be used for credible performance evaluation.

10.3. Mathematical Models

Ref. 9.1. above.

10.4. Initial Assessment of the Ethical and Human Behaviour Aspects

The researchers investigating closed queuing networks of the product form and repeating the erroneous assumptions neglecting existence of flow control mechanisms in any actual computer system or network harmed many people involved in design, development and operation of computer systems and networks through delivering false data for them, that could result in severe economic losses. Therefore, their conduct should be recognised inappropriate and unethical.

On the other hand, the Leader and his team worked hard and developed an approximate tool based on a true description of computer systems and networks, making it possible to perform performance evaluation calculations and thus avoiding sometimes high losses due to adoption of inappropriate solutions. Therefore their conduct should be assessed appropriate and ethical.

11. POWER PLANT DATA BASE PROJECT

This Section describes the project of computerisation of a big coal-fired power plant.

11.1. Description of the Badel Power Plant Computer System and Performance Requirements

11.1.1. Introduction

The Institute for Power System Automation (IASE), Wroclaw, Poland, has been a definite leader in design, development and implementation of Polish pioneering monitoring and control systems for the power industry since the early nineteen-fifties (J. B. Lewoc, M. Rozent and I. Saczuk, 1992). Since the nineteen-seventies, IASE educated numerous experienced staff for the design of system functionality, the selection of the hardware and software structures, the design and development of specialised hardware and software modules (including single-board microcomputers), and the design, development and implementation of complete systems, training, etc.

Due to the reasons described in J. B. Lewoc, M. Rozent and I. Saczuk (1992), the power industry suffered severe financial problems and most of the experienced staff left the Institute during that very low economic period in Poland in the early nineties. However, the rest of them, who stayed with the institute, could undertake the challenge released by the Polish electric and thermal power industry in the late nineteen-nineties and later, and design and develop the most critically needed systems.

It should be emphasized that, after the political transformation of 1989 and after the earlier downturn in the Polish economy, the demand for electric power decreased considerably in Poland instead of pre-planned continuous increase. Therefore, the most experienced organisation in Poland that had developed computer systems for the power industry, had to look for a market for themselves in the thermal and electric power generation industry.

The section will describe the basic planned product for the application range, Badel (from Polish Baza danych dla elektrowni = Data base for power plants), based on the earlier design product, the KSWDB (from Polish Komputerowy System Wspomagania Dyspozytora Bloku = Power Generating Unit Control Engineer Computer Aiding System). For the proposed case-study solution of Badel, an approach to performance evaluation/prediction worked out during development and investigations of the first successful Polish heterogeneous network MSK (from Polish Miedzyuczelniana Siec Komputerowa = Interuniversity Computer Network) (Ref. 4.8), based on the use of the approximate network performance evaluation tool (Anapest (Ref. 4.9), has been described. The Badel project was commissioned in 1988 and the Leader was appointed as the leading designer.

The hardware architecture planned for Badel is shown in Figure 52.

11.1.2. The Badel Network

11.1.2.1. General

A basic problem needing solution in combined Heat and Power Generating Stations (HPGS-s) was connected with monitoring and control of operation of Heat and Power Generating Units (HPGU-s). Due to the huge number of analogue and digital variables (both primary and secondary (calculated variables)), this required the application of advanced computer systems/networks.

The first solution (Badel) intended specifically for monitoring of HPGU's and for management of the complete (heat and) power generating plants was designed and tested on the turn of the eighth decade of the previous century. The schematic diagram of the system is shown in Figure 47.

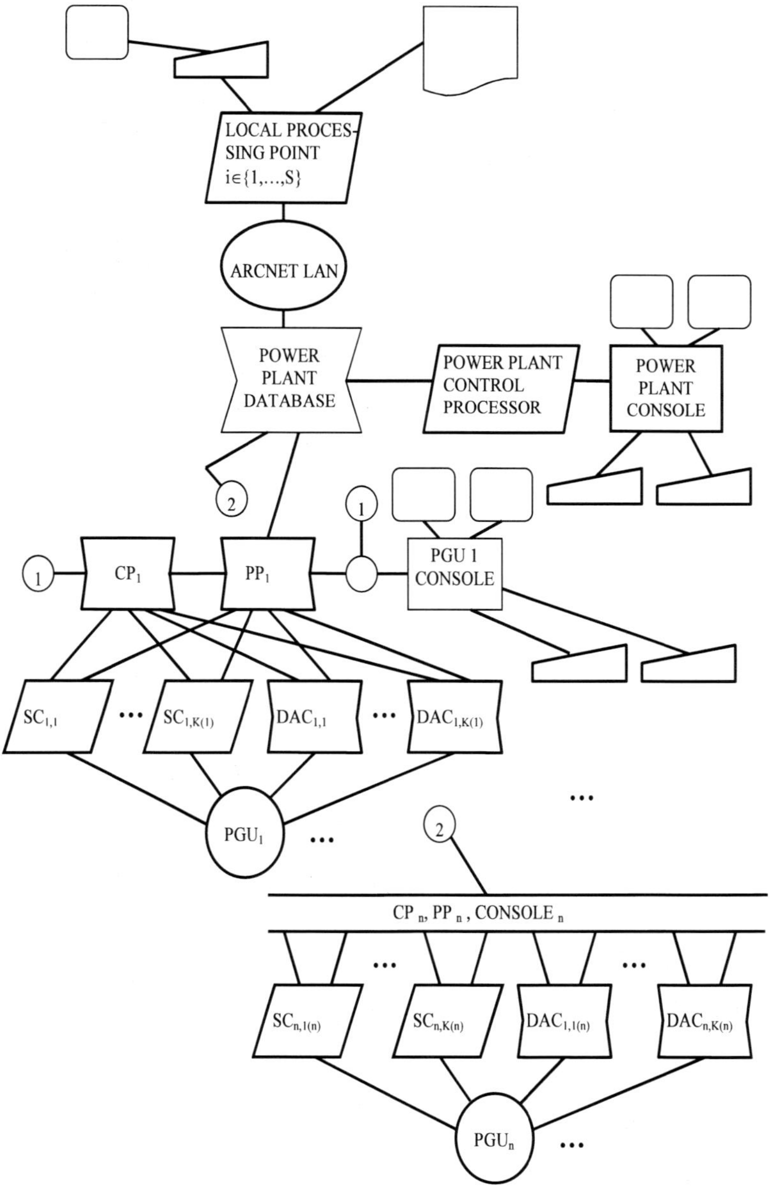

Figure 52. Hardware architecture of Badel.

11.1.2.2. The Process Level

Any of the *n* Process Levels (PL-s) computers was constituted of Intel-based microprocessors (designed and developed, and called the cells), the analogue and two-state Input/Output modules ($CP_{1\text{-}n}$), the communication module ($SC_{1,1\text{-}n.1(n)}$, being a redundant version of CSMA-CD (Ethernet) LAN (Wikipedia, 2017j)) and the power supply circuits required (grouped in so called automation hubs, $DAC_{1,1\text{-}n,K(n)+}$). The LAN Network interconnected the process stations with PL-s, and the Plant Operator Level (POL).

The PL functionality, realised under control of the software platform (a home-made operating system) and of the application software written with use of the specialised, object-oriented programming language REGIN-H, and another home-made program, the graphic editor, covered the following basic tasks:

- the user algorithm executed in a cell,
- transmissions between cells,
- exchange of data with OL,
- buffering of event messages on the level of the cell and hub.

11.1.3. The Plant Operator Level

11.1.3.1. Engineering Subsystems

The Engineering Subsystems (ES) enabled the development of Badel software through customisation, thus facilitating the task and avoiding many possible programming errors. The customising functionality was realised with the following editors of ES:

- The catalogue editor (used to create the sets (called catalogues) of the field variables, secondary variables, operator variables, automatic control systems and direct control systems),
- The secondary (functional) processing editor (more than 30 standard algebraic and logical functions, expandable of special functions developed on the Customer's demand),

- The screen editor (to create screens with plant synoptic schemes, bar-graphs, plots, colours under control, tables, digital values, logic data, etc.),
- The report writer to create report templates for the field and secondary variable data,
- The field signal and the automatic as well as digital control structure processing editor (to create the algorithms with a graphic environment).

11.1.3.2. Supervision and Management Level

It was planned that the Power Plant Database and the Supervision and Management Level (SML) would enable to develop the Computer Integrated Manufacturing and Management (CIMM) systems considered (by the engineering and managerial staff of heat and power generating plants and other plants) as the necessary component for optimal operation of the total plant. For this purpose, the processes in the gateways could transfer data to the WWW servers (basically) and to the other SML level subsystems. In addition, it was investigated if it was feasible to employ, at SML, some specialised expert systems intended for improvement of the working media production profitability.

11.1.3.3. Exemplary Problem Solution

An exemplary solution of the monitoring and supervision problem will be described roughly hereinafter for the case of a combined thermal and electric power generating plant, realised a dozen or so years later, based on the detailed solutions devised for Badel, supplying energy to several hundred thousand inhabitants of towns in the Country.

The plant under control consisted of two Heat and Power Generating Units (HPGU-s) (320 MW each) and two water boilers which were in operation in order to enable fast changeovers of the HPGU's in operation. In total, the plant under monitoring and supervision was described by several thousand two-state and analogue variables (primary or secondary ones).

The process stations (automation hubs) intercommunicated with the OL computers via the LANs at the levels under discussion (and via relevant gateways).

On the Operator Level, there were two computers per HPGU (one for the boiler operator and the other for the turbine operator). In addition, two computers were provided for the water boilers and one for the overall plant Control Engineer.

The graphic wall shared by the authorized operators/engineers enabled a large-scale graphical display of the data acquired, and the control of the process actuating members. It was very useful for the displaying of important plant schemes, especially in emergency conditions when the operators and control engineers should have at their disposal some schema and other display forms of high readability, reliability and robustness.

The problems of the system robustness were of a particular interest for the system designers (A. Izworski and J. B. Lewoc, 2003a; A. Izworski, J. B. Lewoc and S. Skowronski, 2003b). It was rather understandable: in the 21-st century, that system reliability is the basic feature accepted for any solution of major importance, while the novel task of the designers is to maximise the resistance to disturbance, i.e., the robustness.

The OL computers intercommunicated with those of the Supervisory and Management Network (SMN). However, it should be noticed here that the staff operating on this level was not allowed to perform direct control of the plant (for such actions, the Control Engineers and Operators, solely, were authorised); on this level, the customers could select the data they needed for their work, exclusively.

The solution was implemented successfully in several Polish heat and power generating units. Usually, the benefits generated by similar monitoring and supervisory systems in the heat and power industry were assessed as some dozen or so per cent of the thermal and electric energy sold by the plant. Based on this assumption, the system paid for itself many times during the first half year after being commissioned.

A digression: The first stage of the Badel project covered assembly of the hardware configuration, design and development of software, and debugging as well as testing in the testing centre of IASE (Institute for Power System Automation) of a complete set planned for one power generating unit of the power plant under development. The initial Badel project stage was performed in a way that enabled the education and upgrading of as many designers and programmers as possible so that they were able to perform leading designer duties: the Leader drew flow diagrams of one solution after another in front of a team of more than 50 designers, in the presence of the final users. The pilot configuration passed the tests. However, due to a the severe industrial recession in the country after 1989 (the date of the political change in Poland) due to, primarily, the naive and/or intentional liberalism at the initial phase of capitalism in the country, resulting in very harmful effects for the economy of Poland, the demand for electric power decreased considerably and the construction of the power plant, for which Badel was designed, was stopped.

After several years, the economic standing of the Country improved and a demand was generated for solutions similar to Badel. A project was granted to a team of IASE designers/programmers who were educated and upgraded by the Leader at the Badel project. They had to change the computer from SM-4 (PDP 11/40 compatible) to an industrial PC running the QNX operating system (BlackBerry, 2017) but decided to use the solutions devised by the Leader, using the new environment. The solution proved to be amazingly successful: IASE, a small industrial institute, in the condition of the aggressive competition of the world's biggest Hi-Tech corporations, interested very much in computerisation of the power industry in Poland, managed to sell more than 200 different configurations derived from Badel to the country's power industry. In accordance with the official methods of assessment of the benefits generated for the Country, the benefits exceeded 5 billion Euro.

The above was a reason for well-deserved pride for the Leader:

- Due to his methods of educating and improvement of the younger generation, they proved to be successful leading designers of subsequent projects.

- Due to the solutions he had devised several years before which proved to be competitive with those proposed by the world's most recognisable corporations involved in computerisation of the power industry.

The basic questions concerning Badel's performance were:

- What would be the maximum possible round trip delay values of the random variable R_s (ref. 4.9.1) for interrogating mode transfers?
- What would be the throughput, d_s (ref. 4.9.1), for file (bulk) data transfers.

The answers were needed until the completion of the Badel testing phase in the IASE testing centre, i.e., 1989.

11.2. Available Queuing Network and Simulation Tools

The references on application of closed queue networks to performance analysis, available in 1989 were: L. N. Bhuyan, Q Yang and D. P. Agrawal (1989); R. Jain (1989); S. Kundu and I. F. Akyildz (1989); I. F. Akyildiz, (1988 and 1989); and A. E. Krzesinski (1987). These used the same assumptions, omitting the existence of flow-control mechanisms and, thus, the methods proposed by them were inappropriate for investigation of actual computer systems and networks.

11.3. Mathematical Models

For Badel, several connection scenarios (mathematical models) were defined. A typical scenario for the future operation of Badel and the basic results obtained are described below.

The number of the power generating units assumed was 7 (6 actual power generating units and a virtual PGU destined for the environment protection purposes). The connection scenario is defined in Table 6 below.

Table 6. Badel connection scenario (Ref. Figure 47)

Closed route numbers	Connection (virtual call) description
1 - 7	From the first keyboard of the s-th PGU console, via the s-th Presentation Processor PP_s to the power plant database and backwards.
8 - 14	From the other keyboard of the s-th PGU console, via PP_s, the power plant database to the power plant control processor and backward.
15 - 21	From the s-th communication module, $SC_{s,1}$, via the control processor CP_s, the presentation processor PP_s to the power plant database and backward (Note: the closed route was equivalent to operation of all communication modules since they operated alternatingly).
22 - 28	From the s-th automation hub $DAC_{s,1}$, via the control processor CP_s, the presentation processor PP_s, to the power plant database and backward (Note: the closed route is equivalent to operation of all automation hubs since they operated alternatingly).
29	From the first keyboard of the power plant console, via the power plant control processor, the power plant database, to the presentation processor PP_s and backward.
30	From the second keyboard of the power plant console, via the power plant control processor, the power plant database, to the presentation processor PP_s and backward.

11.4. Basic Characteristics Assessed

For the connection scenario defined above, the following additional assumptions were assumed:

- Transmission speed in every link: 40 Kb/sec.
- Window (credit) size: 1 in each closed route, in accordance with the Badel assumptions, in order that file transfers did not prolong

the round-trip delay in closed routes, operating in the interrogating mode, too much.

- Packet data field length: 128 octets.

For the closed routes 1÷14, 29 and 30, operating in the interrogating mode (the man – machine dialogue), the basic performance measure of interest was the maximum possible round-trip delay in the *s*-th closed route, r_S^*. In no case under investigation did this time exceeded 1 s. Therefore it was acceptable that the value of an annoying time was assumed as 2 s.

The closed routes number 15÷28 transferred data between computers, corresponding to file transfer conditions. For all these closed routes, the throughput, d_s, found during the investigations was not less than 500 bytes what was assessed acceptable for the power plant purposes.

A digression: The Badel performance evaluation investigations were included in the project led by the Leader. Various PoPs (Power of People) protested loudly, arguing that research work could not be included in a technical project. The Leader answered: I believe that performance evaluation is a must for such complex and expensive project. If you think otherwise, you have to find another leading designer. And that stopped further discussion about performance evaluation.>>

CONCLUSION

The most popular assumptions of the queuing system and network theories cover the following:

- Poisson input stream, defined by independent random variables, the inter-arrival times, of the exponential distribution;
- Independent service times i.e., independent random variables, often of exponential distributions (exponential servers);
- Investigation of the mean values only.

The assumptions were inadequate for actual computer systems and networks since:

- All properly designed computer systems and networks were provided (then and now) with implemented flow control mechanisms allowing the generation of one only interrupt request from an interrupt source for a computer system (or some credit/window of interrupt requests for an actual computer network). The flow control mechanisms protected the actual computer system or network against congestion and the assumption of the Poisson input stream lead to the investigation results that were very far from reality;
- Especially in computer control systems (See 4.1.3), the distributions of inter-arrival times could be approximated by exponential ones with minimum intervals. The minimum intervals were of a high importance since the computer system designers were to ensure that the intervals were not violated by interrupt request sojourn times, in order that the real-time operation requirements were observed;
- For actual computer systems, individual interrupt requests could be strongly correlated since they reflected the internal relations in the production process and the action of the flow control mechanisms mentioned above;
- For customers (interrupt requests) with implemented flow control, the model where the input variable was not the inter-arrival time but the time between the instant that the previous request was served until the instant that the next request was generated (the model with thinking times – Ref. L. Kleinrock, 1976) should be used instead of that based on inter-arrival times;
- Exponential servers were inacceptable for actual computer systems and networks: well written programs should operate in a way as deterministic as possible; the same refers to length of packets transmitted in packet-switching networks, that defined the transmission (service) times;

- During the comparative performance evaluation studies of Odra 1325 operating under Executive and MINIMOP, and of R-32 operating under OS/MVT and TCAM (See Interuniversity communication network), it was found that the R-32 system operated exponentially as if it were a free human being and the User had to react very fast, as if he or she were a machine, to get a fast response for the system. Such solutions are completely unethical: the servers should be as deterministic as possible while the Users should have as much freedom as possible.
- Investigations limited to mean values only were unacceptable for actual computer systems and networks: for computer control systems, the basic performance requirement was that the interrupt request sojourn times were held within some limits and it was impossible to determine it on the basis of the expected values; this was also a basic requirement for actual computer networks where the throughputs were of import for bulk transfers (file transfers) while for Users operating in the interrogating mode, the maximum possible round-trip delays were important.

The basic reason for crashes of the biggest manufacturers of mainframes in the Country or in the world was an inappropriate or missed performance evaluation of large-scale computer systems, leading to big financial and general losses including the downfall of the former biggest manufacturer of computers and of the large-scale ICT in Poland.

Making light of performance evaluation for large-scale and expensive projects was also a reason for some lower-scale failures but with consequences of high economic and general losses like those borne due to missed implementation of the anti-memory fragmentation idea or premature delivery of the power network control board computer system to an electric power region of the Country.

Perhaps the biggest fault of researchers working in the branch of mathematics, called the theory of queues, were their attempts, regretfully successful, to make up actual computer systems and networks to the capabilities of their branch, which led to erroneous results and, consequently, inappropriate design, developmental and operational decisions.

Conceit and excessive self-assurance could be an equally severe obstacle for proliferation of sound performance-based ICT system and network design and development solutions and methods as omitted or inappropriate performance evaluation.

The computer simulation methods were a good tool for adequate performance evaluation of ICT systems and networks.

Reasonable methods based on experience gained for actual computer systems and networks made it possible to develop in-house solutions enabling approximate but credible performance evaluation systems making it possible to avoid expensive crashes due to inadequate or missed performance evaluation.

REFERENCES

Agrawal S. and Buzen J. (1983). The Aggregate Server Method for Analyzing Serialization Delays in Computer Systems. *ACM Trans. On Computer Systems.* Vol. 1, No. 2. p. 116-143.

Agre J. and Triparhi S. (1982). Modeling Reentrant and Nonreentrant Software. *ACM Sigmetrix Performance Evaluation Review.* Vol. 11, No. 4. p. 163-178.

Akyildiz I. and Bolch G. (1988). *Mean Value Analysis Approximation for Multiple Server Queueing Networks.* Perf. Ev. Vol. 8, No. 2. p.77-91.

Akyildiz I. F. (1988a). On the exact and approximate throughput analysis of closed queuing networks with blocking. *IEEE Transactions on Software Engineering,* Vol. 14, Issue: 1. p. 62 – 70.

Akyildiz I. F. (1989). Product form approximations for queueing networks with multiple servers and blocking. *IEEE Transactions on Computers,* Vol. 38, Issue: 1. p. 99 – 114.

Alderman D. L. (1972). *INSTRUCT – Informational Structures of Instructional Systems*. On-line 72 Conference. Uxbridge.

Allen A. O. (1978). *Probability Statistics and Queueing Theory With Computer Science applications*. Academic Press, New York.

Avi-Itzak B. and Naor P. (1961). On a Problem of Preemptive Queuing. *Opns. Res.* 9, p. 664-672.

Avi-Itzak B. and Naor P. (1963). Some Queuing Problems with Service Station Subject to Breakdown. *Opns. Res.* 11, p. 303-320.

Avi-Itzak B. (1963). Preemptive Repeat Priority Queues as a Special Case of the Multipurpose Server. *Opns. Res.* 11, p. 597-619.

Avi-Itzak B. and Heyman D. P. (1973). Computational algorithms for closed queueing networks with exponential servers. *Opns. Res.* Vol. 21, Issue 6. P. 1212-1230.

Bharath-Kumar K. (1980). Discrete Time Queueing Systems and Their Networks. *IEEE Trans. On Comm.,* Vol. 28, Issue 2. p 260-263.

Bhuyan L. N., Yang Q. and Agrawal D. P. (1989). Performance of multiprocessor interconnection networks. *Computer.* Volume: 22, Issue: 2, Feb. 1989). p. 25 – 37.

Bilski E. (Ed.). (1987). *Protocols in Interuniversity Computer Network (MSK).* Wydawnictwo Politechniki Wroclawskiej. Wroclaw. (In Polish).

BlackBerry. (2017). *QNX Operating Systems*. Available: http://www.qnx. com/content/qnx/en/products/neutrino-rtos/index.html.

Bolopion A. B. and Sabonnadiere J. C. (1975). *An Experiment of Integration of the Computer in Engineering Education*. International Conference on Future Progress of Electrical Engineering. Prague.

Bruell S., Balbo G. and Afshari P. (1984). *Mean Value Analysis of Mixed, Multiple Class BCMP Networks with Load Dependent Service Stations. Perf. Ev. 4*: p. 241-260.

Buslenko N. P. et al. (1966). *The Monte Carlo Method: The Method of Statistical Trials*. Edited by Shreider Yu. A. Pergamon Press.

Buzen J. P. (1973). Computational algorithms for closed queueing networks with exponential servers. *Communications of the ACM*. Vol. 16, Issue 9, Sept, p. 527-531.

Buzen J. P. (1978). A Queueing Network Model of MVS, *ACM Computing Surveys,* Vol. 10, No. 3. P. 319-331.

California Data Processors. (1974). Microprogrammable Minicomputers Provide Hardware/Software Compatibility. *Computer Design,* Vol. 13, 1974, No. 5.

Chandy K. M. and and Sauer C. H. (1980). Computational algorithm for product form queuing networks, *Comm. ACM,* Vol 23, Issue 10. p. 573-583.

Chaudhry M. L. (1981). The queuing system M/GB// and its modifications. *E. J. Operational Research*, Vo. 6, Issue 1. p. 56-60.

Cobham A. (1954). Priority Assignment in Waiting Time Problems. *Opns. Res.* 2, p. 70-76.

Cobham A. (1955) Priority Assignment, A Correction. *Opns. Res.* 2,p. 547.

Coffman E. G. and Denning P. J. (1973). *Operating Systems Theory.* Prentice-Hall, Inc.

Conway A. E. and Georganas N. D. (1986). *J. ACM. Vol.* 33, Issue 4. p. 768-791.

Czajkowski W. et al., Initial Performance Evaluation for a Communication Subnetwork Node. (1984). International Conference on Modelling Techniques and Tools for Performance Evaluation (INRIA, ACM), Paris (North Holland). pp. 6.

Czajkowski W., Lewoc J. B., Slugocki M. and Strzalkowski W. (1985). A communication subnetwork simulation and performance evaluation tool. Modelling Techniques and Tools for Performance Analysis (INRIA, ACM), Paris. pp. 6.

Davis S. (1974) A Fresh View of Mini- and Microcomputers. *Computer Design,* Vol. 13, No. 5.

Doyle J. C. (1982). Analysis of feedback systems with structured uncertainties. *Proceedings of the Institution of Electrical Engineers,* Part D, **129**. p. 42-50

Durr L. (1969). A Single-Server Priority Queuing System with General Holding Times, Poisson Input and Reverse Order of Arrival Queuing Discipline. *Opns. Res.* 17, p. 351-358.

Eisenberg. (1971) Queues with Changeover Times. *Opns. Res.* 19. p. 387-401.

Erlang A. K. (1909). The Theory of Probabilities and Telephone Conversations. Nyt Tidsskrift for Mathematic B, vol. 20.

Farlex. (2017). Yalta Agreement. Available: http://legal-dictionary.thefree dictionary.com/Yalta+Agreement.

Feller W. (1957). An Introduction to Probability Theory and its Applications (Volume 1). John Wiley & Sons Inc.

Feller W. (1971). An Introduction to Probability Theory and its Applications (Volume 2). John Wiley & Sons Inc.

Franasik L. et al. (2001). System Media – a Step toward Computer Integrated Manufacturing and Management systems. *Modelling, Measurement and Control* (AMSE Press). Vol. 22, No. 3. p. 37-46.

Izworski A., Lewoc J. B. and Skowronski S. (2006). Development of Computer Integrated Manufacturing and Management Systems. *Information Control Problems in Manufacturing*, Saint Etienne. p. 6.

Gaver D. P. (1967). Probability Models for Multiprogramming Computer Systems. *Journal of ACM*, July 1967. Vol. 14, No. 3, p. 423-438.

Gaver D. P. and Shedler G. S. (1973). *Opns. Res*. Vol. 21, Issue 2, p. 569-576.

Giffin C. (1978). Queueing: Basic Theory and Applications. Grid. Inc., Columbus, Ohio, USA.

Halfin S. and Whitt W. (1981). Heavy-Traffic Limits for Queues with Exponential Servers. *Operations Research,* Vol. 29, Issue 3. p 567-588.

Hansen P. B. (1973). Operating System Principles. Prentice-Hall, Inc.

Heathcote C. R. (1960). A Simple Queue with Several Preemptive Priority Classes. *Opns. Res.* 8, p. 630-638.

Izworski A. and Lewoc J. B. (1991). Quality comparison for big power plant computer monitors: A case study, RCSDuH&RM, IMC/SERC/ IEE/IEEE. Cambridge. pp. 6.

Izworski A. and J.B. Lewoc. (2003). Approximate Analytical Performance Modelling of a Computer Integrated Manufacturing and Management System. In: I. Troch and F. Breitenecker (Editors), *4-th MATHMOD (IMACS).* Vienna. pp.6.

Izworski A. and Lewoc J. B. (2003a). Robustness Comparison of Enterprise Energy Distributions Systems of Various Topologies. *Robust Control Systems* (IFAC), Milan. pp. 6.

Izworski A., Lewoc J. B. and Skowronski S. (2003b). "Robust Performance Case Study: Topology of System Media. *Control Applications of Automation (IFAC),* Visegrad. pp. 6.

Izworski A., Lewoc J. B. and Skowronski S., Development of Computer Integrated Manufacturing and Management Systems, In: *Information Control Problems in Manufacturing*, Saint Etienne, 2006.

Jain. R. (1989). A delay-based approach for congestion avoidance in interconnected heterogeneous computer networks. *ACM SIGCOMM Computer Communication Review,* Vol. 19, Issue 5. p. 56-71.

Jaiswal N. K. (1961). Preemptive Resume Priority Queues. *Opns. Res.* 9, p. 732-742.

Joandar S., Bhattacharyya S., Bhattacharya A. B., and Datta C. R. (2010). *Progress in Electromagnetics Research B.* Vol. 22, p. 73-102.

Jerzykiewicz K., and Szczepkowicz J. (1970). Odra 1204 computer programming systems: ALGOL 1204. Politechnika Warszawska. (In Polish).

Kleinrock L. (1975). *Queueing Systems.* Volume 1: Theory. Wiley.

Kleinrock L. (1976). *Queueing Systems.* Volume 2: Computer Applications. Wiley.

Kleinrock L. and Finkelstein R. P. (1967). Time Dependent Priority Queues. *Opns. Res.* 15, p. 104-116.

Kleinrock L. (1967). Time Shared Systems, A Theoretical Treatment. *Journal of ACM,* Vol. 14, No. 3, p. 242-261.

Kleinrock L. and Nilson A. (1981). On Optimal Scheduling Algorithms for Time-Shared Systems. *J. ACM*, Vol. 28, Issue 3. p. 477-486.

Kobayashi H. and Konheim A. (1977). Queueing Models for Computer Communication System Analysis. *IEEE Trans. On Communications,* Vol. 25, Issue 1. p. 2-29.

Kobayashi H. (1978). Modelling and Analysis: An Introduction to System Performance Evaluation Methodology. Addison-Wesley, Reading, Mass., USA.

Konheim A. G. and Reiser M. (1978). Fine Capacity Queueing Systems with Applications un Computer Modelling. *Siam Journal on Computing,* Vol. 7, No. 2. p. 210-229.

Krzesinski. A. E. (1987). Multiclass Queueing Networks with State-Dependent Routing. (1987). *Performance Evaluation,* Vol. 7, Issue 2. p. 125-143.

Kuberska A., Lewoc J. B. and Misiura L. (1986). A semi-graphical visual display for power dispatching purposes. Work with Display Units, Stockholm. pp. 6.

Kundu S. and Akyildiz I. F. (1989). Deadlock free buffer allocation in closed queueing networks. *Queueing Systems*, Vol. 4, Issue 1. p. 47-56.

Lam S. S. (1977). Queuing Networks with Population Size Constraints. *IBM Journal of Research and Development*, Vol. 21, Issue 4. p. 370-378.

Lavenberg S. S. and Reiser M. (1980). Stationary state probabilities at arrival instants for closed queuing networks with multiple queueing networks with multiple types of customers. *J. Applied Probability*, Vol. 17, Issue 4. p. 1048-1061.

Lewis P. A. W. and Shedler G. S. (1974). A Cyclic-Queue Model of System Overhead in Multiprogrammed Computer Systems. *Journal of the ACM.* Vol. 18. Issue 2, April, p. 199-220.

Lewoc J. (1971). Analysis of operation of a control system making use of a digital computer. *Graduation work.* University of Wroclaw. (In Polish).

Lewoc J. B. and Sibilski R. (1985). Some Critical Remarks on Studies Limited to Mean Values. *Advances in Modelling and Simulation.* AMSE Press. Vol. 4, No. 2. p.45-53.

Lewoc J. B. (1990). Performance Evaluation Problems for Actual Computer Networks. AMSE Press, Tassin, France.

Lewoc J. B., Rozent M. and Weksej. (1992a). A power system simulator: Participation of people involved, ASBoHS (IFAC), Madison, 6 p.

Lewoc J. B., Rozent M. and Saczuk I. (1992). The computing power and the computer systems for the power industry in Poland. MICC (IFAC). Prague. pp. 6.

Lewoc J.B., Izworski A. and Skowronski S. (2003). Simulation and Modelling of Computer Networks. The 3-rd Int. Conf. on Computational Science, Petersburg. pp. 6.

Lewoc J. B., Izworski A and Skowronski S., ALSIS case study: computer integrated manufacturing and management systems, Applications of Large Scale Industrial Systems, (IFAC), Helsinki-Stockholm, 2006.

Lewoc J. B., and Hersh M. A. (2017). Ethics and Human Behaviour in ICT Development. Springer-Verlag (approved for printing).

Maciejowski J. M. (1989). Multivariable Feedback Design. Addison-Wesley. Wokingham.

Manacher G. K. (1967). Production and Stabilisation of Real-Time Schedules. Journal of ACM, July 1987. Vol. 14, No. 2, p. 439-465.

Masse Ph. and Sabonnadiere J. C. (1975). A Computer Aided Instruction System for Network Engineering Education. Prague.

Mevert P. (1968). A Priority System with Set up Times. *Opns. Res.* 16, p. 602-612.

Miller R. G. (1964).Review: Lajos Takacs, Introduction to the Theory of Queues. *Ann. Math. Statist.* 35 (1964), no. 1, p. 450-453.

Murray D. N. and Enslow P. H. (1984). An experimental study of the performance of a local area network. *IEEE Com. Mag.* 22. p. 48-53

Pawlita P. F. (1981). Traffic measurements in data networks, recent measurement results and some applications. *IEEE Trans. Comm.*, Vol. 29, No. 4. p. 525-535.

Ramaswami V. (1980). The N/G/1 queue and its detailed analysis. *Advances in Applied Probability,* Vol. 12, Issue 1. p. 222-261.

Reiser M. (1978). *Interactive Modelling of Computer Systems J.,* Vol. 15, No. 4, p. 309-327.

Reiser M. and Lavenberg S. S. (1980). Mean-Value Analysis of Closed Multichain Queuing Networks. *J. ACM,* Vol. 27, No. 2. p. 313-322.

Reiser M. (1981). Mean-Value Analysis and Convolution Method for Queue-Dependent Servers in Closed Queueing Networks. *Performance Evaluation* 1. p. 7-18.

Robertazzi, T. G., (2000). Computer Networks and Systems. *Queuing Theory and Performance Evaluation,* Springer-Verlag.

Sakata M., Naguchi S. and Oizumi J. (1970). *Opns. Res.* Vol. 19, Issue 2, p. 371-365.

Saslow S. M. (1975). The "Smart" Terminal. *Telecommunications,* Vol. 9, No. 6. *Telecommunications,* Vol. 9,

Sawicki J., Kowalski A. J. and Lewoc J. B. (1974). Implementation of the Automatic Data Processing for the Power System Control in Poland. Data Processing Conference. Madrid. pp. 8.

Schoch J. F. and Hupp J. A. (1980). Performance of the Ethernet local network. *ACM Comm.,* Vol. 23, No. 12. p. 711-721.

Scott G. (1978). *ACM Computing Surveys,* Vol. 10, Issue 3. p. 219-224.

Shanthikumar J. G. and Yao D. D. (1986). The effect of increasing service rates in a closed queueing network. *J. Applied Probability*, Vol. 23, Issue 2. p. 474-483.

Shemer J. E. (1967). Some Mathematical Considerations of Time Sharing Scheduling Algorithms. *Journal of ACM,* April 1967. Vol. 14, No. 2, p. 262-272.

Skinner C. E. (1967).A priority Queuing System with Server Walking Time. *Opns. Res*. 15, p. 278-285.

Steele J. M. and Mattson R. C. (1973). Architecture of an Universal Communications Processor. *Computer Design,* Vol. 12, No. 11.

Takacs L. (1962). Introduction to the Theory of Queues. Oxford University Press, New York.

Takahashi Y., Miyahara H. and Hasegawa T, (1980). An Approximation Method for Open Restricted Queueing Networks. *Operations Research,* Vol. 28, Issue 3-part-i. p. 594-602.

Techopedia. (2017). Public Networks. Available: https://www.techopedia.com/definition/26424/public-network.

Techtarget Network. (2017). TCP/IP (Transmission Control Protocol/ Internet Protocol). Available: http://searchnetworking.techtarget.com/ definition/TCP-IP.

Towsley D. (1980). Queuing Network Models with State-Depending Routing. *J. ACM*, Vol. 27, Issue 2. p. 323-337.

Takacs L. (1960). Two Queues Attended by a Single Server. *Opns. Res.* 16, p. 639-650.

Tobagi F. A. (1978). Modeling and measurement techniques in packet communication networks. *Proc. IEEE* 66. p. 1423-1447.

University of Cambridge. (1980). Phoenix system technical documentation.

University of Windsor. (2017). History of Queueing Theory. Available: https://web2.uwindsor.ca/math/hlynka/qhist.html.

Unknown author. (2017). Memory partitioning. Available: www.idc-online.com/technical.../pdfs/.../Memory_Partitioning.pdf.

Wikipedia. (2012). JAS. Available: https://pl.wikipedia.org/wiki/JAS (in Polish).

Wikipedia. (2017a). Odra 1325. Available: https://pl.wikipedia.org/wiki/ Odra_1325. (In Polish).

Wikipedia. (2017b). ICT 1900 series. Available: https://en.wikipedia.org/ wiki/ICT_1900_series.

Wikipedia. (2017c). ICT 1900 Series. https://en.wikipedia.org/wiki/ICT_ 1900_series.

Wikipedia. (2017d). Momik 8b. Available: https://pl.wikipedia.org/wiki/ MOMIK_8b.

Wikipedia. (2017e). PDP-11. Available: https://en.wikipedia.org/wiki/ PDP-11.

Wikipedia. (2017f). OS/360 and successors. Available: https://en. wikipedia.org/wiki/OS/360_and_successors.

Wikipedia. (2017g). TCAM. Available: https://en.wikipedia.org/wiki/ TCAM.

Wikipedia. (2017h). MINIMOP. Available: https://en.wikipedia.org/wiki/ MINIMOP.

Wikipedia. (2017i). ICT 1900 series. Available: https://en.wikipedia.org/wiki/ICT_1900_series.

Wikipedia. (2017j). Ethernet. Available: https://en.wikipedia.org/wiki/Ethernet.

White H. and Christie L. S. (1958).Queuing with Preemptive Priorities or with Breakdown. *Opns. Res.* 6, p. 79-95.

Zuber R. (2017). My Elwro Memories. Available: http://www.elwrowcy.republika.pl/strona11.html. (In Polish).

In: ICT Performance ... ISBN: 978-1-53614-916-6
Editor: Józef Bohdan Lewoc et al.

Chapter 5

ROBUST DESIGN OF COMPUTER CONTROL SYSTEMS

Jozef B. Lewoc**, Pasha Bekhrad, Mike Fitzgibbon, Iwona Chomiak-Orsa, Antoni Izworski, Bogdan Kasierski, Antonina Kieleczawa, Eric Leitgeb, Jozef Patkiewicz, Mieczyslaw Rozent, Halina Strzelecka, Andrzej Tomczyk, Wojciech Szubert and Edward Ziaja

1. INTRODUCTION

In the early years of computer automation systems, system performance and reliability were usually chosen as the primary system quality measures (See e.g., Chapter 4 above).

However, after some time of computer control system development, performance and reliability became a *conditio sine qua non* for any system to be considered eligible for any application and the users required more

* Corresponding Author's Email: jblewoc@wroclaw.home.pl.

and more often that the systems operated correctly not only in normal operating conditions but also when some, possibly severe, disturbances occurred.

Therefore, computer automation system designers had to start to think about optimisation of their systems under uncertainties.

This led to the notion of robustness in the sense used in automatic control (J. M. Maciejowski 1989) - this is not in the sense used in artificial intelligence (F. Cozman 1997)).

After J. C. Doyle (1982) and J. M. Maciejowski (1989), the structured singular value for the compensated plant subject to structured perturbations (known as the μ function - see below) is used to analyse the robustness of such plant, in this Book 2.

2. The μ-Function – A Robustness Measure for Computer Systems

In the authors' opinion, computer system designers should think, like their colleagues working in automatic control, how the system will behave not only in normal operating conditions but also when some, perhaps serious, disturbances occur. In other words, they should also think in the category of optimisation under uncertainties.

From the point of view of robustness, there were, in practice, two architectures possible for the computer control systems:

- a star case

and

- a common-medium case.

The basic diagram of the star case is shown in Figure 1. The authors thought that it was not possible to determine the transmittance of the system presented in Figure 1. For instance, G(s) was to describe the operation of the high-level computer and of the System Engineer. And even if we were successful in modelling one System Engineer, another one could behave rather differently. It seemed that it was a proper thing to make use of the actual System Engineers who claimed usually that such systems could be stable if and only if the time delays introduced between the y and Z_k variables did not exceed some t_k values, $k = 1,\ldots,n$.

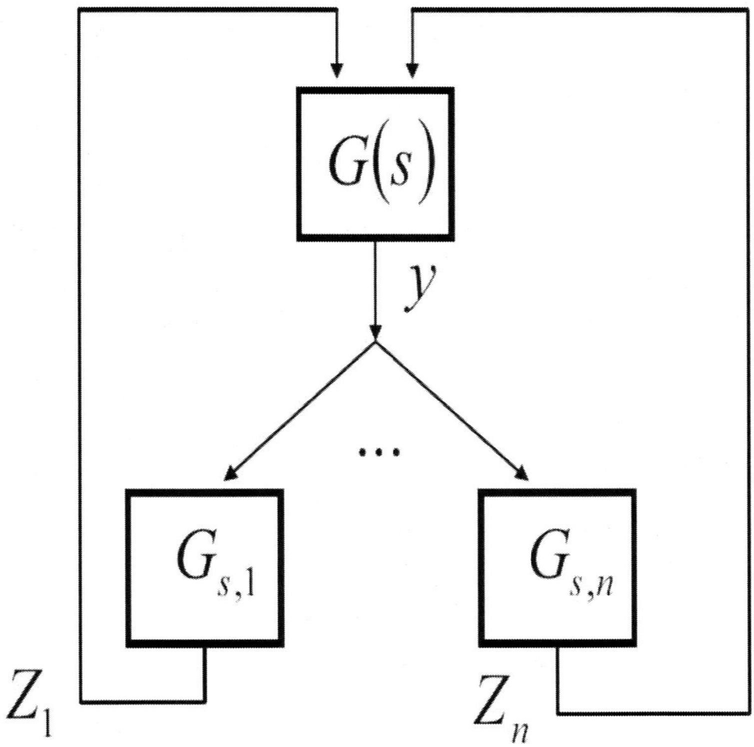

Figure 1. Basic diagram of the star case.

For the purposes of the stability and robustness considerations for computer control systems, it could be assumed that the $G_{s,1}$, …, $G_{s,n}$ (known as data concentrators) introduced some known time delay, only, since:

- the functions of the concentrators were almost the same for both architecture cases,
- the signal processing programs should be the same if the comparisons were to be fair,
- the data transmission aspects were of primary interest.

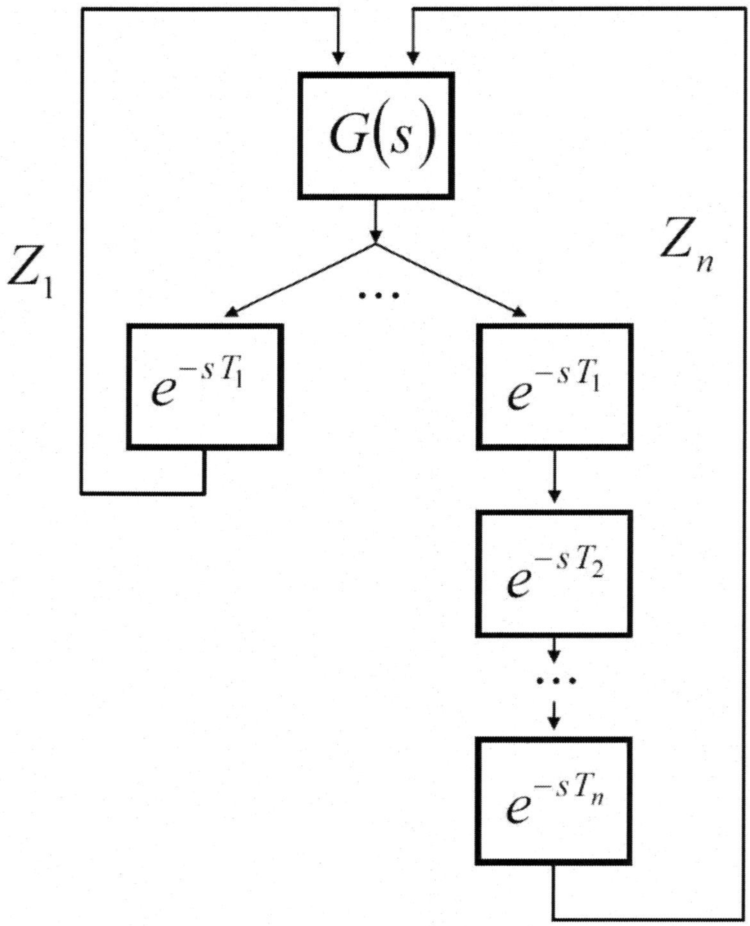

Figure 2. Basic diagram for the common-medium case.

Therefore it could be assumed that:

$$G_{S,k} = l_k\, e^{-sT_k}, k = 1, \dots, n, n = 8, T_k \geq 0 \qquad (29)$$

The basic configuration for common medium case is shown in Figure 2.

In practical implementations of this basic diagram, data items sent via individual branches of the basic scheme had to be transferred one after another.

Thus, the equivalent diagram for this case is shown in Figure 3.

Here, we have:

$$G_{C,k} = e^{-s\sum_{m=1}^{k} T_m}, k = 1, \ldots, n, n = 8, T_k \geq 0 \tag{30}$$

The number of branches, $n = 8$, was accepted as a typical one for the two cases described hereinafter.

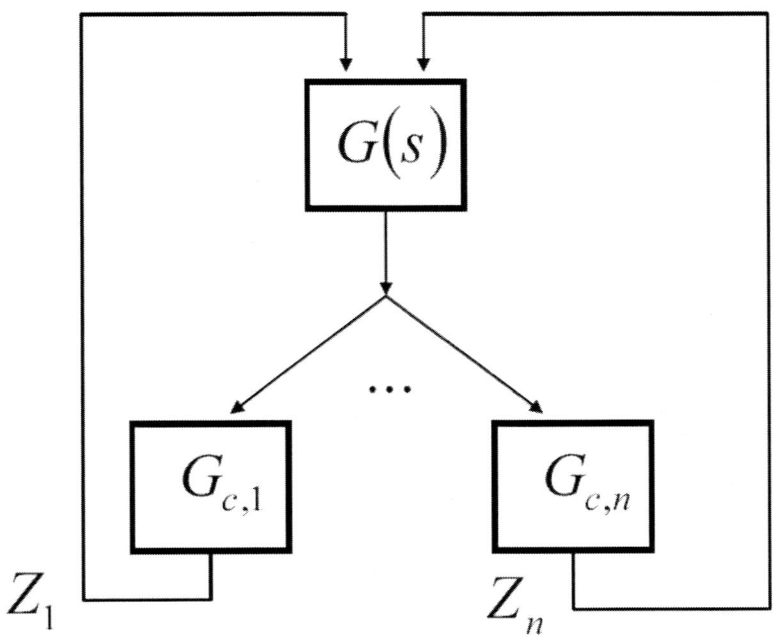

Figure 3. Equivalent diagram for the common-medium topology.

To investigate and compare robustness of the star and common-medium architectures, a disturbance of the multiplicative type, a time delay: e^{-sd}, should be added to each delay of the branches, the disturbance structures, Δ_S and Δ_C, being equal to:

$$\Delta_S = diag\,\{e^{-s(T_k+d_k)}\}_{k=1}^{n}\,, n = 8 \qquad (31)$$

$$\Delta_C = diag\,\{e^{-s\sum_{m=1}^{k}(T_m+d_m)}\}_{k=1}^{n}\,, n = 8 \qquad (32)$$

(J. C. Doyle 1982)

Let us note that, for the unit circle, all values are eigenvalues which makes the computation of the structured singular values (the μ-function) rather easy. For the purpose of normalisation, we can assume (as it is in the real life):

$$G(s) = diag\,\{\frac{\Pi}{2t_k\,s}\}_{k=1}^{n}, n = 8 \qquad (33)$$

Thus, the μ_S function for the star topology and the and μ_C for the common medium topology may be calculated as follows:

$$\mu_S\,(G) = (\min \overline{\sigma}\;(diag\,\{1 - \;e^{-j\omega(T_k+\,d_k)}\}_{k=1}^{n} \qquad (34)$$

$$:\det(\,\mathbf{1} + G\,\Delta_C) = 0\,)^{-1}\,; n = 8$$

$$\mu_C(G) = \left(\min \overline{\sigma}(diag\left\{1 - e^{-j\omega\sum_{m=1}^{k}(T_m+d_m)}\right\}_{k=1}^{n}\right): \qquad (35)$$

$$:\det(\mathbf{1} + G\Delta_C) = 0\;)^{-1}\;; n = 8$$

2.1. Application for a House Appliance Manufacturing Plant

This subsection describes the pilot media control/monitoring system devised for the Computer Integrated Manufacturing and Management (CIMM) system designed for the biggest (at that time) Polish home appliance manufacturing plant. In the authors' opinion, the key for the effective development of CIMM systems was to educate possible designers of such systems in both process control and management problems.

A good example is that the first thread through a CIMM system seemed to be the Chief Working Media Engineer Department, due to: the important role of the media in the total manufacturing costs, the similarity of the problems in any manufacturing enterprise, the similarity of the supervision and control problems to those existing in the power industry, that were quite well known, the fact that the Chief Working Media Engineer served all people employed in the Enterprise, which could be helpful in development of the whole CIMMs (L. Franasik 2001; and A. Izworski et al. 2003b, 2006).

The general star-type architecture of the System Media is depicted in Figure 4.

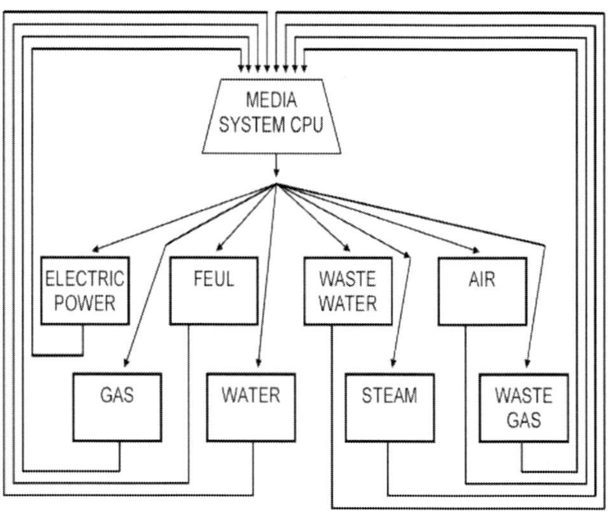

Figure 4. System Media-Polar architecture.

The basic diagram of the case is shown in Figure 1. For the initial stage of investigations, the same immanent disturbance for each controller was assumed:

$$d_k = d \text{ for } k = 1,\dots, n, n = 8 \quad (36)$$

In addition, the data field length was assumed to be the same for both cases.

For the first case, it was assumed that the data transfer rate was the same for both cases. The plots of the structured singular values (μ functions) are shown in Figure 5.

The robustness for the star topology is much higher than that for the common-medium case. The other case was a comparison of the star architecture operating at the transmission rate of ca. 4 Kbps, comparing with the common-medium one operating at a variable speed of up to 10 Mbps (See Figure 6).

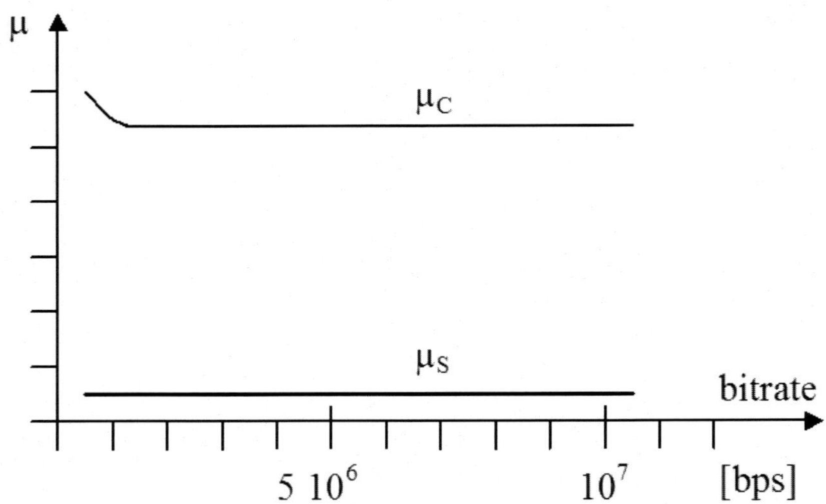

Figure 5. Structured singular values versus data transfer rates (the same for the star and common-medium architectures).

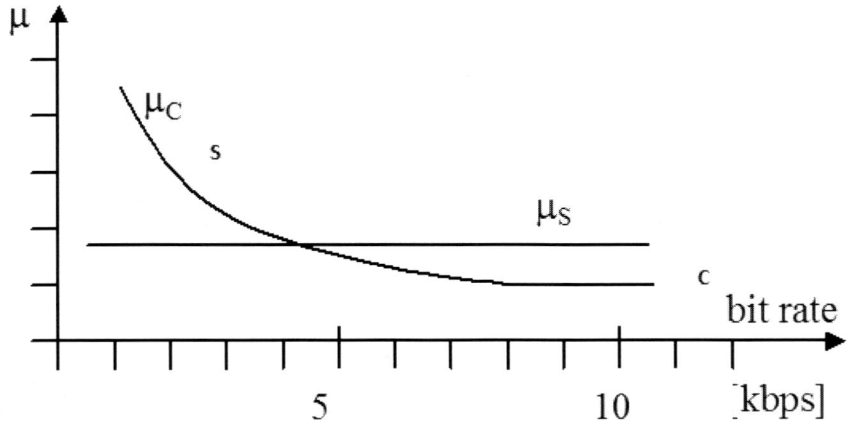

Figure 6. μS versus transmission rate compared with μC up to 107 bps.

It can be noticed that the star configuration operating at 4 Kbps is more robust than the common-medium one operating at 10 Mbps.

A conclusion was that the star architecture operating at a low or moderate data transfer rate could ensure higher robustness than the common-medium one operating at 10 Mbps.

2.2. Application for Power Generation/Distribution Control Systems

The power plant database project was analysed hereinabove (See Chapter 4 Section 10) from the point of view of performance. In the present sub-chapter, the robustness aspects will be investigated.

The basic diagram of the pgu (power generating unit) data acquisition and control system is depicted in Figure 7. For the *p*-th pgu (p = 1,…, 7), there were *k(p)* (*k* = 4) sequential controllers, $SC_{p,k}$, and *n(p)* Data Acquisition Units, *DAC*, *n(p)* = 4 in order that the comparison with the System Media-Polar is more easy.

For the above assumptions, possible for the power generating unit, the basic results for the System-Media are valid also for the pgu case (Ref. 2.1 above).

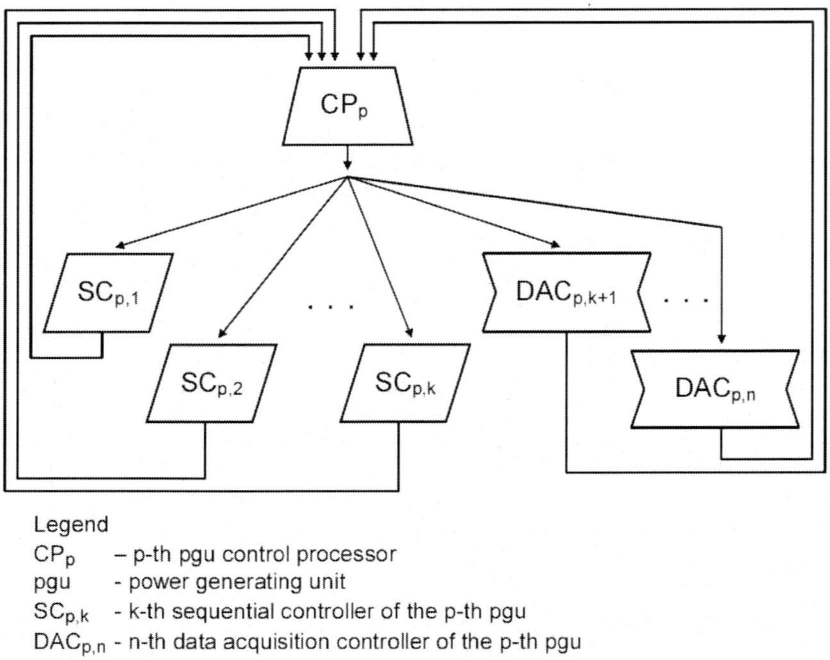

Figure 7. Power generating unit data acquisition and control system architecture.

2.3. Application in Democratic Networking

Many networking experts mention *democratic networking*. However, they refer to *the owners* of the networks than the democratic rules within the networks. The authors of this Book think it is needed and possible to approach the problem of democratic networking in the sense of the internal service of network users. In the authors' opinion, such an emerging approach to assessment of the computer network investigation should be based on an actual case study and proceed to the more complex cases.

For the first step, the case of Polar, the former biggest Polish manufacturer of household appliances has been assumed, described hereinabove (See. Exemplary application of Anapaest, 4.9.1. D.). The basic requirements for the communication network (the Network) for the case study has been defined in A. below:

For any large-scale LAN communication network, the topology should correspond to an isomorphic image of the actual network interconnecting human beings and technical equipment. The Team of network designers (the Team) thought that the requirement should be applied both to the communication network hardware and software topologies.

The general organisation of the management component of the enterprise is shown in Figure 8.

The authors assumed that the network of the Enterprise would be democratic when the equipment would be identical for each User (in the target state) and that the optimisation was based on maximisation of the quality of service for the worst served User.

In accordance with the general approach applied in this Section (5), it was assumed that the network should be optimised from the viewpoint of robustness. These problems have been discussed hereinabove (See 1 and 2).

The general topology (overall structure) of the Network is shown in Figure 9.

It is obvious that the proposed numbers of the Network nodes (sometimes called the switches) located at the extreme right hand branch form the geometric series of the integer quotient q while the numbers of the level l up to n form the partial sum of the geometric series:

$$S_n = \frac{1-q^n}{1-q} \tag{36}$$

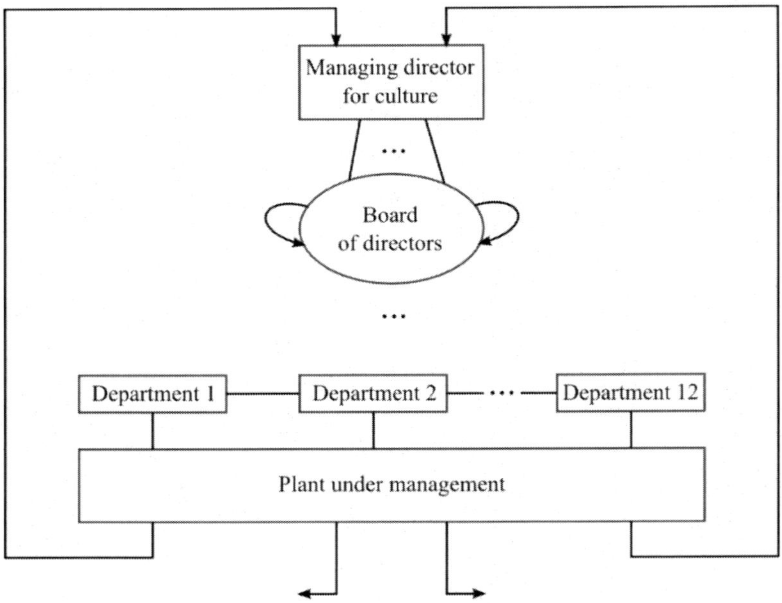

Figure 8. General organisation of the management component of the enterprise.

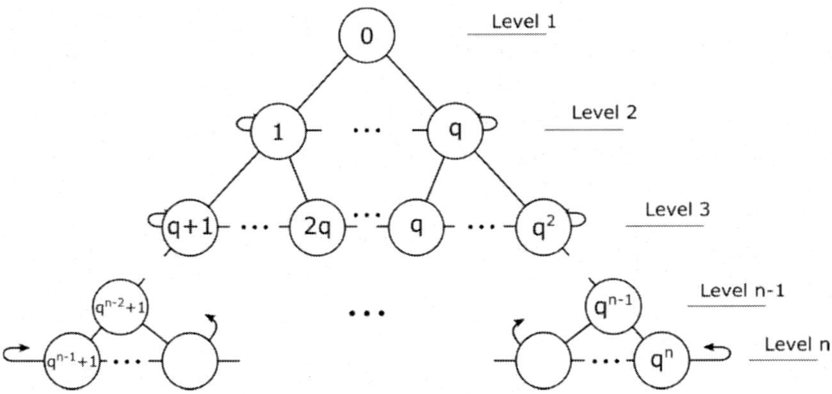

Figure 9. Overall structure of the network.

Individual branches in the Network represent links (sometimes called hops) and are identical. Therefore, without impairing the generality, it may be assumed that they are equal to 1. For optimisation, it is needed to define the optimality criterion:

For any democratic network, any User of the Network should receive the same service quality as any other User of the same class (it was assumed), located on the same level.

Considering the Network homogeneity in normal operating conditions, the objective function should be the biggest distance from the *k*-th node to another node (User) in the Network during the normal operation, i.e., with use of the horizontal links.

2.3.1. Optimal Topology for the Case Study Network

Determination of the optimum network for the case study is equivalent to finding the quotient q for which, for the minimum level number, $n(q)$, such that the number of nodes of the network, i.e., the partial sum of the geometric series:

$$n = n(n,q) = \frac{1-q^{n(q)}}{1-q} \geq 300 \tag{37}$$

where the maximum number of links (hops) between the nodes $q^{n(q)-1}+1$ and q^n, $d(q)$, is of the lowest value which is equivalent to that $q^{n(q)-1}(q-1)$ which is of the lowest value. For the case study, it can be simply verified directly.

Let us note that we may to limit our investigations to $2 < q < 300$. Indeed, for $q = 1$, we have the case of a common media network, disqualified by the robustness investigation results.

On the other hand, for $q > 300$, we have $n(q) = 1$, so that the number of links (hops), $d(q)$, mentioned above equals q and, obviously:

$$\prod_{q>300} d(q+1) > d(q) \tag{38}$$

or $2 < q < 300$; the values of $n(q)$ and $d(q)$ were verified by direct calculations; $d(q)$ assumes the minimum value for $q = 3$.

Thus, considering the democratic criterion and the number of network nodes/switches needed, the optimal communication network for the case study will be that shown in Figure 510.

The above case study was presented by Lewoc (2012). The general case is considered below.

$$d(q,n) = q^{n-1}(q-1) = (N \cdot (q-1) + 1)(q-1) \tag{39}$$

Thesis:

$$\prod_{\substack{N=1,\dots \\ q=2,4,5,6,\dots}} d(N,q) > d(3,q) \tag{40}$$

The thesis will be proven by induction with respect to $N >= 4$:

Assumption:

Let (40) is fulfilled for some $N >= 4$.

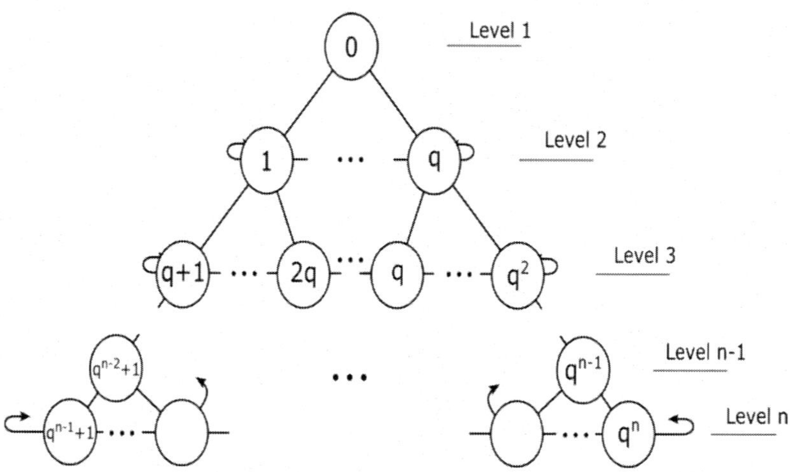

Figure 10. Optimal network for the case study.

We have:

$$(N(q-1)+1)(q-1) > (N(2)+1)2 = 2(2N+1) = 4N+2 \tag{41}$$

Then:

$$d(3, N+1) = ((N+1)(3-1)+1)2 = 2(N+1)2+1 = 4N+6 \tag{42}$$

And

$$\begin{aligned} &d(q, N+1) = ((N+1)(q-1)+1)(q-1) = \\ &(N(q-1)+1)(q-1) + (q-1)^2 \geq 2(2N+1) + \\ &(q-1)^2 = 4N+11 > 4N+6 = d(3, N+1) \end{aligned} \tag{43}$$

Qed.

We have also to consider the case of $q = 2$

$$\begin{aligned} &d(N,2) = N+1 \\ &\textit{and} \\ &d(2, N+1) = ((N+1)+1)(1) = N+1 \end{aligned} \tag{44}$$

Qed.

Conclusions:

Assuming the democratic criterion defined in this Book 2, the three-party communication network is the optimal one for the case study of 300 network nodes (switches), i.e., network Users. as well as for the general case. A hypothesis has been defined that the same holds true for any network of limited size (finite n), observing the democratic criterion in the understanding of this Book 2.

2.3.2. Initial Assessment of the Ethical and Human Behaviour Aspects

Applications of robustness in networking have been developed in a very limited extent and the ethical and HB aspects may not be given for the network designers, developers and users.

The attempts to apply the aspects to networking may be useful and not making any harm to anybody. Thus the ethics an HB of the authors should be assesses as appropriate.

CONCLUSION

Investigation of robustness, in particular, for networks introducing time delays only, seems to be a promising tool for networking. Such an approach may be successfully applied for the designing of robust computer systems and networks. Another application is possible in the design and development of democratic computer systems and networks. For computer systems and networks composed of delay-type members only, it is possible and worthwhile to use the μ function to perform the investigations of robustness.

REFERENCES

Cozman, F. (1997). Robustness analysis of Bayesian networks with local convex of distributions. Uncertainty in Artificial Intelligence. Morgan & Kaufmann. San Mateo.

Doyle, J. C. (1982). Analysis of feedback systems with structured uncertainties. *Proceedings of the Institution of Electrical Engineers,* Part D. 129. Pp. 42 - 50.

Franasik, L. et al. (2001). System Media – a Step toward Computer Integrated Manufacturing and Management systems. Modelling, *Measurement and Control (AMSE Press),* Vol. 22, No. 3. p. 37 - 46.

Izworski, A. and Lewoc, J. B. (1991). Quality comparison for big power plant computer monitors: A case study, RCSDuH&RM, IMC/SERC/IEE/IEEE. Cambridge. pp. 6.

Izworski, A. and Lewoc, J. B. (2003a). Robustness Comparison of Enterprise Energy Distributions Systems of Various Topologies. *Robust Control Systems (IFAC),* Milan. pp. 6.

Izworski, A., Lewoc, J. B. and Skowronski, S. (2003b). "Robust Performance Case Study: Topology of System Media. *Control Applications of Automation (IFAC),* Visegrad. pp. 6.

Izworski, A., Lewoc, J. B. and Skowronski, S., Development of Computer Integrated Manufacturing and Management Systems, In: *Information Control Problems in Manufacturing*, Saint Etienne, 2006.

Lewoc, J. B. et al. Optimal Management Network Topology in a CIMM System. A Case Study. (2012). In: Stapleton, L. (Ed.), SWIIS 2012. Waterford, pp 21 - 26.

Maciejowski, J. M. (1989). Multivariable Feedback Design. Addison-Wesley. Wokingham.

In: ICT Performance … ISBN: 978-1-53614-916-6
Editor: Józef Bohdan Lewoc et al.

Chapter 6

Case Studies of Ethics and Human Behaviour under Investigation: The Line of the ICT Systems and Networks

Jozef B. Lewoc*[*]*, Pasha Bekhrad, Mike Fitzgibbon, Iwona Chomiak-Orsa and Eric Leitgeb

1. Introduction

A survey of available references searched for with the keywords computer system and network performance evaluation ethical issues was done. Unfortunately, no references were found concerning the ethical issues for the main actors playing in the domain of designing and development of performance evaluation methods. Typical references found in the search and omitting consideration of the ethical issues for such actors may be: J. Yerby (2013), B.C. Stahl et al. (2014), H. T. Tavani

[*] Corresponding Author's Email: jblewoc@wroclaw.home.pl.

(2016), G. S. Alder (1998). Considering the fact that poorly designed and developed performance evaluation methods resulted in many very serious computer system and/or network failures, it was decided to consider here the case studies of the ethical issues of the performance evaluation method design and development actors. In order that the ethical issues for various actors included in design (and also the performance evaluation research work) of the computer systems under investigation in this Book, the same approach has been adopted in all of them.

While recognizing that some of these actors behaved ethically, whereas others did not, it is important to try to avoid classifying them as 'heroes'/'goodies' and 'villains'/'baddies.' Instead, it is preferable to try to understand and analyse the factors which affected their behaviour, as well as to apply the lessons of the example to your own situation. Most people face temptations and pressures at some time in their lives. These temptations and pressure may explain, but do not justify, acting in ways that harm others. It should also be noted that it can be difficult to stand against the ethos of the surrounding society and that it is easier to behave ethically when the ethos of the wider society encourages this.

At the simplest level, the Leader and his Team, generally, behaved ethically in carrying out their work to a high standard, whereas the researchers working in the theory of queues, a branch of mathematics, or in robust control systems, a branch of automation, generally behaved unethically in forcing the former to investigate the systems under design and development in their own ways to verify if they were capable of observing the requirements for the useful work. In most cases, such work was unpaid, voluntary work (or a work for the society, as it was called in this country).

On the other hand, the researchers working in the queuing theory branch of mathematics behaved unethically by neglecting the actual requirements imposed by real-life computer applications. This led sometimes to gigantic losses suffered by the society of this Ccountry and of the world.

Other actors taking part in the development of computer systems included, first of all, researchers working in the domain of computer simulations. In general, they behaved ethically and developed simulation aids and methods enabling effective investigations of computer systems and making it possible to verify whether the solutions designed met the requirements for real time operation.

Other actors involved in the computer system development process were the technical and political Authorities in the country and in the computer system manufacturers. They also behaved sometimes unethically, leading to big losses suffered by the societies involved.

2. Ethical Evaluation of Performance Evaluation Case Studies

2.1. Actions of the Queuing Theory Researchers

The basic assumptions adopted by the queuing theory researchers from the very beginning of this branch of mathematics till now have been as follows:

A. The description of the input process as a collection of independent arrival times, often of the Poisson input stream character;
B. Independent exponential service times;
C. Determination of mean values of the system characteristics only.

Concerning the assumption A, let us consider the steel-bar mill traffic control system (See Chapter 4 Section 1). The input processes are the software interrupt requests received by the material traffic control system. If the interrupt requests were of the Poisson input stream character, of exponential and independent inter-arrival times, individual realisations could be very low, violating the basic real-time operation condition requiring that no single request could be lost since at such conditions, the steel-bar mill control system could not pay back. Fortunately, the inter-arrival times of IR-s (Interrupt Requests) were not independent random variables, but they were defined by operation of mechanical machines and devices, much slower than the computer hardware and software. And the basic job of the system designers was to ensure that the IRs could be served successfully, without any input signal loss.

In fact, the main input signals in the steel-bar mill could not occur earlier than after the instant that a previous billet or bar passed through a material processing station (e.g., a steel mill) + some technological break between sequential material items. Considering that the maximum material travel speed could not exceed 3 m/s, the spacing between two successive photo-sensors (detecting material travel direction) could not be shorter than 0.3 m and the technological break could not be shorter than 1 s, the inter-arrival times of photo-relay IRs should be approximated by some random value distribution (the exponential distribution concentrated in an interval <1.2 s, 600 s> could be good, considering that inter-arrival times exceeding 10 minutes denoted major breaks in the steel-mill operation, not of interest from a performance evaluation aspect). In no case could the minimum interval of 1.2 s sbe neglected; on the contrary, the prime job of the system designers was to ensure that all material travel control calculations for all high priority system IR-s could be completed in this minimum interval.

In the steel-bar mill material travel control system and in all computer systems and networks designed and developed with use of good design practices (not only the real-time computer systems), the computers are protected against too short IR inter-arrival times: the IR-s are disabled till the previous ones are served. Examples: A scale could not accept a lot of bars for weighing till the previous lot is not weighed and the result is processed; an operator must not read a paper tape till the previous one is read and processed; a teletype will not generate an IR till the previous message is output. Such a solution protect the computers against losing signals. In such cases, the input stream is not defined by IR inter-arrival times but by times between the instant that the previous request is served and the next request arrives.

The MSK interuniversity communication network (See Chapter 4 Section 8 above) and other communication/computer networks popular nowadays should be designed and analysed as collections of a finite number of closed routes (connections/calls) shown in Figure 41. In such closed routes, the subscriber opening such an s route thinks for the thinking time, M_s, and may send a transmission entity (a packet) into the network. The server receiving the packet provides a service for the message received and sends a response packet which, after reaching the closed route opening subscriber, makes it possible to send the next packet into the network.

Note: To optimise transfers via the communication network, the opening subscriber and the server are allowed to send w_s (window or credit) packet for each packet received.

It is usual to describe the computer networks and the communication networks as composed of several parts called layers. It must be emphasised that the flow control mechanism depicted above may be implemented in various layers but, nevertheless, it is operable and protects the computer or communication network against overloading called saturation.

Concerning the assumption B, let us remind ourselves that, in actual computer systems and networks, the basic service was given by programs run on the Central Processing Units (CPUs) and it was very clear that the service times of reasonably written and debugged programs had to be concentrated on finite intervals. The lower and upper limitations of the concentration intervals of programs must have been taken into consideration if the queuing theory researchers were really interested in useful investigations of computer systems and networks. The programs (or hardware units) that violate some finite maximum service times are erroneous ones and such servers must be eliminated, and there is no need to investigate performance of queuing systems including such errors.

Concerning the assumption C, basing on performance evaluation investigations on the expected values only was severely criticised e.g., by the world best experts in probability calculus (Feller 1957, 1971) (See Chapter 4 Section 1.4). The opinion was that the high variance values in comparison with the means made the use of the theory of queues for investigation of practical cases very doubtful. In the specific cases of computer systems and networks, in particular of computer control systems, the use of expected values only could not be taken into account since this could lead to unlimited cases of service or sojourn times which excluded the systems under investigation from possible application in a real practice.

It should be noted here that expected values may be useful characteristics of actual computer systems, including real-time computer control systems, describing the degree within which the computer systems could be expanded to cover other computing jobs. However, the first task of a performance study should be to prove that the system under investigation could meet the time requirements defined by the application and the possible expansion of the system functions should be a secondary system characteristic only.

In the opinion of the authors of this book, such an approach to performance evaluation of actual computer systems (in particular the real-time computer control systems) should be called unethical. Usually, it is assumed that research work may not be unethical since, after a time, the results may prove to be useful for some actual future applications. But here, the problems were quite different: the theory of queues was claimed, by the researchers, an applied and not pure branch of mathematics and the possible users were cordially invited to apply its results to investigate the results achieved.

It was especially unethical since the researchers often claimed or suggested that their models and methods could be used for computer systems, which was not true at all. Such unethical approach is summarised best for the case study of the SOSAPI operating system, (See Chapter 4 Section 4); theoreticall, the reference book devoted to computer applications of the theory of queues. In practice, the reference book neglected basic computer system mechanisms, and flow control; the results proposed for possible computer system designers, developers and users were completely different from the behaviour of actual computer systems. Such an approach was not only unethical but also could be harmful if the performance evaluation aids proposed were applied in the design process, since it would be theoretical studies on models, on not existing systems.

In the initial era of the heterogeneous computer networks designed and developed by prospective network users (mostly from academia, see e.g., Chapter 4 Section 8 above), many computer network designers and developers involved in computer network performance evaluation strongly believed that the references on so called closed queuing networks were decidedly good steps towards adequate investigations of computer networks. However, it was recognised soon that there was no needed isomorphism between closed computer networks and queuing networks, and the proposals of applying the Mean Value Analysis (MVA) to investigation of actual computer networks were unethical.

2.2. Actions of the Leader and His Teams, and Other System Designers

In general, the actions of the Leader may be assessed as highly ethical. He undertook performance evaluation studies to avoid failures due to inadequate throughput or time delays, though such work was unpaid in most cases. For instance, performance evaluation for the steel-mill traffic control system (See Chapter 4 Section 1) was done within the framework of his graduation work in mathematics and for the radio-astronomy centre control system (See Chapter 4 Section 2) – within the framework of his PhD dissertation. The project of the interuniversity communication network (See Chapter 4 Section 8), including the internal network measuring system and Approximate network performance evaluation tool (Anapaest) (See Chapter 4 Section 9.1), realised on the Wroclaw University of Technology, covered also the topic 'Development of new computer network design and operation methods', and provided some financing for performance evaluation.

For the power plant data base project, the Leader included a network performance evaluation project in the overall project (See Chapter 4 Section 10). This resulted in severe protests of the so called local PoPs (Power of People), i.e., political circles appointed (formally or not) to supervise the project. The Leader answered: I do believe that performance evaluation is a must for such complex and expensive system; if you believe otherwise, you must appoint another leading designer. In addition to being substantially right, he had to show considerable courage to do so.

The research work of the Leader was unpaid completely since the domain of design and development of the large-scale computer system collapsed in the Country and there was no job available for a leading designer like him. So he continued his work as a researcher, financing it from translation. He chose the topics for his projects from the Country. First of all, he knew them best. But, more important was his motivation: In order that he became a leading designer needed in the Country and this meant much more than in any democratically ruled, well developed country, of ICT on a higher level, each citizen had to pay a contribution equivalent to several loaves of bread for his toys, computer hardware and software needed to develop the steel-bar mill traffic control system and the Regional Power Control Board system; it was due to this contribution that he was able to reach the computer system design level making it possible to make fun of the big-heads of Cambridge. The Leader believed that he could never pay back his debt to the people of the Country irrespectively of the benefits generated by his systems.

All this leads to recognition of the Leader's conduct as highly ethical.

2.3. Actions of Other Actors

2.3.1. Actions of Other Computer System Designers and/or Developers

It should be emphasised that the above case of the Leader (See 6.2.2.) could not be considered as typical for computer system designers and developers. The case was possible for realisation due to the unusual education and experience of the Leader: an MSc. in Computer Ccience; an MSc. in Mathematics with Distinction, received by him for his graduation work on performance evaluation of the steel-bar mill traffic control system (See Chapter 4 Section 1) and granted at a time when the Wroclaw School of Mathematics was led by Prof. Hugo Steinhaus and was ranked on the top level of the World Mathematics; a PhD. in Automation granted mainly due to his research work on a radio-astronomy centre control system performance evaluation; and also leading several dozen practical and/or theoretical projects in the area of computer systems and networks. Such a combination of scientific education and practical experience could very rarely be met in typical projects.

However, computer systems and networks (and the internet) have been designed successfully for several dozen years. This means that various computer system and network designers and developers must have dispensed with the fake scientific results of the queuing theory researchers and designed their projects in accordance with the reasonable thinking rules. However, if they did not, their projects resulted, sometimes, in slow and extremely expensively operating systems. To operate within the characteristics typical of earlier computers, they needed, simply, the rebuilding of software and, sometimes, hardware.

Here, the example of the major actors involved in the design and development of the Interuniversity communication network (See Chapter 4 Section 8), the University of Cambridge Computer Laboratory must be mentioned. The Laboratory corrected, step by step, many computer system faults and improved the operating performance characteristics by a high factor, making the operating Systems OS MVT and OS VS useful and not extremely expensive tools for the System /360 and /370 mainframes.

It should also be mentioned here that the researchers designing and developing Monte Carlo methods behaved, in general, very ethically and their results helped a very lot in developing the simulators used effectively for the investigation of the steel-bar mill traffic control simulator (See Chapter 4 Section 1.) and the radio-astronomy centre control system one (See Chapter 4 Section 2.).

2.3.2. Technical and Political Authorities

Most of the systems discussed above were designed and developed in the times of Komuna (Communist period) in the Country (Poland). In that time, the Country was ruled by the system WPR (Who has got Power is Right). This meant that so called PoP (Power of People) could arbitrarily implement its own decisions, whatever they were. In order that the people did not protest or struggle with such decisions, a lot was done to convince society that the decisions were beneficial for the nation.

However, while some or many such decisions were beneficial for the country, usually, PoPs rarely looked for actual support of the society for such decisions.

2.3.2.1. Steel-Bar Mill Traffic Control System

The steel-bar mill traffic control system was tuned several times in response to changed operating conditions of the mill and passed the acceptance trial run. However, the local PoPs were afraid of operating the system and the case was referred to the competent Arbitrage Authority. It should be noted that, at that time, arbitrage courts were under so strong an influence of the political Authorities that their decisions could be identified with decisions of the political power. In this connection, the decision that the Elam (the supplier of the system) won the dispute irrespective of the fact that the Warsaw Metallurgical Plant was the apple in the eye of the Central Committee of the Polish United Workers' Party (since the metallurgical plant was developed in Warsaw mainly to create so called Highly Industrialised Working Class there) should be considered a highly ethical and a brave one.

2.3.2.2. Radio-Astronomy Centre Control System

The Copernicus birthday anniversary was to be celebrated by two projects: the traditional optical telescope of the biggest then diameter and the radio-astronomy one. The first project proved to be unfeasible and resulted in high penalties for the Country. This made angry the First Secretary of the Polish United Workers' Party, who cancelled financial subsidies for both projects. The decision of the First Secretary to cancel the radio-astronomy centre control project was arbitrary, incompetent and highly detrimental to the radio-astronomy and science areas in general of the Country, and of the entire world, since it made it impossible to observe the sky from another point of the world, i.e., from the Country. Therefore, it should be considered highly unreasonable and unethical, i.e., a typical decision of PoPs under the WPR system.

2.3.2.3. Regional Power Control Board System

The first version of SAPI ODM was sent to the Southern Region of the Polish electric power network only after a few days that the industrial control peripherals, SMA, became available for the SOSAPI ODM authors, with SOSAPI subprogram 2 (the priority one), the very new part of the software of SAPI ODM, not tested anywhere for similar applications, and almost completely not debugged in the actual hardware environment. The debugging process in the ODM premises was much more difficult than in the computer system development centre in IASE (the Institute of Power System Automation) and while the Southern Region were personally interested in buying a Western SAPI system, this resulted in the SAPI ODM South failure. Similar decisions to prematurely send systems that had not been put in motion were common for the Authorities of the Country at that time, when they would boast groundlessly of their work, and resulted in many failures of emerging systems. Such actions should be considered incompetent and highly unethical.

2.3.2.4. SOSAPI Operating System

The first version of the operating system SOSAPI was implemented successfully in the Polish Central Power Network Region (ZEOC). The system was home-made and the operating staff could not account for special benefits (e.g., foreign training courses organised by international suppliers); in implementation, the technical Authorities responsible for SAPI ODM presented a very friendly approach to the SOSAPI system, emphasising, for instance, to the control engineers that they would be provided with very good English visual display units, and initiating modification projects of SAPI ODM solutions (e.g., the clock unit), executed by their technical maintenance staff, to better fit local conditions. In this way, they created a SAPI ODM-friendly atmosphere and created understandings prior the system commissioning, and the latter phase was smooth and faultless.

Such an approach proved to be very successful (faultless implementation and very high benefits generated by ZEOC SAPI ODM) and should be considered as very reasonable and highly ethical.

2.3.2.5. Power Industry Training Simulator

The managerial and technical Authorities of the Southern Region Power Industry Training Centre showed a very engaged approach to the power network simulation project. They were very helpful during the design phase, organising technical meetings of the design and development staff residing in various locations: Warsaw, Wroclaw and Bielsko-Biala; and preparing the rooms necessary for the training sessions. When it became clear that the standard simulation programs might not be applied due to the Odra 1325 computing power limitations (and, in fact, of any computer that was tried for the big object training simulator at that time), they did not resign from the project but delegated their most experienced trainer, a former very skilful power network control engineer, to help the programmers developing the simulator to change over from the standard complete power system models to responses to the trainee actions, defined by the trainer.

Such an approach proved to be very successful: more than 90% of the power network control engineers in the Country were successfully trained on the simulator during, roughly, 10 years of operation and this should be considered to be highly ethical. This was even more so, given that at that time, many computer training simulator projects failed due to the inadequate computing power of the computers available. Thus, it should be called highly reasonable and ethical.

2.3.2.6. Microprocessor-Based Power Control Board System

From the technological point of view, when Martial Law was introduced at the end of 1981 in the Country, it resulted in a severe recession there. The demand for electric power in the Country sank to a large extent, and the lack of demand resulted in the abandoning of many projects, including those that were successfully designed and developed for the power industry. These included the microprocessor based Power Control Board system and no small-scale system were proposed to lower level electric power system hierarch levels in spite of the fact that they were really needed there. Such action should be assessed as a highly thoughtless and unethical one.

2.3.2.7. Interuniversity Computer Network

The highest power (the Rector) of the university designing and developing the MSK (Interuniversity) computer network was very seriously interested in the actual success of this computer network. However, many other PoPs, the research workers of the university, were very envious of the Leader's working successes and tried to hinder his work and private life. The Rector intervened on the Leader's behalf thus enabling him to work successfully. However, when the Rector's term finished, the opponent PoPs attacked the Leader very strongly trying to block his passport and to get rid of him. Such actions of the research workers were not only unethical but simply disgusting.

Surprisingly enough, the Leader got an effective help from the political police of the Country, who were very intent on seeing that the Leader had good conditions in his work. The reason was that the political police knew that he led the most important technical project of the Solidarity underground in the Country, called TV Solidarity (adding moving Solidarity texts to the signals of the governmental TV). The police unit involved in following him (called the Hunting Dogs) were highly interested in his success since, then, they would be highly rewarded for their successful work (in keeping the Leader of the successful TV Solidarity project). Due to their actions, he could go to Paris for an important conference on computer networks and was not sacked from the university, and could complete his project of the communication network of the interuniversity computer network, and continue his work on the TV Solidarity (till the instant that political amnesty was announced in the Country and the need for the underground project ceased). These actions of the Hunting Dogs were not safe for them and should be called ethical and even brave.

2.3.2.8. Power Plant Database Project

The Badel system was designed during the period that the WPR (Who has got Power is R) system was changing into the democratic one, at least in in theory the WRP (Who is Right that has got Power). However, there were the two phenomena hindering the change:

- the force of habits of people accustomed of living long under the old, WPR system, that led to unethical actions,
- the naive (or sometimes purposefully implemented) liberalism that made it possible to implement unethical actions in an often unpunished way.

The first phenomenon led to objections of the employer of the Badel system and the authorities of the institute developing the design to including the performance evaluation part in the overall Badel project. Considering the unethical actions of the queuing theory researchers, such an approach was understandable. However, it was an action similar to the one described, in the Country, as: "throwing the baby out with the bathwater," and that could not be called ethical. However, the decided position of the Leader who was in danger of dismissal if the performance evaluation issues were not included in such big and expensive project was enough to eliminate the problems.

The other phenomenon led to much bigger problems for the Country and for the Badel project. Due to often thieving actions led by the representatives of the new power, the normal development of the Country severely collapsed. This was reflected in the conditions of the power industry of the Country: the demand for electric power decreased and the need of the new big power plant became very doubtful. The actions of the representatives of the new power was highly unethical and resulted in several years delay of the power plant database project (realised by other enterprises).

After many years passed, the Badel project was resumed for various power and heat and power plants, based on the work that had been led by the Leader. His successors, educated and upgraded on the power plant database project, decided to continue his work and won: until the present, more than 200 systems have been successfully implemented in the Country, and have generated the economic benefits of several billion Euro, proving that the unethical action of the new power in the Country and not the lack of knowledge or experience were the actual reasons behind the Badel project history.

3. Human Behaviour of the Performance Evaluation Case Studies

3.1. Introduction

Similar to the ethical aspects, the behavioural ones of the main actors operating in the domain of the development of the analytical performance evaluation methods (the theory of queues) are not investigated in the references known to the authors of this book. For instance the basic reference on ethical and human behavioural investigations of ICT system design and development (J. B. Lewoc, M. Hersh *et. al.*) mentions only the system design, development and operating aspects, missing the problems of design and development of the mathematical tools needed for reliable performance evaluation methods necessary for responsible evaluation (and, even more, optimisation) of computer system and network characteristics, and for the avoiding of very serious losses due to development of inadequate system solutions.

The most probable reason of this fact was that the Human Behaviour (HB) investigators assumed that queuing theory was a branch of pure and not exact branch of mathematics and the HB aspects were not of interest in this case. However, this was not true, which was proved by high losses due to application of inadequate methods and tools proposed by the branch of mathematics and the conducts of the main actors involved in the basic projects described hereinabove will be discussed below.

3.2. Conduct of the Queuing Theory Researchers

Researchers of the theory of queues were motivated by their conviction of the importance and infallibility of this branch of mathematics. They made light, often, of the actual features of the systems to be investigated and proposed studies of them at assumptions far from the actual reality, e.g., Poisson input streams, exponential servers, independent arrival times, examination of mean values only. This conduct consisted in matching the systems under investigation to what the researcher could study and, thus, should be considered highly inappropriate; when applying such approaches, the theoretical results were often quite far from the actual ones and the use of the theoretical results implied wrong conclusions and resulted in substantial and financial losses.

Some mathematicians claimed that even when less than one per cent of pure mathematical discoveries may sometimes applied in the real life, it will be still profitable (A. Rybarski, 1964, Private message). However, it seems impossible that theoretically applied investigations on models of not existing systems can ever belong to that 1% of the mathematical discoveries and the losses suffered due to inadequate models of real systems have been enormous, e.g., billions dollars for the case of the poorly designed computer systems based on the OS MVT operating system (Wikipedia 2018a).

Therefore, it may be safely assumed that such conduct of the creators of the queuing theory applications in computers will remain for ever theoretical investigations on models of non-existing systems, and the recommendations proposed by the creators will lead directly to inappropriate HBs. Even more that that, the queuing method "experts" tried to convince possible computer system and network designers that the experts' methods could be applied directly into investigation of e.g., the steel-bar mill traffic control system in the late nineteen-sixties, while the basic questions asked could not be answered by the theory till now (See Chapter 4 Section 1).

It must be stated clearly here that the authors of methods and tools of approximate methods of performance evaluation (e.g., (A.P. Buslenko et al., 1967) worked in very appropriate ways, and their proposals could be applied directly to investigation of the computer systems and networks described in this Book.

3.3. Conduct of the Leader and His Teams

3.3.1. Steel-Mill Traffic Control System

The Leader being one of two co-designers of the very first computer control system in the Country organised and conducted the performance evaluation investigation for the steel-bar mill material traffic control system. He started from the detailed survey of various mass service systems and found that the questions asked by its designers could not be answered by the queuing system theory of that time (this remains the case today). He realised that approximate investigations of real systems and conditions may ensure results useful for the design and development of the system under study while even accurate results of investigation of non-existing systems and conditions may not, and developed an approximate Monte Carlo model.

The approach produced results valuable for the designers of the material traffic control system since the basic assumptions of the theory of queues could be omitted and actual conditions in the system could be modelled.

For instance:

- The input stream must not have been modelled by inter-arrival times of exponential distributions: the most frequent, in practice, truncated exponential distributions, given good mapping of the time limits (lower and upper) of actual computer systems (of real-time computer control systems, especially), were applied, describing rather well the actual conditions in the production process and in the computer system.
- The basic assumption of the inter-arrival time independence could be eliminated, making the model adequate for the actual conditions

in the production process and in the computer system. For instance, the second photo-relay (of a pair) signal arrival instant was generated as a random variable after the first photo-relay signal arrival; a read request for the tape reader was simulated after a random time from the instant that the former request for the reader was generated; the weighing action complete signal from the scales was modelled after a constant time from the instant that the material lot involved was sensed at the scales.

In this way, the traffic control input stream was mapping well the actual conditions in the steel-bar mill and in the control system, instead of the suppositions of the queuing theory experts' assumptions (See 6.3.1 A) which had no reasonable reference to the actual conditions.

The similar approach of the Leader and his teams was applied with respect to the service times: the assumptions used often by the queuing theory researchers was that the service times could and should be approximated by independent random variables of the exponential distributions (See 6.3.1. B). In the Monte Carlo simulation models, actual distributions of service times could be modelled and investigated.

The assumption of the exponential service times distributions was not met in any computer system and, in particular, in computer control systems, since that led to unlimited realisations of sojourn times of IR-s in the service systems, that were inadmissible, in practice, in any computer system. The Leader assumed that the service time distributions were concentrated on some finite intervals; the concentration intervals made it possible to design and develop the material traffic computer control system, capable of meeting the real-time operation requirements in real practice.

The assumption of independent service times could (and should) also be omitted in cases such as, e.g., the clock subroutines operating with service times dependent on the number of IR-s being served. In this way, the actual service times could be modelled when investigating the steel-bar mill material traffic control system.

In particular note is due to the use of expected values as the basic performance measures of mass service systems (See 6.3.1. C). Such approach has been severely criticised in various sections of this Book 2. However, the Leader and his teams assessed the expected values of IR sojourn times in the steel-bar mill Material Traffic Computer Control System (MTCCS). In this case, the assessments were done at the actual system assumptions ensuring correct approximations of the mean values. Considering that, and when it was validated that the basic real-time operation requirements were met, this ensured that MTCCS was capable of the real-time operation; the sojourn time expectances could approximate the computer busy time and assess the intensity of extra system load that could be charged onto the system; this could forecast the possible extra load introduced to the system, e.g., on some lower priority level.

The Leader behaved as described above for the very first application of computer control systems in the Country when the actual knowledge of operation of such systems was very limited and, to avoid high possible losses, was really needed. In addition, he designed and developed the MTCCS in the form of volunteer work (work for the society), as a graduate work within the Mathematical Faculty. This should be considered a very appropriate approach, enabling investigation of MTCCS when it was actually needed to avoid high economic losses due to inappropriate solutions adopted when very little real knowledge was available, and at the lowest possible investigation costs. Such an approach of the Leader should be recognised as a very appropriate HB conduct.

The conduct developed some sound bases for development of performance evaluation methods and tools for future computer systems and, in particular, computer control systems and networks. Therefore, it should be assessed as highly appropriate from the point of view of HB.

3.3.2. Radio-Astronomy Centre Control System (RACS)

The Leader investigated RACS as a computer control system operating on several pre-emptive resume priority levels. The reason was that the system, in addition to real-time control actions, had to perform long radio-astronomy calculating procedures (aperture super-synthesis) on the data received by the dishes. Therefore, though the computers applied were the same (Odra 1204), the simulation routines were different, enabling to investigate, in practice, allconfigurations of centralised computer control systems (other than computer networks). The Leader designed and developed the simulation model of computer control systems and presented to the radio-astronomers material evidence proving that the computer could be applied for RACS. He won the contest for design and development of the system.

The Leader and his team worked out the simulation models and tested the results within the framework of his PhD dissertation thesis, thus limiting the cost consequences on the RACS design work. Such work was highly appropriate and made it possible to undertake the reasonable decision with respect to the contest results.

3.3.3. Regional Power Control Board (RPCB) System and SOSAPI Operating System

The RPCB system and SOSAPI operating system projects did not include a performance evaluation and/or prediction phase. Therefore, the Leader and his teams used approximate performance evaluation models to verify whether the solutions adopted observed the real-time requirements imposed by the RPCB under design and development. This approach proved to be appropriate (during system development and operation period, no bottlenecks were found for the systems and the benefits achieved by the Country exceeded several billion Euros in total for some six applications).

Therefore, the conduct of the Leader and his teams should be recognised as highly appropriate, ensuring very high economic and scientific results.

3.3.4. Power Industry VDU Project

The Leader led successfully this project, which required detailed knowledge of the visualisation devices (semi-graphic and alphanumeric visual displays), the ICL cluster control unit, computer-computer cooperation and relevant operating system and application software. To verify the real-time operation of the unit (operating at the then high speed of a million bps), he developed (voluntarily) an approximate performance model of the solutions and tested the feasibility of the project. This conduct made it possible to apply the VDU-s in some power industry applications in the Country (e.g., training of the RPCB control engineers) with very valuable results without big financial outlays.

3.3.5. Power Industry Training Simulator

The Leader led successfully an extended feasibility study for the simulator that its enabled successful design and development and educated the staff as needed for the emerging ICT application. He knew that, due to the success of RPCB system, he would have to leave the training simulator design and development team in order not to enter conflicts with the PoPs (Power of People) interested in depriving him of the benefits (money, promotion, system creator glory). Under the communist system or, in general, the WPR (Who has Power is Right) system, in the case of such conflicts, the Leader would be deprived of leading other projects. Therefore, in such cases, the Leader trained and educated his successors and left the team, department or even the employer.

Such conduct proved to be successful many times. In this case, while many training simulator projects failed around the world, the power industry proved to be very successful, and his work made it possible to train more than 90% of the Country control engineers.

3.3.6. Microprocessor-Based Power Control Board System

For the microprocessor based version of SAPI ODM (See subsection C above in the present section), the Leader and his team performed the performance evaluation study, it being a sub-study of SAPI ODM. It was shown that the microcomputer system based on the Intel's 8080 processor could meet the real-time operation requirements for the data acquisition and presentation within the scope of visualisation of measurements and digital signals in lower-level power control boards. These criteria made it possible to design and develop the visualisation tool that could be applied in lower level power control boards where the possible benefits could be much lower than in Regional Power Control Boards and cooling systems were not available to make it impossible to use external memories (at this time, disks).

3.3.7. Interuniversity Communication Network

The communication network of the Interuniversity computer network MSK was a project led by a University of Technology as a scientific one. Due to that, the Leader and his team decided that they should and could carry out performance studies for the MSK network and for future computer networks in the Country and elsewhere. The performance studies commenced with the designing and developing of an internal network performance measuring tool Sitwa, and taking measurements of the communication network performance for various scenarios of the traffic within the network. This work was supplemented by simulation studies of the network performance: a computer network simulator was designed and developed based on those simulators validated for the steel-bar mill material traffic computer control system and for the radio-astronomy dish control system.

The work made it possible to design, develop and fine-tune the Approximate network analytical performance assessment tool (Anapaest) that proved to be an effective performance assessment tool for various network configurations (see subsection H below).

The conduct of the Leader and his team, who treated seriously the scientific goals of the MSK network and designed and developed a useful tool for design, development and operation of future networks, should be considered as a valuable outcome of their work and very appropriate conduct from the point of view of the human behaviour aspects.

3.3.8. Anapaest Performance Assessment Tool

For performance evaluation of computer networks with end-to-end acknowledgement, the Leader and his teams designed and developed and approximate model based on description of such networks as collection of closed routes (See Chapter 4 Section 8 above). The models proved to be appropriate for investigation of various computer networks in the Country and elsewhere (See e.g., J. B. Lewoc 2010a,b.c).

The method worked out during the MSK computer network project proved to be useful for other actual networks as well as for investigations of scientific projects. Therefore, the conduct of the Leader and his teams should be recognised as highly appropriate and useful.

3.3.9. Badel Database for Power Plants

The Badel (from Polish Baza danych dla elektrowni – A database for power plants) database was to be a very large-scale system covering both on-line data processing (for electric power generation) and off-line calculations (for the managerial sphere of the power plant). This implied the need of accurate performance evaluation schemes and the Leader included such investigations in the design phase. The unexpected counter-actions performed by so called PoPs (Power of People) made the Leader to offer his resignation if the performance evaluation aspects were not taken into account in the project.

He won, and led the project till the end (which happened with the suspension of the power plant project due to the low power demand in the Country, resulting from naïve liberalism that led to a serious industry collapse after the very positive political change there). A convincing proof that his conduct was appropriate was that, after a dozen or so years, the Badel design would be implemented successfully in more than 200 power plants and heat and power plants around the Country. A part of this big success, considering the very severe competition of the most important world computer automation corporations in the power industry domain, was that the successors of the Leader, leading the new projects, had a good knowledge of the performance evaluation aspects and could avoid such inappropriate phenomena as saturation in their work.

4. Ethical Evaluation of the Robustness Evaluation Case Studies

4.1. Introduction

The Leader and his teams found that the μ-function, i.e., the structured singular value for the compensated plant subject to structured perturbations, may be successfully used for the robustness of such plants. The primary reason for that is that two architectures are possible for actual computer control systems (see 5 above):

- the star architecture (topology) and
- the common-medium topology.

For the plants that may be modelled with use of delay-members only (as in actual cases), the μ-function can be evaluated rather easily, since, in that case, very cumbersome calculations of the Eigen values are not necessary. This leads to the results described below (See sub-section B).

4.2. Case Study 1: House Appliance Manufacturing Plant

The authors do not know models of the plants of a simplicity similar to that proposed by the Leader and his teams. From the very beginning, robustness investigators have analysed the μ-function cases needing very complex calculations (R. P. Bratz et al., 1994), thus making it impossible to study the actual computer control system cases. This has led to many studies analysing the computer control systems in a way much too complex to calculate actually needed results.

4.3. Case Study 2: Power Generation/Distribution Control Systems

In this case, the approach described above was used and similar data was obtained. Thus, in this case, the simple and straightforward calculation of the μ-function was possible, and comparison of the systems of various topologies could be carried out. The results showed that the "old fashioned" star topology was much better for actual applications than the "modern" one (it should be called a 'new' one since the new needs to prove to be better than the old to be called 'modern').

4.4. Case Study 3: Democratic Networking

This case study was aimed towards finding the optimal structure of the really democratic computer network. It was shown that the network should be represented by the three-part topology applied, among others, in military topologies. In the case study, it was proven that such topology was the optimal one when the quality criterion adopted was the maximisation of the services provided for the worst-served network user which, in opinion of the authors, was a really democratic one.

4.5. Human Behaviour of the Robustness Evaluation Case Studies

Involvement into too complex calculations of the μ-function instead of using rather simple ones ensuring the needed results seems to be an inappropriate conduct from the human behaviour point of view and, thus, should be eliminated from the design work.

4.6. The Relationship between Ethics and Human Behaviour for the Case Studies

For the case studies described in this book, it was assumed that the non-maleficence rule was adopted for ethical conduct while behavioural not-needed unnecessary work was assumed as appropriate conduct from the point of view of the Human Behaviour. In many cases, the examples of ethical conduct were the same as those appropriate ones from the point of view of the human behaviour. This reflects the conviction of the authors that the simple and straightforward approach to any research and technical work is both ethical and appropriate from the point of view of the Human Behaviour, since it does not harm anybody and does not imply extra time and money to get the results promised.

4.7. Lessons to Be Learnt

Perhaps the most important lesson to be learned from the ICT system case studies presented here is that of the simplicity and straightforwardness in the approach to looking for the best solutions needed by real users. Any extravagance in scientific or technical solutions is, usually, a sign that the authors are interested in their private glory of being acquainted with complex formulae, rather than in solving actual user problems. And, in such a case, the solutions may not be called ethical or appropriate from the point of view of the Human Behaviour.

Scientific or technological publicity should not be used as a reason to apply an approach to the investigation of actual computer systems, computer control systems in particular. For instance, the works of Kleinrock or Riser received very many citations, while they had not made it possible to investigate reliably actual ICT systems, including computer control systems.

An example: During the process of the interuniversity communication network design and development, an *ad hoc* measurement of time performance characteristics was organised, comparing the R-32 computer (compatible with IBM /360 mainframe with the TCAM access method) and Odra 1325 (equivalent to ICL 1902a with George 3 and multiplexer). The results were astonishing: on-line computing costs were some hundred times higher and off-line computing costs – at several times higher on the R-32 computer, for similar tasks of student program debugging and processing. This was to herald the downfall of Polish computers after the transition to the IBM /360 compatibles.

A curiosity found during the *ad hoc* measurements was that the students who were fast enough received fast computer response. The other users get the long, exponentially distributed sojourn times. It looked as though the mainframe tried to recognise its colleague, another computer, and provided a better service to it. Most probably, such a mode was a result on the operating system programmers' tricks based on the exponential service times.

Another lesson to be learnt was that you could never guess what was old (obsolete) and what was new (novel). For instance, the examples of performance evaluation based on the open system approach (Kleinrock for computer systems) may seem obsolete. The example below contradicts that:

Example: In the present century, the Leader was a reviewer of several IEEE Transactions and Journals. He was sent a submission for review of a performance evaluation of some computer memory systems, proposing performance evaluation which used the open system approach that was assumed unfeasible a few dozen years earlier. He got angry and recommended rejection of the paper; the editorial board accepted the recommendation. Later, he found other papers on performance evaluation of computer networks, using erroneously the same approach. This confirms that this Book 2 investigates a problem that continues to recur even now.

CONCLUSION

The simplicity and straightforwardness of work on technological and scientific applications is a must for obtaining models that are reliable and easy for applying, for actual computer systems and networks.

The performance and robustness evaluation systems that use inadequate assumptions concerning the models of the systems being investigated may lead to completely erroneous results and should not be used for the investigation of actual computer systems and networks since they may lead to conclusions resulting in very high losses. This may be considered a truism but is valid for rather expensive computer systems and networks.

Historia est mater studiorum and historic surveys may be useful for understanding the rules governing even the most current solutions; in particular, this refers to performance evaluation problems for which some researchers and practitioners try to apply the open system approach that has been found inadequate several dozen years ago.

REFERENCES

Alder G. S. (1998). Ethical Issues in Electronic Performance Monitoring: A Consideration of Deontological and Teleological Perspectives. *Journal of Business Ethics,* Vol. 17, 1998, p. 729-743.

Bratz R. P. et al. (1994). Computational Complexity of Au Calculation. *IEEE Trans. Aut. Control.* Vol. 39, No. 5, p. !000-1002.

Buslenko N. P. et al. (1966). *The Monte Carlo Method: The Method of Statistical Trials.* Edited by Shreider Yu. A. Pergamon Press.

Hersh M. (Ed.). (2015). *Ethical Engineering for International Development and Environmental Sustainability.* Springer-Verlag London. ISBN 978-1-4471-6617-7, Library of Congress Control Number: 2015934010.

Kleinrock L. (1976). *Queueing Systems. Volume 2: Computer Applications.* Wiley.

Lewoc J. B. et al. Network Modelling Technique: A Case Study. CSNDSP (IEEE, IET), Newcastle, 2010b, *IEEE Xplore,* pp. 250-255.

Lewoc J. B. (2010c). *A Case Study: Performance Evaluation for a Computer Integrated Power Plant Network.* Eurosim 1010 Congress, Prague. p 6.

Lewoc J. B. and Hersh M. et al. (2016). Human Behaviour Case Studies for the ICT and Automation Industry in Poland. In.: R. Bednarik (Ed.) (2016). *Understanding Human Behavior. Theories, Patterns and Developments.* p. 211-260.

Lewoc J. B. et al. (2010a). An Approximate Actual Network Performance Evaluation Method. L. Alamitos et al. (Eds.) UKSim/AMSS First International Conference on Intelligent Systems, Modellimg and Simulation, ISMS 2010, Liverpool, United Kingdom, IEEE CS Press, 2010, *IEEE Xplore* DOI: 10.1109/ISMSA.2010.74, pp. 380-384.

Reiser M. and Lavenberg S. S. (1980).Closed Multichain Queueing Network. *J. ACM*, Vol. 27, No. 2. p. 313-322.

Stahl B. C., Eden G., Jirotka M., Coeckelbergh M. (2014). From computer ethics to responsible research and innovations in ICT: The transition of reference discourses informing ethics-related research in information systems. *Information and Management,* Vol. 51, September 2014, p. 810-818.

Wikipedia. (2018a). OS/MVT and Successors. Available: https://en. wikipedia.org/wiki/OS/360_and_successors.

Yerby J. (2013). Legal and ethical issues of employee monitoring. *Online Journal of Applied Knowledge Management,* Vol. 1, Issue 2, 2013.

In: ICT Performance ... ISBN: 978-1-53614-916-6
Editor: Józef Bohdan Lewoc et al.

Chapter 7

CONCLUSION

Jozef B. Lewoc*[*], Pasha Bekhrad, Mike Fitzgibbon, Iwona Chomiak-Orsa, Antoni Izworski, Bogdan Kasierski, Antonina Kieleczawa, Eric Leitgeb, Jozef Patkiewicz, Mieczyslaw Rozent, Halina Strzelecka, Andrzej Tomczyk, Wojciech Szubert and Edward Ziaja

This Chapter presents the conclusions drawn from this Book, in the form of a resume.

1. RESUME

The Book emphasises the fact that researchers are thought of as working for society and are low paid. However, in the practice of science and technology, they should work, first of all, for system designers needing their help. To present this, the Book describes the design and implementation experiences for some line of computer systems and networks, gained in Poland.

---

[*] Corresponding Author's Email: jblewoc@wroclaw.home.pl.

The country and the line of the computer systems and networks were chosen purposefully: after World War II, the country was given as the most desired present to Stalin, the then head of the Soviet Union Communist Party and, in accordance with the Cold War rules, Poland was covered by embargo regulations, in particular, in the area of computers. The clear unjustness of the regulations generated understandable opposition of ICT designers and developers, most of whom become furious, claiming: they may put their computers into their ****; we shall design and develop our own ones, better than theirs. And the computer industry in Poland developed fast, with a delay of just a few years in comparison to the best developed countries of the West.

The ICT system and network designers and developers, having no access to Western computer hardware and, even more, to the ICT science of the Western world, must have done far greater work than their counterparts of the West, and their conduct has been compared with that of the Wild West Pioneers and, therefore, it was not a heresy to suggest that a successful Polish designer or developer must have learned more than a Western designer. The Leader was the most successful ICR application designer in the Country which explains the fact that his experiences were discussed in the Book.

The topics discussed in the Book should in no way be called obsolete or historical. First of all, history is the mother of students, which should explain such historical surveys. Secondly, in the domain under study, there many papers have been published proposing the open system approach to performance evaluation in various applications (e.g., performance evaluation for external memories or for network traffic the network layer), assuming the Poisson input stream and omitting the fact that such stream is inadequate due to the flow control mechanisms implemented at other levels of the traffic in the systems or networks. Therefore, the lessons given in the Book are up-to-date in the domain of current-day ICT systems and networks.

The Book covers the area of ICT performance evaluation, since the lack of, or inadequate, solutions in the area may lead to very costly system failures. To provide the classification needed, some methods of ethics and human behaviour (HB) have been employed. The line of the ICT systems and networks of the Wroclaw province and the development of ICT solutions in Wroclaw are described.

Chapter 4 describes the lines, specifying the denotations used in the Book.

For the steel-bar mill material traffic control system, the system description and the analytical model are presented and the basic performance characteristics as well as available queuing system aids are described. The system performance was investigated using a simulation model, mapping well the system and its operating environment. The basic simulation subroutines are discussed and the simulation results are presented together with the initial assessment of the ethical and HB aspects.

For the radio-astronomy centre control system, the queuing system and simulation aids available at that time are described, and a simulation model is presented together with the ethical and HB aspects.

For the Regional Power Control Board system, the Book covers the system description and the system aids available, together with the mathematical model of SAPI ODM (Automatic Data Processing for Regional Power Control Boards) and the performance evaluation project complete with the results obtained, including the initial assessment of the ethical and HB aspects, as they are in each case study.

For the SOSAPI operating system, for the power industry VDU project as well as for the microprocessor-based Power Control Board system, the system architectures (hardware and software) are presented, complete with the mathematical model of the system environment. The computer speed including hesitations is presented and the computing power available for user programs is computed.

The communication network was one designed and developed in Wroclaw for the Interuniversity Computer Network (MSK) in Poland. The Book describes the communication network, the performance requirements and the measuring aids available then. The measuring/testing tool is described together with mathematical models, exemplary internal network measurements and the initial assessment of performance tests/ measurements is presented.

The *A*pproximate a*na*lytical network performance *a*ss*es*sment tool (Anapaest) is a tool for approximate performance evaluation of computer/communication networks with end-to-end acknowledgement, analysed as collection of closed routes. Such a standard computer network and typical performance requirements are described. The Anapaest method complete with validation of the method are described, including internal measurements and network simulation. An application is shown for a CIMM (Computer Integrated Manufacturing and Management) system.

For the Badel (from Polish Baza danych dla elektrowni = Database for power plants) network, the Book describes the metropolitan network covering the Process Level, the Plant Operator Level, the Engineering subsystems, and the Supervision and Management Level. Available queuing network and simulation tools as well as the mathematical models and basic Badel characteristics are presented together.

For the robust design of computer control systems (Chapter 5), the Book proposes the use the μ-function as the robustness measure for computer systems, computer control systems included. The applications of the μ-function are proposed for a big house appliance manufacturing plant, power station monitors and democratic networking (here, it is shown that the three-part topology is the optimal one).

The case studies which feature ethics and HB under investigation for the line of the ICT systems and networks, propose the general information and the ethical evaluation of the case studies covers the actions of queuing theory researchers, the Leader and his Teams and other actors, complete with the ethical evaluation for the robustness case studies.

The relationship between ethics and HB for the case studies discussed is that research and technical work is performed in a simple and straightforward way is, usually, both ethical and appropriate from the HB point of view. On the other hand, any work that is *unduly* complicated, is, usually unethical in its consequences and inappropriate from the HB point of view.

2. Lessons to Be Learnt

The non-maleficence ethical theory seems to be a reasonable approach to ethical assessment of research and technical projects.

The assessment of any research and/or technical projects, led in a simple and straightforward way, is proposed as appropriate from the HB point of view, and seems to be an appropriate method for the case studies discussed in the Book.

The fury generated by unjust policy may be a very strong motif for development of own products and systems instead of buying foreign ones.

It was possible to design and develop, in the severe conditions of embargoes for hardware, software and knowledge, such complex and difficult systems as: the steel-mill material traffic control systems, radio-astronomy centre control system, regional Power Control Board system (SAPI ODM), SOSAPI operating system, power industry VDU clusters, power industry training simulator, microprocessor based Power Control Board system, MSK Interuniversity communication network, approximate network performance assessment tool (Anapaest), Badel database for power plants, μ-function based applications for a house appliance manufacturing plant, power station monitors, and democratic networking.

ABOUT THE EDITORS

Jozef B. Lewoc

Jozef Bohdan Lewoc graduated from the I LO Grammar School in Legnica, the Electronics Faculty (the Mathematical Machine Specialty) of the Wroclaw Technical University and from the Mathematical Faculty of the Wroclaw University (with distinction). He received his PhD degree (Automation Specialty) from the Warsaw Technical University.

During his professional carrier, he was with numerous entities of the ICT and automation branch, including: the computer manufacturer Elwro, the automation manufacturer Elam, the Institute for Power System

Automation IASE, Wroclaw University of Technology, Zielona Gora University of Technology, University of Wroclaw, Home Appliance Manufacturer (Polar), the design and translations agencies Leader and BPBIT Leader LLC. The frequent changes of the employing unit made it possible for him to be granted a high number of application projects (the highest in his Country).

Dr. Lewoc led several dozen ICT design projects, most of which were developed in the branch of automation. The most important were: the first Polish computer control system for a steel bar mill (participation in a two-designer team), and the projects he lead: the regional power control board data processing system SAPI ODM, the power industry oriented operating systems SAPI and SOSYM, the power plant database Badel, the communication network of the Interuniversity Computer Network MSK, computer system and the network performance evaluation approximate analytical and measuring tools. The systems and networks designed and developed under control of Dr. Lewoc resulted in many billion Euro benefits for the Country and many non-financial benefits.

Dr. Lewoc published close to 300 publications including 2 monographs.

Likes: skiing, sailing, gardening, picking berries and mushrooms, occupations with his twin granddaughters.

Eduard Babulak

Professor, Computational Sciences
Department of Computer Science
School of Business
Liberty University
Lynchburg, VA, 24502, USA

Education

D.Sc. in Information Technology, University of Pardubice
Ph.D. in Computer Science, Staffordshire University
M.Sc. in Information Systems, University of East London

Biography

Professor Eduard Babulak is accomplished international scholar, researcher, consultant, educator, professional engineer and polyglot, with more than thirty years of experience. He served as Editor, reviewer, Conference Chair, has successfully published, his research was cited by scholars all over the world. He served as Chair of the IEEE Vancouver Ethics, Professional and Conference Committee.

He was Invited Speaker at the University of Cambridge, MIT, University of Surrey, Purdue University, Penn State, Yokohama National University & University of Electro Communications in Tokyo, Japan, Shanghai Jiao Tong University, Sungkyunkwan University in Korea, Czech Technical University, Graz University of Technology, Austria, and other prestigious academic institutions worldwide.

His academic and engineering work was recognized internationally by the Engineering Council in UK, the European Federation of Engineers and credited by the Ontario Society of Professional Engineers and APEG in British Columbia in Canada. He was awarded higher postdoctoral degree DOCENT - Doctor of Science (D.Sc.) in the Czech Republic, Ph.D., M.Sc., and High National Certificate (HNC) diplomas in the United Kingdom, as well as, the Diploma Engineer (MSc and BSc in Electrical Engineering) in Slovakia.

He is Fellow of the Royal Society RSA, London, UK; Chartered Fellow, Mentor and Member of the ELITE Group of the British Computer

Society, London, UK; 2013-2014 Invited Panel Member for the DoD & National Science Foundation Graduate Research Fellowship Program, USA; Expert Consultant for HORIZON 2020 & CORDIS FP6 - FP7 European Commission, Brussels, Belgium; Mentor and Senior Member of the IEEE and ACM, USA; Nominated Fellow of the Institution of Engineering and Technology, London, UK and Distinguished Member of the ACM, USA; Chartered Member of the IET, London, UK;

His biography was cited in the Cambridge Blue Book, Cambridge Index of Biographies and number of issues of Who's Who.

Orcid: http://orcid.org/0000-0003-2450-090X
Copernicus: http://my.indexcopernicus.com/babulak
Researchgate: https://www.researchgate.net/profile/Eduard_Babulak

David Al-Dabss

School of Computing and Technology
Nottingham Trent University
Nottingham
NG11 8NS
United Kingdom.

My research interests include nature inspired models of architecture and algorithms for hybrid intelligent systems. It focuses on the development and application of real time recurrent hybrid networks to semantic mining to model emergent behaviour. Specific application areas of these techniques have recently covered behaviour parameter discovery for economic model dynamics and semantics mining for opponent strategy estimation in games play. Current work attempts to extend these ideas to semantic web intelligence through dynamical models of ontologies.

Prof Emeritus Dr David Al-Dabass, PhD.
BSc(Eng), Imperial College, London University, UK.
ACGI: Associate of the City & Guild Institute, UK.
CEng: Chartered Engineer, UK
FIET: Fellow of Intitute of Engineering & Technology, UK.
FBCS: Fellow of British Computer Society, UK
FIMA: Fellow of the Institute of Mathematics & its Applications, UK
President, UK Simulation Society.

About the Contributors

Pasha Bekhrad

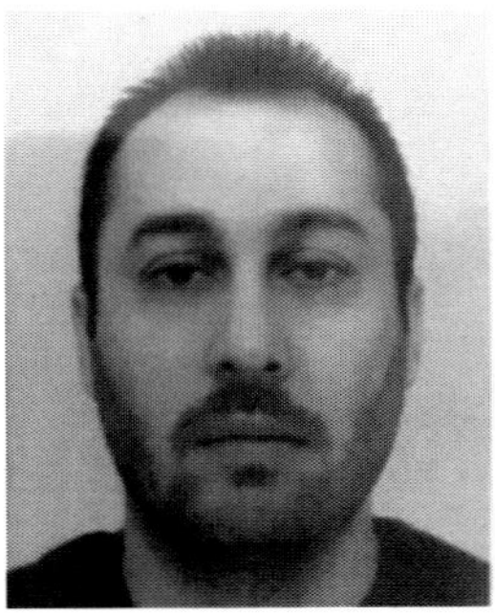

Pasha Bekhrad was born in 1983 in Tehran, Iran. He graduated from the Razi High School, Tehran, and received his bachelor degree from Esfahan Azad University in 2008 and his master degree from Multimedia University (MMU) in Telecommunication in 2013. He is currently pursuing his PhD degree with the title of "The suitability and evaluation of fibres and fibre optics component in free space applications for future communication scenarios'' from institute of Microwave and Photonic Engineering at Graz University of Technology under supervision of Professor Erich Leitgeb.

From 2006 to 2009, he worked at Petro Sadian Consulting Engineers Company in Tehran, Iran as a head of their instrument department. From 2014 until 2015, he worked with 20% dedicated work portion in Space

Research Institute, Department Satellite Geodesy at Austrian Academy of Sciences (IWF) in Graz, Austria. Since 2016 he has worked as a Project scientist PhD student in the European Space Agency, ESA, Project HybridPDT with 30% dedicated work portion.

In 2015, he attended the KORUZA workshop for scientific applications in Maribor, Slovenia, after which he was participating at the International training school on Fiber Laser/Optical Fiber Technology 2016 in Prague, the Czech Republic. In March 2017, he attended the Short Term Scientific Mission for Improvements on Optical Wireless Communication Systems to prevent transmission failures caused by Weather-based disruptions in Ilmenau, Germany with the support of Professor Mike Wolf.

Pasha Bekhrad is the author and co-author of 4 papers in IEEE and SPIE conferences. He also was a member of a local support team for international IEEE conferences (ICTON 2014 and CoBCom 2016 and, currently, CoBCom 2018) in Graz.

Likes: playing piano and table tennis

Iwona Chomiak-Orsa

Iwona Chomiak-Orsa graduated from the College of Economics in Srem and received her MSc. and PhD degrees in Information and Communication Technology from the Wroclaw Academy of Economics (AE) and from the Wroclaw University of Technology. In 2017, she was granted the Wroclaw University of Economics Professor title.

Professor Chomiak-Orsa acquired her knowledge from the Wroclaw firms: ASPA SA, AE, ZEH, YARD, Denmark Co. Ltd., Rynek 13, and Omega Systems. Presently, she is with the Wroclaw University of Economics, and is a researcher employed by the Chair of Business Intelligence in Management.

She was a coordinator of many educational subjects including: Modelling of ICT needs, Modelling of enterprises, Business bases and organisation, Business process modelling languages.

Professor Chomiak-Orsa has participated in numerous research programs, including national ones: Controlling information system determinants, Computer tools aiding insurance agency activity, Key probationer, Mozart probation project, etc., and International projects: Service Oriented Engineering Systems and Management, Translational LOGistics' Improvement through Cloud computing and innovative cooperative business models, IFAC Working Group for Non-technological Aspects of ICT and Automation (Nota), Accelerate Transversal Competences, ActGo-Gate, etc.

Likes: Bridge, hiking, snowboard.

Antoni Izworski

Antoni Izworski graduated from the Electrical Technical College in Nowy Sacz.

He received his scientific degrees: MSc. Electronic Eng. and PhD. from the Wroclaw University of Science and Technology.

During his professional carrier, he was with the Wroclaw University of Science and Technology.

Basic scientific interest areas of Dr Izworski include: the optimisation problems for controls in industrial processes and design of industrial control systems. He is an author or a co-author of more than a hundred papers presented at international scientific conferences and published in journals of the international reach.

Dr Izworski was also involved in applications of the control theory. He has developed and implemented control system designs in the industrial, military, research installations and intelligent buildings.

Dr Izworski has been leading educational courses in the electronics and measurement bases, sensor technology, actuation system technology, embedded systems, PLC controller programming, electrical installations in intelligent buildings, embedded systems, programming of PLC controllers, electrical installations in intelligent buildings provided with the KNX bus.

Dr Izworski has cooperated with the Polish National Education Ministry within the scope of the development of the educational programs, designing didactic units and developing national examinations for the professions: electrician, mechatronic and power engineer.

For some sixteen years, Dr Izworski has co-operated with the International Federation for Automatic Control and other Research organisations in the domain of the non-technological aspects of automation and ICT (ethical and Human Behaviour issues).

Likes: Mountain hiking, sailing.

Bogdan Kasierski

Bogdan Kasierski graduated from the Nicolaus Copernicus Grammar School in Torun and received his MSc. Electronic Eng. Degree

(Mathematical Machine Specialty) from the Warsaw Technical University. He completed also the following major professional courses: ICL 1900 logic architecture, IBL 360/370 logic architecture, CII computer system manufacture organization, ERP Mapics system, Sun Solaris 8 operating training course.

During his professional carrier, he was with several ICT enterprises: the former Polish biggest manufacturer of computers Elwro; Rex Wroclaw, Winuel Wroclaw, PMT Wroclaw and KASMA Wroclaw.

Bogdan Kasierski participated in the following major ICT projects: the design, prototype commissioning and launching of production of Odra 1204 computers as well as of Odra 1304 and 1305 computers (awarded with the National Prize); and led similar projects for the R-32 and R-34 Unified System Computers; implementation of ERP Mapics in ZNTK Ostrow Wlkp.; managing a team designing, manufacturing and implementing digital measuring and transmission devices for the power industry; implementation of the Local Market Operator internet application ORL in the Opole Power Utility.

Likes: Following of scientific and engineering work records, journeys.

Antonina Kieleczawa

Ms Antonina Kieleczawa graduated from the Grammar School in Szprotawa and from the Faculty of Electronics of the Wroclaw University of Technology. She has been with the Institute for Power System

Automation since 1977, presently holding the position of a senior research/technical specialist.

During the years 1983-1988, Antonina Kieleczawa was delegated for work in the United Nuclear Investigation Institute in Dubna, the nuclear reaction measurement analysis and informatics processing conducted in the Nuclear Reaction Laboratory, including a specialty in the real-time system domain.

She is a co-creator of the Polish Automation System, DCS MASTER, and the disturbance logging system, RZ-SPEEDY4, as well as of very many implementations of the above mentioned systems in various facilities, first of all in Poland, including complex turnkey installations in the heat and power generating plants EC Wrocław and EC Gdynia. She has specialised in the domain of the conceptual solutions at the operator level of the MASTER system, and of the communication and time synchronisation module. She performs, among other things, the work connected with the development, designing and implementation of new DCS MASTER system installation.

Antonina Kieleczawa has been a member of the Scientific Council of the Institute since 2012 and a member of the Working Group 03, the Technical Committee 9.5 of the International Federation of Automatic Control. She is a co-author of several dozen research and technical papers published in the Polish and international press, and presentations during Polish conferences.

In 2009, she was decorated with a national honour award "Deserved for the Power Industry".

Likes: Music (various kinds), poetic prose and other literature, theology (among others: Old-Slav language literary output, Orthodox music, iconography), hiking (in forests, mountains, sea-coasts).

Erich Leitgeb

Erich Leitgeb finished his secondary school education in Jennersdorf (Burgenland, bordered to Hungary) with excellent Abitur honours. In 1994 he received his masters degree at the University of Technology Graz. From 1982 to 1984, he attended military service and he is still active as an expert in military communications (current military rank Lieutenant-Colonel). In 1994, he started his research work in Optical Communications at the Department of Communications and Wave Propagation (TU Graz). In 1999, he received his PhD-degree with honours. Since January 2000, he has been the project leader of international research projects in the field of optical communications.

At the end of 2003, he submitted his research work for the post of Associate Professor. Since 2011, he has been a Professor for Optical Communications and Wireless Applications at the Institute of Microwave and Photonic Engineering at TU Graz. He gives lectures in Optical Communications Engineering, Antennas and Wave Propagation, and Microwaves.

Erich Leitgeb had research stays at the Institute of Telecommunications (FER) at the University of Zagreb (Croatia), at the University of Ljubljana and the Jozef Stefan Institute (IJS) in Ljubljana (Slovenia). He gave guest lectures in "Optical Wireless" at the University of Patras and at the University of Zagreb. He is a Visiting Professor at the Northumbria University in Newcastle (UK) and a Member of IEEE, SPIE, OSA and

WCA. Since the EuCAP 2012, he has been a representative of "Optical Wireless" at EurAAP, and since 2011 – the Austrian delegate of URSI Commission B (Fields and Waves).

Since 2003 he has been a reviewer for IEEE and SPIE conferences and journals, and acted as a member of Technical Committees and Chairpersons on these conferences. Since 2007, he has organised international IEEE conferences (e.g., CSNDSP 2008, ConTEL 2011, NOC 2013, ICTON 2014, ConTEL 2015, CoBCom 2016 and, currently, CoBCom 2018) as alocal organizer in Graz.

Erich Leitgeb is the author and co-author of 5 book-chapters, around 40 Journal publications, 140 reviewed Conference papers, around 40 Invited Talks and more than 60 international scientific reports.

Likes: Erich Leitgeb likes to organize conferences and the networking with colleagues and students. His hobbies are the family, friends and walking.

Jozef Patkiewicz

Jozef Patkiewicz graduated from the Secondary School No. 1 in Wroclaw in 1963 and from the Mathematical Faculty of the Wroclaw University in 1969. He received his PhD degree in Physical Culture Sciences from the Physical Education Academy in Wroclaw in 2013.

Jozef Patkiewicz is with the Polish Society for Rehabilitation of the Disabled, the Provincial Branch in Wroclaw, holding the President position since 1991. Earlier, he was Editor-in-Chief of the Disabled Persons

Bulletin – Lower Silesia "POMOST" (PIER) since 2005, was employed by the Wroclaw Province Office as the Wroclaw Voivode Proxy for disabled persons (1995-1996). He was with the Institute for Power System Automation (IASE) in Wroclaw as a research adjunct, the Head of the Operating Laboratory of the IASE System Automation Testing Centre, holding the positions of mathematician, a designer of computer and minicomputer operating systems, and a designer of production process control in ELWRO-Wroclaw (the former Polish biggest manufacturer of computers) and IASE-Wroclaw (1972-1991). He was also a programmer and edp system designer in 1972 in the Provincial Oil Product Turnover Enterprise (CPN) in Wroclaw, Corporate Managerial Computing Centre, a lecturer of the Post-Secondary Digital Computer Programming and Electronic Technical College (1970-1974), and a computer programmer in the Provincial Statistic Technique Station (1969-1971).

Jozef Patkiewicz was an organiser of a series of general Polish and international scientific conferences and symposia, including the Scientific Conferences: The Nationwide Child Rehabilitation Day (each year since 1975), The Provincial Conference: The Worldwide Disabled Person Day (after each year since 1970), TOP – The Non-Governmental Organisation Meeting (1998, 1999, 2001), The International Scientific Conference concerning Motoric Activity of Disabled Persons (2003, 2005, 2007, 2008, 2010, 2012, 2014, 2016, 2018)] as well as of touristic and cultural events for disabled persons.

He is the author or co-author of 221 scientific, academic for general public and columnist publications, including 40 books.

Likes: Diving, sailing, tourism, books.

Mieczyslaw Rozent
(Consultant on computer control system software)

Mieczyslaw Rozent graduated from the Grammar School in Walbrzych. He received his scientific degree: MSc. of Mathematics (Specialty: Applications of Mathematics) from the Wroclaw University.

During his professional carrier, he was, from 1972 to 1994, with the Institute for Power System Automatics (IASE). Next, he established his own business, Insofter, active in computer aided automatics.

The basic scientific interest areas of M. Rozent include: the design of industrial control systems complete with implementation and support for the users. He is an author or a co-author of 4 publications presented on international scientific conferences and published in journals of the international reach.

In IASE, he worked in the team which developed and implemented control systems for electrical network control centres and led the project of the power network computer training simulator.

Insofter created and implemented complex hardware – software projects such as: road system monitoring (1995 -2002), auxiliary devices for the investigations conducted in the Physical Education Academy and in the Electro-technics Institute in Wroclaw, a footfall count system for big objects and dispersed networks, selective delivery of technical information to automated manufacturing stands.

Likes: Skiing, manual work.

Halina Strzelecka

Halina Strzelecka graduated from the Secondary School in Ostrow Wielkopolski in 1963 and from the University of Wroclaw, the Mathematical Faculty, in 1968.

She commenced her professional carrier in the Experimental Division of the former Polish biggest Manufacturer of computers, Elwro, holding the position of a programmer of the Odra 1304 computer. Next, she joined IASE (the Institute for Power System Automation) and held the position of a Senior Expert Engineer.

She participated the following major operating software projects:

The operating system for the TUROW power plant CRPD (Central data logging and processing) system, 200 MW power generating unit;

The operating system for SAPI ODM (Regional Power Control Board Automatic Data Processing System);

The KON-10 minicomputer control operating system;

The operating system for the ProSter-Master computer system intended for the power stations as well as the heat and power stations.

Likes: skiing, swimming, hiking.

Wojciech Szubert

Wojciech Szubert graduated from the Wroclaw University of Technology, the Electrical Faculty, and was granted the MSc Electrical Eng. degree (the Electriv Power Systerm Specialty). In addition, he completed his MBA studies on the Wroclaw University of Economics in 2012, at the Management, Informatics and Finance Faculty. He was granted his PhD degree from the Wroclaw University of Technology, the Electric Power Institute in 2008.

Since 2004, Dr Szubert has been employed by the Institute for Power System Automation. Presently, he holds the position of Technical Director. Working in the Institute, he is responsible, in a particular way, for realisation of contracts, is involved in acquisition of contracts and supervises them until their completion.

Doctor Szubert is a specialist within the scope of the power facility automation, in particular of the turbine sets.

He was decorated with the honour award "For merits for the power industry".

Dr Szubert is an author or a co-author of a dozen or so scientific papers.

Likes: Keen runner and sailing lover.

Andrzej Tomczyk

Andrzej Tomczyk graduated from the Stefan Czarniecki Grammar School in Chelm and from the Electrical Faculty of the Wroclaw Technical University. He received his PhD Degree from the same Faculty (Dissertation title: An adaptive data model for the purposes of assistance of the electric power operation).

He commenced his professional carrier in the Institute for Power system Automation in Wroclaw, where he worked until 2007, fulfilling the research adjunct function and holding the positions of a laboratory head, division manager, the Leading Specialist and the Coordinator for the Station and Network Supervision.

Presently, Dr Tomczyk participates in the work of the Electric Power Institute of the Wroclaw University of Technology. His main areas of interests are: the electric power automation, the measuring systems: sensors, the operating research, databases, the data exploration and the BPL-PLC transmission applications aimed towards increasing safety in mine conditions.

Likes: jogging, swimming and listening to classical music.

Edward Ziaja

Edward Ziaja graduated from the Mechanical College in Stalowa Wola and from the Electrical Faculty of the Wroclaw Technical University, being granted the MSc. Eng title (Specialty: Automation).

For 10 years, he was with the Electric Machine Institute of the Wroclaw Technical University as a research assistant and senior assistant.

Via the Polservice Warsaw Foreign Trade Agency, he was employed as the principal engineer of the Algerian Company EPBTP SAIDA near Oran and the USA.

Since 1989, he has been with IASE as: an automation designing specialist, Marketing Department Head, Director's Proxy for Marketing, Deputy Director for Development and Marketing, Director for development and Key Customers, Director and President of the Institute.

For his invention activities, he was awarded with the Invention Commodore's Cross and the Invention Order Officer's Cross of the Kingdom of Belgium.

He published ca. 60 publications and 16 patents, and registered designs. He has been active as a member of numerous scientific and technical organisation and was awarded with many professional decorations.

Likes: classic music, non-typical collections including the collection of right-legged elephants with trunks oriented upwards (250 pcs.), collection of well-known wine sorts, etc.

Willy Wojsznis
(Consultant on computer control system)

Willy Wojsznis was a member of the Emerson DeltaV research team and has been involved in the development of advanced control products for nearly 25 years, focusing on the model predictive control, optimization, auto timing, adaptive control and data analytics.

Over the previous years of his career, he worked on developing computer control systems and applications. His professional work resulted in a number of successful and innovative advanced control products, over forty patents, and over fifty technical papers. He graduated from the Kamienna Gora Grammar School, received a control engineering degree (EE) from Kiev Technical University in 1964, an M.S. in Applied Mathematics from Wroclaw University in 1972, and a Ph.D. from the Warsaw University of Technology in 1973. He co-authored the ISA bestselling books *Advanced Control Unleashed* (2002), *Advanced Control Foundation* (2012) and *Wireless Control Foundation* (2014). In 2010, he was inducted into *Control Magazine's* Process Automation Hall of Fame. Willy is an ISA Fellow and IEEE senior member. He retired in 2015 after 52 years of the professional activity, still continuing to be active.

Likes: Gardening, skiing.

INDEX

μ

μ function, 164, 228, 235, 244

A

actors, 248, 249, 255, 256, 263, 285
Anapaest, 12, 179, 180, 185, 186, 198, 199, 238, 254, 271, 272, 284, 286
are eigenvalue, 233
automation, xv, 16, 17, 22, 68, 87, 102, 103, 107, 130, 131, 132, 138, 146, 201, 205, 207, 208, 211, 219, 227, 228, 245, 248, 256, 258, 273, 279, 287, 288, 295, 296, 298, 301, 304, 305, 306, 307, 308, 309
autonomy, 2

B

badel, 201, 202, 203, 204, 205, 206, 208, 209, 210, 211, 212, 261, 262, 272, 273, 284, 286, 288
beneficence, 2
book 2, xv, 228, 243, 267, 277
branch, 32, 88, 98, 105, 152, 215, 239, 248, 249, 253, 263, 264, 287, 288, 301

C

call, xii, 163, 164, 170, 177, 210
CIMM, 180, 186, 187, 188, 189, 190, 192, 206, 234, 245, 284
commandment, 6, 7
common-medium case, 229, 231, 235
communication network, 155
computer, viii, xi, xii, xiii, 11, 13, 19, 22, 23, 24, 25, 30, 31, 34, 36, 38, 39, 41, 43, 44, 58, 59, 64, 65, 66, 67, 69, 72, 73, 86, 87, 88, 89, 92, 94, 98, 99, 101, 102, 103, 104, 105, 106, 108, 109, 117, 118, 120, 121, 129, 130, 131, 135, 136, 137,138, 139, 141, 142, 143, 145, 146, 152, 153, 154, 158, 159, 160, 162, 163, 164, 165, 167, 168, 174, 177, 178, 179, 180, 185, 186, 192, 193, 197, 198, 199, 200, 201, 202, 203, 206, 208, 210, 212, 213, 214, 215, 216, 217, 218, 219, 220, 221, 222, 223, 227, 228, 229, 230, 234, 238, 244, 245, 247, 249, 250, 251, 252, 253, 254, 255, 256, 258, 260, 261, 263, 264, 265, 266, 267, 268, 269, 271, 272, 273, 274, 276, 277, 278, 279, 281, 282, 284, 288, 289, 290, 291, 295, 297, 301, 303, 304, 305, 308, 309

computer system, xi, xiii, 13, 23, 24, 30, 31, 34, 36, 38, 92, 98, 118, 129, 135, 137, 145, 152, 167, 178, 185, 198, 199, 200, 202, 203, 210, 212, 213, 214, 215, 221, 228, 244, 247, 249, 251, 252, 253, 255, 256, 258, 263, 264, 265, 266, 267, 268, 276, 277, 278, 281, 282,284, 288, 297, 305
conduct, 1, 67, 69, 88, 89, 102, 152, 178, 179, 200, 201, 255, 264, 265, 268, 269, 270, 272, 273, 275, 282
connection, v, 70, 90, 174, 176, 177, 210, 211, 257
control system, 12, 23, 32, 33, 38, 40, 41, 42, 44, 54, 58, 59, 63, 64, 65, 66, 67, 69, 70, 73, 74, 75, 86, 87, 88, 92, 103, 118, 139, 163, 164, 179, 186, 193, 199, 201, 205, 213, 214, 221, 228, 230, 248, 250, 251, 252, 253, 254, 255, 256, 257, 265, 266, 267, 268, 271, 273, 274, 276, 283, 284, 285, 288, 296, 303, 308, 309
Country, xi, xii, 11, 12, 22, 68, 89, 145, 152, 165, 206, 208, 214, 215, 248, 249, 255, 257, 258, 259, 260, 261, 262, 265, 268, 269, 270, 271, 272, 273, 282, 288

D

data acquisition and control system, 237, 238
data concentrator, 17, 230
data transmission, 96, 123, 198, 230
database, 12, 191, 192, 193, 206, 210, 211, 237, 261, 262, 272, 284, 286, 288
decalogue, 5, 6, 7
democratic computer network, 275
democratic criterion, 242, 243
democratic networking, 238, 284, 286
deontological approaches, 2
disturbance, 207, 232, 298
disturbance of the multiplicative type, 232
disturbance structure, 232

E

enterprise, 188, 189, 194, 219, 234, 239, 240, 245, 301
equivalent diagram, 232
Ethics, vii, viii, 1, 2, 3, 5, 6, 7, 13, 14, 222, 244, 247, 275, 278, 279, 283, 285, 289
ethics of care, 2
existence, 2, 200, 210
exponential, 19, 27, 28, 29, 32, 33, 34, 37, 47, 65, 72, 84, 85, 86, 92, 94, 97, 118, 121, 124, 135, 193, 212, 213, 214, 216, 217, 219, 249, 250, 264, 266, 267, 277

G

geometric series, 239, 241
growth, 3, 197

H

hardware, xii, 13, 40, 58, 67, 69, 87, 102, 103, 104, 106, 119, 124, 130, 138, 139, 140, 141, 143, 146, 147, 148, 151, 153, 154, 155, 162, 169, 187, 188, 189, 190, 201, 202, 204, 208, 217, 239, 250, 252, 255, 256, 258, 282, 283, 285, 303
harm, 2, 6, 67, 88, 103, 106, 145, 152, 244, 248, 276
HB, 1, 244, 263, 268, 283, 285
hierarchy of needs, 2
House Appliance, 234, 274
Human Behaviour, vii, viii, 2, 5, 7, 14, 222, 244, 247, 263, 275, 276, 279, 296
hypothesis, 243

I

IBM /360, 276
ICT, 1, iii, vii, viii, xi, xii, xiii, xv, 9, 11, 12, 13, 14, 15, 20, 36, 117, 152, 187, 215, 222, 224, 225, 247, 255, 263, 270, 276, 279, 282, 283, 285, 287, 288, 295, 296, 297
immanent disturbance, 235
Independent, v, 2, 32, 47, 49, 58, 65, 92, 118, 199, 212, 249, 250, 264, 267
induction, 242
input stream, 19, 27, 29, 32, 37, 43, 47, 48, 49, 50, 51, 58, 64, 92, 97, 98, 118, 119, 122, 125, 135, 167, 199, 212, 213, 249, 250, 251, 264, 266, 282
integer quotient, 239
inter-arrival time, 32, 33, 48, 60, 65, 77, 85, 92, 93, 95, 118, 119, 120, 122, 123, 167, 199, 212, 213, 250, 251, 266
Interrupt Request, 16, 17, 18, 19, 20, 25, 32, 47, 48, 73, 75, 77, 87, 91, 93, 111, 118, 119, 147, 149, 213, 214, 250
interuniversity communication network, 12, 214, 251, 254, 256, 276, 286

J

justice, 2

L

large-scale LAN, 239
leader, 12, 37, 38, 40, 41, 64, 67, 74, 86, 87, 89, 92, 96, 98, 103, 118, 129, 130, 138, 145, 146, 151, 152, 153, 160, 161, 162, 163, 164, 165, 168, 170, 178, 200, 202, 208, 209, 212, 248, 254, 255, 261, 262, 265, 266, 267, 268, 269, 270, 271, 272, 273, 274, 277, 282, 285, 288

M

management, 106, 113, 140, 144, 187, 203, 222, 234, 239, 240
Martial Law, 152, 260
Maslow, 2, 3
material traffic, 23, 28, 30, 32, 33, 40, 41, 42, 44, 54, 58, 63, 64, 65, 73, 87, 88, 118, 250, 265, 267, 271, 283, 285
mean value, 27, 34, 35, 118, 165, 167, 174, 175, 176, 182, 183, 184, 185, 212, 214, 250, 264, 267
Metallurgical Plant, 23, 257
minimum interval, 20, 27, 28, 29, 33, 34, 47, 65, 72, 94, 98, 118, 120, 121, 125, 213, 250
MSK, 153, 154, 155, 158, 159, 160, 161, 162, 167, 168, 178, 179, 185, 193, 194, 197, 202, 217, 251, 260, 271, 272, 284, 286, 288

N

narrative ethics, 2
network designer, xi, 168, 177, 186, 198, 239, 244, 253, 256, 264, 282
network nodes/switches, 242
non-maleficence, 2, 275, 285

O

operating system, 12, 106, 108, 109, 119, 130, 137, 138, 139, 140, 141, 146, 149, 155, 160, 162, 169, 174, 179, 205, 208, 253, 256, 259, 264, 269, 270, 277, 283, 285, 288, 301, 304, 305
optimum network, 241

P

partial sum, 239, 241
performance evaluation, xiii, 12, 27, 28, 37, 38, 41, 67, 70, 88, 92, 100, 103, 129, 160, 169, 175, 177, 180, 185, 186, 187, 192, 193, 198, 199, 200, 202, 212, 214, 215, 218, 247, 250, 252, 253, 254, 256, 262, 263, 265, 268, 269, 271, 272, 273, 277, 278, 282, 283, 284, 288
pgu, 237
PGU, 210
poisson, 37, 39, 59, 72, 92, 118, 135, 212, 213, 218, 249, 250, 264, 282
PoP, 67, 257
power generating unit, 102, 111, 121, 137, 208, 210, 237, 304
Power Generation/Distribution Control Systems, 237, 274
power industry, 12, 90, 91, 92, 94, 97, 102, 103, 106, 121, 129, 130, 131, 135, 137, 138, 139, 140, 145, 146, 152, 164, 201, 202, 208, 209, 221, 234, 259, 260, 262, 269, 270, 273, 283, 286, 288, 297, 299, 306
power of people, 67, 102, 162, 212, 254, 257, 270, 272
power plant, 12, 201, 202, 206, 208, 210, 211, 212, 219, 237, 245, 254, 261, 262, 272, 273, 279, 284, 286, 288, 304

Q

queuing theory, 35, 36, 66, 67, 91, 129, 137, 170, 198, 249, 252, 256, 262, 263, 264, 266, 285

R

radio-astronomy, 12, 68, 70, 71, 73, 74, 75, 86, 87, 89, 91, 163, 254, 256, 257, 258, 268, 271, 283, 285
random variable, 27, 28, 29, 33, 35, 38, 39, 40, 64, 66, 94, 121, 159, 165, 167, 174, 180, 192, 198, 209, 212, 250, 266, 267
real-time, 30, 31, 33, 35, 44, 60, 62, 63, 66, 71, 73, 75, 86, 87, 88, 92, 93, 97, 98, 100, 101, 105, 107, 111, 119, 121, 125, 127, 128, 135, 137, 141, 143, 144, 151, 185, 186, 193, 213, 250, 251, 252, 253, 266, 267, 268, 269, 270, 271, 298
regional power control board, 12, 89, 103, 130, 136, 138, 141, 146, 255, 258, 269, 271, 283, 288, 304
relatedness, 2
reliability, 28, 54, 207, 227, 228

S

SAPI ODM, 89, 90, 91, 92, 95, 96, 97, 98, 99, 101, 102, 103, 104, 106, 108, 109, 111, 117, 119, 122, 123, 125, 126, 127, 128, 136, 137, 139, 141, 145, 146, 258, 259, 270, 283, 285, 288, 304
sequential controller, 237
service, v, 16, 18, 20, 25, 26, 27, 29, 30, 32, 33, 34, 37, 38, 42, 43, 44, 46, 47, 52, 53, 54, 58, 60, 62, 63, 64, 65, 66, 71, 73, 75, 77, 78, 79, 80, 81, 85, 86, 92, 93, 94, 95, 96, 98, 99, 100, 104, 110, 111, 112, 117, 118, 119, 120, 121, 122, 123, 124, 125, 126, 127, 135, 151, 165, 166, 170, 172, 174, 182, 191, 192, 193, 212, 214, 216, 217, 223, 238, 239, 241, 249, 251, 252, 265, 266, 267, 277, 295, 299
signal processing, 110, 163, 230
simulation, 13, 38, 39, 40, 41, 42, 43, 47, 48, 49, 50, 51, 52, 53, 54, 55, 56, 57, 58,

59, 61, 63, 64, 67, 73, 74, 77, 78, 86, 87, 88, 89, 92, 98, 140, 141, 144, 176, 177, 185, 186, 193, 194, 199, 209, 215, 218, 221, 222, 249, 259, 267, 268, 269, 271, 279, 283, 284, 291
software, xii, 13, 23, 26, 40, 58, 70, 73, 100, 101, 102, 105, 106, 119, 124, 128, 139, 141, 142, 151, 156, 157, 163, 169, 171, 201, 205, 208, 216, 217, 239, 250, 255, 256, 258, 270, 284, 285, 303, 304
SOSAPI, 12, 17, 92, 96, 97, 103, 106, 109, 111, 112, 113, 115, 116, 117, 119, 122, 124, 125, 128, 130, 137, 138, 139, 140, 141, 146, 149, 253, 258, 259, 269, 283, 285
stability, xv, 230
star case, 229, 230
star-type architecture, 234
steel-bar mill, 12, 20, 21, 22, 32, 34, 35, 37, 38, 44, 54, 59, 60, 88, 250, 251, 255, 256, 257, 265, 266, 267, 271, 283
structured singular value, 228, 233, 235, 236, 273

T

team, xi, 74, 86, 87, 99, 103, 105, 106, 129, 131, 136, 138, 140, 143, 145, 151, 152, 161, 170, 179, 187, 200, 208, 239, 248, 269, 270, 271, 272, 288, 294, 297, 303, 308
three-party, 243
time, xiii, 10, 16, 17, 18, 19, 22, 23, 25, 26, 27, 28, 29, 30, 31, 32, 33, 34, 35, 38, 41, 42, 44, 46, 47, 49, 54, 58, 60, 61, 62, 63, 64, 65, 66, 68, 70, 71, 72, 75, 77, 78, 79, 80, 81, 82, 84, 85, 86, 87, 88, 89, 90, 93, 94, 95, 96, 97, 99, 100, 101, 102, 105, 106, 108, 110, 111, 113, 118, 119, 120, 121, 122, 123, 124, 126, 127, 134, 135, 136, 137, 138, 141, 142, 143, 144, 149, 151, 163, 170, 171, 172, 174, 175, 176, 178, 181, 182, 183, 184, 185, 188, 192, 193, 194, 195, 198, 211, 213, 216, 217, 220, 222, 223, 228, 229, 230, 232, 234, 244, 248, 249, 251, 253, 254, 256, 257, 259, 260, 265, 266, 267, 271, 276, 283, 291, 298
time delay, 90, 229, 230, 232, 244, 254
training simulator, 12, 137, 138, 140, 141, 142, 260, 270, 286, 303
transmittance, 229

U

unit circle, 233

V

VDU, 12, 18, 129, 130, 133, 134, 135, 136, 137, 138, 139, 154, 269, 270, 283, 286
virtue ethics, 2, 3
voluntary work, 248

W

working media, 206, 234
WPR, 257, 258, 261, 262, 270

Related Nova Publications

Quantum Image Watermarking

Authors: Ri-Gui Zhou, PhD, Gaofeng Luo and Wenwen Hu

Series: Computer Science, Technology and Applications

Book Description: This book offers various schemes related to watermarking techniques for quantum images in spatial and frequency domains.

Hardcover ISBN: 978-1-53616-099-4
Retail Price: $160

Vehicular Networks: Applications, Performance Analysis and Challenges

Editors: Peter Chong and Ivan Ho

Series: Computer Science, Technology and Applications

Book Description: This book provides an overview of vehicular networks on the performance analysis, potential applications, and existing challenges.

Hardcover ISBN: 978-1-53615-978-3
Retail Price: $230

To see a complete list of Nova publications, please visit our website at www.novapublishers.com